Ina C

At the age of 50, Ina Crawford's life fell apart. She divorced her husband after 26 years of marriage, her hard earned financial "security" disappeared overnight and she was in poor health. It took her two years to get her life together again, and then she had a nervous breakdown. There was nothing in the world worth living for and she often felt suicidal, but had to keep going because her two sons needed a home base.

During this painful period she clung desperately to the memory of a psychic happening – experienced twelve years before – which pointed to the possibility of another dimension where perhaps a reason for going on could be found.

She emerged from this state thirteen months later with her feet consciously on the Path (the inward journey), and subsequently learned that what she had experienced was one of the classic spiritual awakenings, which is through what we term a nervous breakdown, or crisis, when nothing in the material world has any attraction.

For the next thirty years her home and her time were devoted to the dissemination of the good news about the spirit of the New Age – the evolutionary breakthrough into new perspectives – and particularly about the mysteries and revelations leading to transformation to be found in the exploration of the Ageless Wisdom teachings.

She focalised study groups, discussions, meditation meetings, workshops, seminars, helped with the distribution of the Alice Bailey books and always had an open door and sympathetic ear for those faced with any of the problems of the Path.

Although she always read widely in this field, her inspiration always came *from*, and her questions were always answered *by*, the Alice A. Bailey books which are a series of bridging treatises between the material knowledge of man and the science of the initiates.

This book is the outcome of these experiences.

Confusion may bring order harmony, establish peace, set up relations (ship) between countries etc our job is to re-imagine a healthy world

"Change the world, one word at a time"

A GUIDE TO THE MYSTERIES

An Ageless Wisdom Digest
for the New Age

by Ina Crawford

First published 1990 by
The Lucis Press
Suite 54
3 Whitehall Court
London SW1A 2EF

ISBN 0 85330 140 9

Design and typography:
Peter Wyart,
Three's Company, London WC2

Typesetting:
Saxon Printing Limited, Derby

Printed in England by
Biddles Ltd, Guildford

CONTENTS

PART 3: FOR DEEPER REFLECTION

CHARTS

INTRODUCTION

I will praise thee; for I am fearfully and wonderfully made: marvellous are thy works; and that my soul knoweth right well.

Psalm 139 : 14

When searching for the truth I was pointed in what *for me* was the right direction, to esotericism – the study of the world of energies, moving and working under the Law of Cause and Effect – and more particularly to the teachings contained in the series of books by Alice A. Bailey. Increasingly, as the years went by and more and more people called at my house to ask questions and discuss the problems they had encountered in *their* search for truth, I found myself thinking of how immeasurably they could be helped if only they knew something of the Wisdom Teachings and the miracle of their own equipment; of how we are, each of us, an aggregate of energies, living and moving in an ocean of energies.

Then, when talking to various groups recently on "The Seven Rays and the Human Energy Field" I found that their immediate and enthusiastic response was "wonderful! We'd love to know more, but where do we begin?". I decided to write this book as an attempt to help such beginners who have read somewhat in this field and know something of the terminology, but are unsure of their next step ahead or of how to evaluate the quality of the many books, teachers and groups that are encountered on the Path.

It is meant to be read more than once; the first time a quick "run through" is sufficient – even of those parts not easily understood at first reading, particularly the first three chapters which are the most difficult. On going over it again, slowly, the reader should be able to find what is most useful to him.

The study of this and all allied subjects is made much easier if the fact is kept firmly in mind that everything in the universe, from an atom upwards, is electrical and should be thought of as frequencies.

The major reference books used are the Holy Bible (King James version) and the Alice A. Bailey books. Most of the latter were dictated by The Tibetan, Djwhal Khul, a Master of the Wisdom, who is often referred to by his students as D.K.

At the end of the book is an extensive glossary of the specialised terms used, and readers may find it helpful to refer to this.

T.S. Eliot bemoaned "the intolerable confusion of words". Lyall Watson wrote that when he tried the new E type English it made everything, even Hamlet's soliloquy, sound very silly.

I found myself in sympathy with them when I tried, in deference to the women's movement, to use words like person, human and humankind instead of man and mankind. The results sounded very silly indeed. So I had to fall back on the use of such words as "man" and "mankind" as a matter of expediency.

The women's perspective is further discussed on pages 47–49 in Chapter 5, "Evolutionary Sequence and the Chakras".

Another example that illustrates the "intolerable confusion of words", is the word "God". There is only one God. The confusion arises because of the personalisation of the energies of His never-ending immeasurable universe, which are embodied and wielded by great Entities, and even these are so awesome that they are referred to as Gods, i.e. those Great Entities, the Gods of solar systems, planets, the wind, the sea, etc..

A much abused word today is the word "occult". It means "hidden, kept secret, mysterious, beyond the range of ordinary knowledge". "Occult" is often used interchangeably with "esoteric". In this work it relates to knowledge about the energies of the Universe. These subjective incoming and outgoing energies are neutral. They are used for good by the white occultist in serving God. The black occultist uses them in serving his own selfish personal ends. Unfortunately some religious groups are promoting the idea that all occultism is black.

Occultism, or *esotericism*, is practical mysticism. It adds the intelligent use of the mind to the heart approach.

Although this work bears my name as author, it could not have been written without the permission of the Lucis Trust to use some of their invaluable material and without the help of several companions of the Lighted Way.

I wish to express my sincere thanks to Rose de la Hunt for the beautiful artwork on the cover; to Dr. Wim Ahlers, who, by giving so cheerfully and unstintingly of his time, truly walked that "extra mile" with me while helping with the preparation of this book; and to Dierdre Hughes for the loving care with which she produced the charts.

Acknowledgements

I wish to acknowledge with gratitude and to record my sincere thanks to the following for permission to quote from various works:

To The Lucis Press Ltd. for permission to quote from any of their published works. The titles of the twenty-one books used for this purpose are listed in the bibliography on page 205.

To DeVorrs & Company, Publishers and Book Distributers, for permission to quote from *Breakthrough to Creativity,* by Shafica Karagulla, from *Through the Curtain,* by Viola Petitt Neal and Shafica Karagulla, and from *Everyone is Right: A New Look at Comparative Religion and its Relation to Science,* by Roland Peterson.

To the Agni Yoga Society, New York, for permission to quote from *The Agni Yoga Series* and *Letters*, by Helena Roerich, for which they hold copyright.

To The C.W. Daniel Company Ltd, Publishers, for permission to use a chart from *Radionics and the Subtle Anatomy of Man*, by David V. Tansley. To Dr Fritjof Capra for permission to quote from his book, *The Tao of Physics.*

To The Churches' Fellowship for Psychical and Spiritual Studies for permission to quote from *Testimony of Light* by Helen Greaves.

A Note from D.K.

"The superficial student or the mystically inclined person is apt to feel that all these technicalities are of minor importance. The charge is often made that the "jargon" of occultism and its academic information is of no true importance where knowledge of the divine is concerned. It is claimed that it is not necessary to know about the planes and their various levels of consciousness, or about the Law of Rebirth and the Law of Attraction; it is an unnecessary tax upon the human mind to study the technical foundation for a belief in brotherhood, or to consider our distant origin and our possible future. It is nevertheless just possible that if the mystics down the ages had recognised these truths we might have had a better managed world. It is only today that those forces are being set in motion which will lead to a truer understanding of the human family, a wiser comprehension of the human equipment, and, therefore, to an effort to bring human living into line with the basic spiritual truths. The sorry condition of the world today is not a result of the intellectual unfoldment of man as is often claimed, but it is the working out of the unalterable effects of causes, originated in the past of the Aryan race.

That good can come from evil, that the bad effects of man's mental laziness can be transmuted into teaching points in the future and that humanity is now intelligent enough to learn wisdom will be the result of the widespread dissemination of the academic truths of the esoteric teaching (the Ageless Wisdom) and its correct interpretation by the trained minds in the Occident. The East has had this teaching for ages and has produced numerous commentaries upon it – the work of the finest analytical minds that the world has ever seen – but it has made no mass use of the knowledge, and the people in the Orient do not profit by it, as a whole. It will be different in the West and is already modifying and influencing human thought on a large scale; it is permeating the structure of our civilisation and will eventually salvage it."

Esoteric Psychology Vol. II, pages 510, 511.

WHAT IS THE AGELESS WISDOM?

*But we speak the wisdom of God in a mystery, even the hidden wisdom, which
God ordained before the world unto our glory . . .*
I Corinthians 2:7

The Ageless Wisdom, also known as the Ancient Wisdom, or the
Wisdom Teaching, or esotericism, is the name given to those ancient
Mystery Teachings which contain the secrets of the *reality-of-that-
which-is-not-seen*, this reality being the ever-pulsating energies of our
Creator's universe and His evolutionary plan. These energies are the
causes responsible for the effects in the universe, the effects being the
myriad diverse forms which compose the sum total of all that is.

All that transpires on the physical plane is due to subjective forces.

This knowledge has had to be kept secret because mankind *has not
been*, and *is not now* responsible enough to be entrusted with the
power that this knowledge brings: for instance, the power that comes
with the formulas and mantrams that manipulate matter.

Consider the power that came with the knowledge of the splitting of
the atom. This has been sadly misused for aggression and pollution
instead of for the benefit of the planet.

This is why, although these Teachings have been with us since
Lemurian times – about 18 million years ago – only gradually, little by
little, have the secrets of the Ageless Wisdom been unfolded to those
who have been ready.

Those who have been ready are those who have discarded dogmatic
separatist beliefs, who are free from conceit and selfishness and who
accept this unbroken oral tradition of the Ageless Wisdom revealed by
living divine men during the infancy of the race. The Masters of the
Wisdom are thoroughly versed in the science based on such uninterrupted teachings.

These teachings are not in text books with numbered pages, but are
a decree of life. Webster's dictionary describes the word decree as "an
order usually having the force of law".

So this Ageless Wisdom teaching, this expression of divine law, this
Law of Life, is today entirely appropriate to the present state of
consciousness of those ready to receive it.

This divine law is steadily bringing man to become aware of the great
issues. When, through contact with his own higher self, he comes to the
realisation that a law is the spiritual will, impulse, incentive and life

manifestation of the Being-in-Whom-he-lives-and-moves-and-has-his-being, he learns that that impulse is demonstrated as intelligent activity and based on love.

He then himself begins to direct lovingly, wisely and intelligently through himself as much of the spiritual life impulse as his frequencies can resonate to and transmit. He opens the door to spiritual energy.

As above, so below. The macrocosm, the microcosm. This vibratory impulse of the One Life is repeated down through everything in creation from Gods, angels, men and the myriads of little lives expressing themselves in all the forms of nature through the process of evolution.

He learns that the Ageless Wisdom teaches that the One Life, manifesting through matter, produces consciousness. This consciousness is the soul of all things, underlying all forms, whether of a man, an atom, a planet, or a solar system.

The unfoldment of this consciousness is the revelation of the soul, or the evolution of light. Veiled and hidden in every form is light and, as evolution proceeds, matter becomes increasingly a better conductor of light.

It teaches too that all life manifests cyclically. This is the theory of reincarnation. Man, made in the image of God, through the process of reincarnation, unfolds his consciousness step by step.

Such are some of the great underlying truths which form the foundation of the Ageless Wisdom – the existence of Life, and the development of consciousness through the cyclic taking of form.

It is essential that the old processes – profoundly useful in their day – should be forgotten and the newer methods and techniques should be substituted. This is essential now on account of the surprising unfoldment of human consciousness.

Through the chaos of the recent great world war (precipitated by humanity itself), there is developing a structure of truth and a paralleling responsiveness of the human mechanism which guarantees the perpetuation and the rapid unfoldment of the next stage of the Ageless Wisdom.

From *A Treatise on White Magic*, pages 331 to 333:

If it is true that there is being gathered together in the background of our present world-state a group of mystics who are distinguished by knowledge, vision, and a power to work on mental levels, unseen and unrecognised by men, it could also be noted that this band is not confined to the strictly religious types. Men and women in every branch of human thought are found among this group including scientists and philosophers.

Like all else at this time, science itself is in process of transformation, and little as it is realized by many, their work with what they call matter, and their investigations of the atom are entering into a new field. In this field the older techniques and mechanisms will gradually be discarded and a new approach and a different fundamental concept as to the nature of matter will mark the new age. . . . The truth of certain basic premises of the Ageless Wisdom will be demonstrated. . . .

All great scientists and workers in the realm of objective nature have worked as souls, and all the most amazing of the developments in the realm of physics and chemistry, as in other departments of human knowledge, have been made when the worker in any particular field has launched forth with faith in some hypothesis he has formed, and has investigated and progressed his work forward stage by stage until he has contacted an aspect of the truth hitherto unformulated by man. Then, having through the use of his intuition entered into a new realm of thought, he takes the knowledge there discovered and formulates it in such way by theory, principle, experiment and mechanical contrivance that it becomes the possession of the group, and in due time is understood and utilized by the world. But in its genesis it has been mystical work and based on a mystical intuition.

D.K. introduces himself as a teacher of the Ageless Wisdom in the following extract from "A Statement by the Tibetan", published in August 1934, by the Lucis Trust:

I am a brother of yours, who has travelled a little longer upon the Path than has the average student, and has therefore incurred greater responsibilities. I am one who has wrestled and fought his way into a greater measure of light than has the aspirant who will read this article, and I must therefore act as transmitter of the light, no matter what the cost. I am not an old man, as age counts among the teachers, yet I am not young or inexperienced. My work is to teach and spread the knowledge of the Ageless Wisdom wherever I can find a response, and I have been doing this for many years. I seek also to help the Master M. and the Master K.H. whenever opportunity offers, for I have been long connected with Them and with Their work. In all the above, I have told you much; yet at the same time I have told you nothing which would lead you to offer me that blind obedience and the foolish devotion which the emotional aspirant offers to the Guru and Master whom he is as yet unable to contact. Nor will he make that desired contact until he has transmuted emotional devotion into unselfish service to humanity — not to the Master.

The books that I have written are sent out with no claim for their acceptance. They may, or may not, be correct, true and useful. It is for you to ascertain their truth by right practice and by the exercise of the intuition. Neither I nor A.A.B. is the least interested in having them acclaimed as inspired writings, or in having anyone speak of them (with bated breath) as being the work of one of the Masters. If they present truth in such a way that it follows sequentially upon that already offered in the world teachings, if the information given raises the aspiration and the will-to-serve from the plane of the emotions to that of the mind (the plane whereon the Masters *can* be found) then they will have served their purpose. If the teaching conveyed calls forth a response from the illumined mind of the worker in the world, and brings a flashing forth of his intuition, then let that teaching be accepted. But not otherwise. If the statements meet with eventual corroboration, or are deemed true under the test of the Law of Correspondences, then that is well and good. But should this not be so, let not the student accept what is said. . . .

The following summary of D.K.'s work, as a teacher of the Ageless Wisdom for the New Age, consists of extracts from *The Tibetan Master's Work* published by The Arcane School (Lucis Trust).

Hierarchy, the planetary heart centre
Towards the end of the nineteenth century the Master Djwhal Khul, head of one of the subsidiary ashrams within the major second ray ashram of the Master K.H., accepted responsibility for presenting a sequence of three new interpretations of the Ageless Wisdom teaching intended "to precede and condition the new age". D.K.'s present work and teaching is therefore hierarchical – in origin and scope.

He has also undertaken the task of training for discipleship many aspirants associated with the various ray ashrams, so relieving the Masters concerned from this necessary function and releasing them for other vitally important hierarchical activities during these years of preparation for the externalisation of the ashrams and the reappearance of the Christ.

Teaching planned by the Hierarchy
The first in the series of three interpretations of the Ageless Wisdom teachings planned by the Hierarchy and entrusted to the Tibetan Master, was given to the world through H.P. Blavatsky between the years 1875 and 1890 – fifteen years. This D.K. called the "preparatory" phase of the teaching. The second was given over a thirty year period through Alice Bailey – from 1919 to 1949. The third and final aspect in the series will be given early next century by D.K. through a prepared initiate for, as he puts it, "this series of bridging treatises between the material knowledge of man and the science of the initiates has still another phase to run."

Two major ideas
The Tibetan Master has stated that he was responsible to the Hierarchy for bringing *two major ideas* to the attention of humanity everywhere. These two are: 1) the announcement of the existence of the new group of world servers as an effective group of workers intermediate between humanity and the spiritual Hierarchy; and 2) the statement in connection with the reappearance of the Christ and the immediate work of preparation.

D.K. comments that "these constitute by far the most important aspects of the work which I have done in the service of the Hierarchy. . . . All else is of secondary importance to those two statements of spiritual fact."

In connection with the function of the new group of world servers, we are told that "all disciples and initiates are at this time members of that group, which is the focal point of the present effort being made by the Hierarchy." Through it spiritual energy from five of the ashrams is flowing:

a) the ashram of the Master K.H., particularly in regard to the work of education.

b) the ashram of the Master D.K., particularly in regard to aspirants for initiation.

c) the ashram of the Master R., particularly in regard to the reorganising and reconstruction of Europe from the economic point of view.

d) the ashram of the Master Morya, as he seeks to find, influence and direct activities in the political field throughout the planet.

e) the ashram of the Master Hilarion, as he supervises the discoveries (and their application) of the scientific movement in the world.
(See pages 54 to 59 of *Initiation, Human and Solar*)

The "newer truths" in the Tibetan's teachings

The Tibetan gives us in some detail what he considers to be the "newer truths" for which he was responsible through the teachings. He lists them as follows:

1) *The teaching on Shamballa*, including:
a) the nature of the will aspect;
b) the underlying purposes of Sanat Kumara;
c) the building of the antahkarana, the first step towards monadic consciousness and the Way of the Higher Evolution.
2) *The teaching on the New Discipleship*, including:
a) the new attitude of the Masters to their disciples;
b) information on the constitution of the Hierarchy, with its various ashrams, as the Ashram of Sanat Kumara.
c) the newer type of meditation emphasising visualisation and the use of the creative imagination, with its keynote of group fusion and of service.
3) *The teaching on the Seven Rays*, emphasising the psychological angle, because the new psychology is in the making. If esoteric teaching is eventually to be public in its presentation, it will be given out along the lines of psychology because esotericism concerns the consciousness aspect of man and God.
4) *The teaching on the new astrology*, which provides sufficient information to establish the coming astrology on a firm basis.
5) *Information about the new group of world servers*, including:

a)   recognition of the group as *intermediate* between Hierarchy and
      humanity.
b)   the nature of their work *as it influences the human soul* and, through
      the instrumentality of men and women of goodwill, *determines the*
      period in which we live.
c)   the Triangles work which embodies the network of light and goodwill
      as a channel of communication between Hierarchy and humanity.
6)   *The attempt to form an exoteric branch of the inner Ashram.*
      Instructions to this group are published in the two volumes of
      Discipleship in the New Age.
7)   *The teaching on the new world religion*, emphasising the three major
      spiritual festivals at the time of the Aries, Taurus and Gemini full
      moon periods; and the nine lesser festivals. The full moon meditation
      work is thus of first importance. It establishes a relation between the
      work of the Christ and the Buddha, leading to a broadening of human
      aspiration.

The Mystery Schools of the future.
The Tibetan Master states that at the end of this century, or soon after, the
new Mystery Schools of the future will come into existence. These will be
established by experienced, senior initiates from the ashram as the
externalisation of the Hierarchy actually gains momentum. The Schools will
be established in two groups – preparatory and advanced, for applicants and
for initiates. D.K. informs us that the *Fourteen Rules for Applicants* (given in
the book *Initiation, Human and Solar*) and the *Fourteen Rules for Disciples*
and Initiates (given in the book *The Rays and the Initiations*, the fifth and
final volume of *A Treatise on the Seven Rays*) will form the foundational
teaching for these two grades of Schools.
    The Science of Meditation and the conscious building of the antahkarana
will be the first two preliminary stages in the esoteric curriculum of all true
esoteric schools. This develops the sense of wholeness, of synthesis which is
occult vision, and a necessary faculty for those trained in the new Schools
who will be "the builders of the new world and the trainers of future public
opinion". This is the purpose of esoteric teaching – correct interpretation
and full application to the reconstruction of the world along new age lines.

In his perceptive book, *Everyone is Right – A New Look at*
Comparative Religion and its Relation to Science, Roland Peterson, a
distinguished electrical engineer, shows that references to the Ageless
Wisdom appear in many traditions and cultures.
    He continues on page 94:

The esotericists use the term *Ancient Wisdom* or *Ageless Wisdom* to describe
their teachings, which they claim to be of very early origin, of a fundamental
nature, and universally taught by esotericists in all times and places. It is
interesting to note that St. Paul, whom the esotericists regard as a high

"initiate" and therefore intrinsically aware of a portion of this teaching, speaks also of such a wisdom:

"There is, to be sure, a certain wisdom which we express among the spiritually mature. It is not a wisdom of this age, however, nor of the rulers of this age, who are men headed for destruction. No, what we utter is God's wisdom: a mysterious, a hidden wisdom. God planned it before all ages for our glory . . . Of this wisdom it is written:

Eye has not seen, ear has not heard, nor has it so much as dawned on man what God has prepared for those who love him.

Yet God has revealed this wisdom to us through the Spirit. The Spirit scrutinizes all matters, even the deep things of God. (I Cor. 2:6-10). (Quoted from *The New American Bible.*)"

The aspects of the Ageless Wisdom introduced in this book are divided into three parts. May you enjoy the discovery of this knowledge, and may it add a new dimension to your life.

Part 1
ALL IS ENERGY

Energy is a life fluid circulating throughout the entire body of the universe, giving life to even the tiniest atom.

In Part One we trace the flow from our solar system down through our planet Earth, on to humanity, and then, in greater detail, to the miracle of the energy equipment of each one of us.

As children of the universe, our energy fields are copies – in minute form – of the energies of the universe: as above so below; the macrocosm and the microcosm.

MAN
KNOW THYSELF

"So you and I are the problem and not the world because the world is a projection of ourselves, and to understand the world we must understand ourselves. Self knowledge is the beginning of wisdom and therefore the beginning of transformation and regeneration."
Krishnamurti

"Man's whole life is lived within a concentration of cosmic forces and, like a magnet, he attracts to himself conditions and powers like those he has awakened in himself."
White Eagle

"And beside this, giving all diligence, add to your faith virtue; and to virtue knowledge"
II Peter 1:5

CHAPTER 1
The Seven Rays and the Solar System

Throughout the whole of the cosmos constantly flow seven powerful, interacting rays of energy, each with its own quality, colour and sound.

These are wielded by great Lives or Entities known as the Lords of the Rays, named in the Christian bible the Seven Spirits Before the Throne (*Revelation* 1:4) who use the constellations of the zodiac and the planets as transmitting agents.

These seven streams of energy are the seven channels through which all life in the solar system flows and are the cause of the predominant characteristics or modifications of all life. There is nothing in the whole solar system which is not a part of, and has not always been a part of, one or other of the seven rays.

They are not all active at the same time, but our many civilisations, past and present, are the result of the particular qualities of the particular rays transmitted to our planet at a particular time.

We are told that They influence our planet through two time cycles. There is the annual cycle that is used for compiling astrological birth charts. We are actually referring to the qualities of the ray energies when we discuss the characteristics conveyed through the zodiacal sign of the month, such as Aries in April, Leo in August, or Capricorn in January.

The second, grander, cycle is governed by the zodiacal position of the sun at the northern hemisphere Spring equinox. The position of the sun advances slightly every year with the sun taking over two thousand years to move through just one sign of the Zodiac. This is known as the precession of the equinoxes. As the sun moves through each sign, the characteristics and modifications of the dominant rays being transmitted through that sign are active, and affect everything on our planet from the smallest atom upwards – in the mineral, vegetable, animal and human kingdoms, and indeed, all the kingdoms in nature. The full cycle takes approximately 26,000 years.

The effects on our civilisations of the dominant ray energies of each of these zodiacal signs as our sun passes through each in turn, are very evident. In religion, for instance, approximately 6000 years ago, during the Age of Taurus, the 4th Ray through *Taurus the Bull* brought to us the religion of Mithras, the bull dancers, and the bull in the Maze of Crete.

Then the 1st Ray through *Aries the Ram* brought the Jewish religion and the blowing of the ram's horn. The Bible tells us that Moses was very angry when he came down from the mountain and found his people worshipping the golden calf. As a child in Sunday school I thought that this meant the worshipping of gold as wealth. Now I know it means that the people had in fact reverted to the old religion, Mithras, established under the influence of Taurus.

Next came the Age of *Pisces, the joined fishes*, through which the 6th Ray brought us the Christian religion. The secret sign of the early Christians when they were being persecuted in Rome was the fish. This 6th ray energy of devotion brought us saints such as the beloved St. Francis, as well as the opposite – the 6th ray fanaticism of Torquemada and the Inquisition. This age is now receding and we are moving into Aquarius (7th and 5th ray), depicted as the man bearing the waterpot. The keynote of this sign is "Water of Life am I, poured forth for thirsty men". The Aquarian energy will be with us for about another 2300 years. The Water of Life is symbolised for us in the water that poured from Jesus' side when the Roman soldier pierced his side with the spear.

What caused the worship of the bull in Taurus? Not the bestial nature of humanity that took the bull as a symbol of the animal nature and deifie it, which is what the average human being who investigates the mysteries says. It is because there were subjective forces playing upon our planet as our sun passed through the sign Taurus. The lesson for man is that under the symbol of the bull he had to wrestle with the animal in himself.

Then our sun passed into Aries, the Ram, and we had the sacrifice of the lamb, showing that the *sacrifice* of the animal nature was beginning to succeed the concept of *wrestling* with the animal nature.

Then the sun passed into Pisces, the Fishes. The forces that played upon our planet at that time brought into the consciousness of man his essential duality and the link between the two parts of himself, two fishes linked by a band. This consciousness, on a large scale, began to make its impact upon the human being i.e. that he is soul *and* body. Christ came in Pisces to demonstrate to us perfectly what would be our ultimate achievement when we had linked those two together, the fish, the symbol of the second person the fish Avatar, and the fish swimming in matter, the symbol of the human being in incarnation. There you have the story.

Having traced that wonderful idealistic, evolutionary teaching down the last five to six thousand years as a result of subjective forces playing upon humanity, we are now passing into the sign Aquarius where, through symbolism of water and purification, we shall learn how *to be* the soul and not the human being. That is what is going to happen in Aquarius.
The Labours of Hercules, pages 87, 88 (Italics by author).

There are three decanates in each astrological sign. We are now in the first decanate of Aquarius which is governed by Saturn, the disciplinarian. Hence our present turmoil. Saturn restricts us and presents difficulties which, when rightly confronted and worked through, are opportunities for growth and expansion.

The second decanate of Aquarius is governed by Mercury, and out of the present time will come illumination . . . In the third decanate, governed by Venus, we have the emergence of inclusive love.
The Labours of Hercules, pages 89,90.

It is only through the relinquishing of outdated ideals that we are released into a new life, by the Spirit of Resurrection. The purpose of the destruction of worn out ideas and habits is to allow in new light and life. "No man putteth new wine into old bottles." (*Mark* 2:22) We must learn, as Moses' people did, that we cannot revert to the past. We cannot put new Aquarian wine into old Piscean bottles!

The most important event to which all people of all races and religions look forward in the New Age of Aquarius, is the reappearance of the Christ. Christians have to learn that He belongs not only to them but, known by different names in different parts of the world, to everyone (Krishna, the Bodhisattva, the Lord Maitreya, the Imam Mahdi, the Messiah). As Jesus said, "Other sheep I have, which are not of this fold." (*John* 10:16) (See Chapter 9, "The Reappearance of the Christ", page 84)

We don't know when He will come, or where or how, but "be ye also ready: for in such an hour as ye think not the Son of man cometh". (*Matthew* 24:44)

He will bring with him a number of the Masters and Initiates and we are told that many of these are going to stay and work among us on the physical plane. This is referred to as the "externalisation of the Hierarchy". They will help us restructure our whole civilisation so that we live every minute of every day according to God's plan for us and not, as one of my friends so graphically puts it, "Go to church on Sunday and kick the dog for the rest of the week".

There will have to be a more equal distribution of the world's resources. For instance, the incoming 7th ray is the ray of money and finance, and 3rd ray people (active intelligence) are best suited to deal with this. D.K. tells us that very advanced 3rd ray initiates are going to incarnate in the near future in order to change and improve our monetary system.

So, in Aquarius we will develop a new, better measure of organisation, sharing and caring.

The following excerpts are from the mass of information given by D.K. about the reappearance of the Christ and the externalisation of the Hierarchy.

Six of the Masters, as yet quite unkown to the average occult student by name, have already sought physical incarnation . . .
A Treatise on Cosmic Fire, page 758

It is only in the later stages, and when the time has come for the return into recognised physical expression of the Christ, leading to the definite restoration of the Mysteries, that certain of the senior Members of the Hierarchy will appear and take outer and recognisable physical control of world affairs.
The Externalisation of the Hierarchy, page 570

He is now waiting to descend . . . This time, He will play His part, not in obscurity as He previously did, but before the eyes of the entire world. Because of the smallness of our little planet, and because of the prevalence of the radio, television and the rapidity of communication, His part will be watched by all . . .
The Externalisation of the Hierarchy, page 607

I myself, in these difficult times, when in need of reassurance that God *is* in His Heaven and all is right with the world, turn to pages 450 to 452 of *Esoteric Healing*:

A great upheaval in all the kingdoms in nature has characterised this day and generation; a stupendous destruction of all forms of divine life and in every kingdom has been the outstanding note of this upheaval. Our modern civilisation has received a death blow from which it will never recover, but which will be recognised some day as the "blow of release" and as the signal for that which is better, new and more suitable for the evolving spirit, to make its appearance. Great and penetrating energies and their evoked forces have met in conflict which has, figuratively speaking, elevated the mineral kingdom into the skies and which has brought down fire from heaven. I am talking to you factually and not just symbolically. The bodies of men, women and children as well as animals, have been detsroyed; the forms of the vegetable kingdom and the potencies of the mineral kingdom have been disintegrated, distributed and devastated. The coherent life of all the planetary forms has been temporarily rendered incoherent. As an ancient prophecy has put it: "No true united Sound goes out from form to form, from life to life. Only a cry of pain, a demand for restitution and an invocation for relief from agony, despair and fruitless effort goes out from here to There."

All this upheaval of the "soil" of the world – spiritual, psychological and physical – all this disruption of the forms and of the familiar contours of our planetary life, *had* to take place before there could come the emergence of the Hierarchy into the public consciousness; all this had to do its work upon the souls of men before the New Age could come in, bringing with it the Restoration of the Mysteries and the rehabilitation of the peoples of the Earth. The two go together. This is one of the major points which I am seeking to make. The disruption, disintegration and the completely chaotic conditions existing for the past five hundred years within all the kingdoms of nature have at last worked their way out into paralleling physical conditions. This is good and desirable; it marks the prelude to a better building of a better world, and the construction of more adequate forms of life and of more correct human attitudes, plus a sounder orientation to reality. The best is yet to be.

Everything is being rapidly brought to the surface – the good and the bad, the desirable and the undesirable, the past and the future (for the two are one); the plough of God has nearly accomplished its work; the sword of the spirit has severed an evil past from the radiant future, and both are seen as contributory in the Eye of God; our material civilisation will be seen as giving place rapidly to a more spiritual culture; our church organisations, with their limiting and confusing theologies, will soon give place to the Hierarchy with its emerging teaching – clear, factual, intuitive and nondogmatic.

Having read this, I return with renewed confidence to my little tasks for the world, knowing that all is according to God's plan, and the best *is* yet to be.

THE RAYS
THREE MAJOR RAYS

1st Ray	Will
2nd Ray	Love-Wisdom
3rd Ray	Active Creative Intelligence

FOUR MINOR RAYS

4th Ray	Harmony through Conflict
5th Ray	Concrete Knowledge
6th Ray	Devotion
7th Ray	Ceremonial Order

THE SEVEN PLANES

or

THE SEVEN ELECTRICAL FREQUENCIES

or, as described in DK's writings,

THE CONSTITUTION OF MAN

or

THE PLANES OF CONSCIOUSNESS

or

THE BODY OF THE PLANET

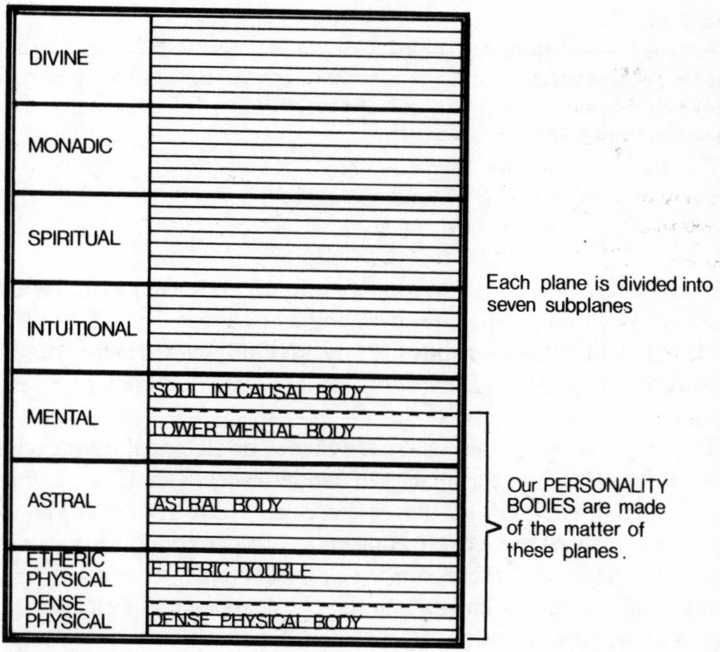

DIVINE	
MONADIC	
SPIRITUAL	
INTUITIONAL	
MENTAL	SOUL IN CAUSAL BODY
	LOWER MENTAL BODY
ASTRAL	ASTRAL BODY
ETHERIC PHYSICAL	ETHERIC DOUBLE
DENSE PHYSICAL	DENSE PHYSICAL BODY

Each plane is divided into seven subplanes

Our PERSONALITY BODIES are made of the matter of these planes.

CHART 1

CHAPTER 2
The Seven Rays and our Planet Earth

The One God shines forth as God the Father, God the Son, and God the Holy Spirit, and these three are again reflected through the Seven Spirits before the Throne, or the seven Planetary Logoi.
Initiation, Human and Solar, page 3

There are different names for the Seven Lords of the Rays:
The Seven Heavenly Men.
The seven planetary Logoi or Spirits.
The seven Lords of the Rays.
The Dyhan Chohans.
The seven Spirits before the Throne.
The seven Archangels.
The seven Logoi.
The seven Builders.
A Treatise on Cosmic Fire, page 233

It is not generally known that what we refer to as Heavenly Bodies are, literally, just that: bodies, used *as* bodies by great Cosmic Entities.

Our planet Earth is the body used by our God, known in the Bible as "the Ancient of days" (*Daniel* 7:9). In the East He is known as Sanat Kumara.

This body of our planet has seven planes or electrical frequencies, often referred to by us as planes of consciousness (see Chart 1, page 25), and the energies of the seven rays which reach us via the constellations and planets are transmitted to permeate the matter of these planes as " . . . the informing essence and active energies in all that is manifested and tangible on the physical plane as well as on the planes of divine expression". (See Chart 2, page 30)

The personal experience of incoming energy can sometimes come as a revelation, as Light did to Saint Paul on the road to Damascus. For instance, physicist Dr. Fritjof Capra recounts an experience in which he no longer merely believed in a dynamic universe, based on his intellectual understanding, but KNEW it to be so. He recalls that he was sitting by the ocean one late summer afternoon, watching the waves, feeling the rhythm of his breathing, when he suddenly experienced the whole environment as a cosmic dance – not just as a concept of physics but as an immediate, living experience:

I "saw" cascades of energy coming down from outer space, in which particles were created and destroyed in rhythmic pulses; I "saw" the atoms of the elements and those of my body participating in this cosmic dance of energy; I felt its rhythm and I "heard" its sound, and at that moment I KNEW that this was the Dance of Shiva . . .
The Tao of Physics, page 11

In our study groups it has been found that a simple exercise of the imagination helps lead to an understanding of this experience. The steps are as follows:

Step 1. Find a quiet place, compose your body comfortably, close your eyes for a few minutes and relax; then, keeping the eyes closed -
Step 2. Picture one of those famous Russian dolls which, when opened, reveals a smaller one inside and a still smaller one inside that, and so on to the last and smallest.
Step 3. Feel yourself on the moon looking at our Earth, seeing it as the astronauts saw it, a beautiful blue sphere floating serenely in space.
Step 4. Imagine that, like Fritjof Capra, your inner eye has been opened because you now see that this earth sphere is, like the Russian doll, surrounded and encompassed by other spheres (six in number) that grow progressively more splendid and bright, the outermost being the most splendid and the brightest. However, these six finer spheres, being of the fourth and higher dimensions, it follows that they interpenetrate. Consequently, on the surface of the earth they co-exist, with the finer ones extending further and further. The principle of interpenetration makes it clear that these different realms of nature are not separated in space.
Step 5. See that, pouring into and through these spheres, there is a constant stream of energies. You see their colours and you hear their sound and you are then, like Fritjof Capra and the astronauts, filled with wonder at the beauty and glory of this world of which you are a part.

What you are seeing is our planet earth with its seven "planes" being permeated by the energies of the seven rays which are transmitted through the constellations of the zodiac and the other planets of our solar system.

In her book *From the Mundane to the Magnificent*, the writer Vera Stanley Alder longed to experience these inner worlds of higher dimensions instead of just read about them. Her teacher, Raphael, adjusted her eyes, awakened a few extra brain cells, taught her how to leave her physical body and then took her into outer space from where she had a clear view of our planet and these spheres or planes surrounding it. She describes them as being like the skins of an onion, as bubbles or as the aura, and as being very beautiful.

She goes on to give a very clear, easily understood and enthralling picture of how this fits into the solar system; of the activity of the seven rays, and of how every living creature, from a rock, a plant, an insect, animal, human being and fairy, up to the great Spiritual Entities, fits into God's stupendous Plan.

Of these seven planes, or spheres, on the *divine plane*, or frequency, is the Father's House, known in the East as Shamballa; on the *buddhic or intuitional plane*, or frequency, is the Ashram of the Hierarchy, the Masters of the Wisdom, known in the Bible as "the spirits of just men made perfect"; (*Hebrews* 12:23) on the *four lowest planes*, or frequencies, the mental, astral, physical-etheric and physical-dense, humanity is still evolving. (See Chart 2 page 30).

Again, use your imagination and compare the following in terms of electrical power:

The Father's House,	to	a main power station;
The Ashram of the Masters,	to	a powerful sub-station;
The world as we know it, where humanity is still evolving,	to	four lower feeder stations all of lesser voltage.

Or, in modern business terms, compare

the Father and Lords of the Rays	to	the Chairman and the Board of Governors;
the Hierarchy of Masters,	to	the Board of Directors;
the New Group of World Servers and people of goodwill,	to	junior executives and all other personnel.

(See Chart 3, page 31)

It is interesting to note here that D.K. tells us humanity is so far advanced that, for the first time in the history of our evolution, there is within us at these lower levels a group capable of carrying out what might be termed a reflection of some of the Hierarchy's work. This task is to work out God's Plan for humanity and the planet earth. This group, which he has named "The New Group of World Servers", is characterised by a non-sectarian spirit, unwavering goodwill and an intelligent commitment to right human relations. (Marilyn Ferguson has written an excellent book, *The Aquarian Conspiracy*, about this Group of New Age World Servers.) It does not, as in the past, consist of a few large organisations, but rather of numerous small organisms spread all over the world on every continent and in every nation, working in medicine, psychiatry, education, religion, politics, finance and science. Most of these workers are unaware of the New Group of World Servers or of their own particular involvement in it, but all are intent on making our world a better place to live in, thereby helping to work out God's Plan for planet Earth.

THE BODY OF THE PLANET WITH ITS SEVEN PLANES OR ELECTRICAL FREQUENCIES.

DIVINE	Here in THE FATHER'S HOUSE or SHAMBALLA, THE ASHRAM of SANAT KUMARA	dwells THE FATHER THE ANCIENT OF DAYS or SANAT KUMARA	together with THE SEVEN SPIRITS BEFORE THE THRONE who are THE LORDS OF THE SEVEN RAYS .
MONADIC	THE DIVINE SPARKS (MONADS) remain here .		
SPIRITUAL or **ATMIC**	We are capable of working with this very high frequency only on the later stages of the return to THE FATHER'S HOUSE .		
BUDDHIC or **INTUITIONAL**	Here in THE ASHRAM of THE MASTERS of THE WISDOM .	dwell THE SPIRITS OF JUST MEN MADE PERFECT who are . THE HIERARCHY , THE MASTERS OF THE WISDOM.	
MENTAL	HIGHER MENTAL ; also known as THE SOUL , CAUSAL or EGOIC PLANE or LEVEL . LOWER MENTAL		
ASTRAL			
PHYSICAL **ETHERIC**			
PHYSICAL **DENSE**			

THE LOWER PLANES ON WHICH HUMANITY IS STILL EVOLVING .

CHART 2

		POWER or ELECTRICAL FREQUENCIES	MODERN BUSINESS TERMS
DIVINE	From here 'THE FATHER' watches over us and THE LORDS OF THE RAYS direct on to the planet, the 7 RAYS	MAIN POWER STATION	THE CHAIRMAN and THE BOARD of GOVERNORS
MONADIC			
SPIRITUAL			
BUDDHIC or INTUITIONAL	From here THE HIERARCHY works for GOD'S PLAN ON EARTH	POWERFUL SUBSTATION	THE BOARD OF DIRECTORS
HIGHER MENTAL			
LOWER MENTAL			
ASTRAL	Four lower PLANES on which HUMANITY is at present evolving	Four lower FREQUENCIES or FEEDER STATIONS	JUNIOR EXECUTIVES and all other PERSONNEL
PHYSICAL ETHERIC			
PHYSICAL DENSE			

CHART 3

CHAPTER 3
The Evolution of Humanity

God made man in his own image – ". . . in him we live, and move, and have
our being . . ."
Acts 17:28

INDIVIDUALISATION is the emergence of the soul upon the path of outgoing,
through the medium of a form. Thus through the use of a form, expression in
the three worlds becomes possible.
Esoteric Psychology Vol. II, page 208.

Man's bodies are made of the substance of planet Earth, for the conditions
of planet Earth.

You will notice that the chart of the Constitution of Man (see Chart 1)
is also the chart of the body of the planet, for we do indeed "live and
move and have our being" in Him. He did indeed make us "in His own
image". To suit the conditions of His planet Earth, we are made from
the substance of all the planes of His planet Earth. Never forget that
these are planes of consciousness or electrical frequencies. As above,
so below.
  D.K. tells us that the tale of the prodigal son as told in the New
Testament in *Luke* 15:11-32, is the story of the evolution of humanity.

But we must remember that, when Christ was relating this story, He made it
abundantly clear that there was no impulse to return until the pilgrim in the
far country had come to himself or to his senses, as a result of satisfied
desire, through riotous living. This was followed by consequent satiety and
loss of contentment, and then by a period of intense suffering, which broke
his will to wander or to desire. (*This is a description of the classic spiritual
awakening*.) A study of this story will be found revealing. In no Scripture is
the sequence of events (as they deal with the pilgrim's existence and life in a
far country and his return) so concisely or so beautifully treated. Seek out
your Bibles, and study this tale, and read for yourselves the pilgrim's way.
Esoteric Psychology Vol.II, pages 165, 166

So the Pilgrim (humanity) left the Father's House (on the divine plane), went "down" (*in*volution; see chart 4, overleaf) through denser and denser frequencies to the "far country" (the dense physical plane) and there developed a physical body, and on the continent of Lemuria, approximately 18 million years ago, individualised.

This means that the physical body had developed sufficiently to be fit for being "taken over" and used by the soul on the path of return to the Father's House (*e*volution).

On this evolutionary path back to the Father's House, humanity, on the astral emotional plane and on the continent of Atlantis, developed the astral or emotional body.

Humanity is now emerging, in the Aryan race, into mental consciousness, but most of us are still Atlantean in consciousness, that is, we are emotionally polarised. Of our minds, Lyall Watson says, "It is as if God had given us a large mansion and we are only using the service flat in the basement". Incidentally, there are Aryans of every colour in every race on every continent. They are not only white, and in the West, as Hitler would have had us believe.

As of now, this is the picture:

Those who are Lemurian in consciousness (3rd root race)
A very small remnant of humanity, with their consciousness centred in the five senses.

Those who are Atlantean in consciousness (4th root race)
Most of mankind – with consciousness still polarised in the astral emotional body.

Those who are Aryan in consciousness (5th root race)
The many who are emerging into mental consciousness. A very small number of the *6th root race* are already with us, and they will increase in number until, thousands of years hence, they will supersede the 5th root race. In the 6th root race, intuition will show real and general signs of existing.

Those who are Perfected Men – Masters of the Wisdom
A very, very few have reached this stage. The reading public is becoming familiar with the names of some of these perfected men, for instance, the Masters Morya, Maitreya, Koot Hoomi, Djwhal Khul, and Rakoczi (who is also known as the Comte de St. Germain).

There are seven root races in a world period. We are now in the fifth, co-existing with some of the fourth, a few remnants of the third and the first few of the sixth. It will be noted that although each race gives birth to the succeeding race, the two will overlap in time, co-existing for many ages. The Seventh root race, millions of years hence, will demonstrate Love in Activity.

We must never forget that evolution is the growth of consciousness. The highest points of evolution are:

in the mineral kingdom	–	the brilliance of crystals and gemstones;
in the plant kingdom	–	the perfume of the flowers;
in the animal kingdom	–	the affection of a domesticated animal for its owner;
in humanity	–	radiation.

We can indeed, and *in fact*, radiate more light. We can indeed, and *in fact*, lighten our bodies. By aspiring to God, by studying and meditating, by serving humanity and all life on the planet, we can *in fact* throw out the heavy atoms from our bodies and draw in lighter ones thus becoming brighter lights in the world, radiating helpful thoughts, emotions and actions. (In this context *heavy* and *light* are used in the esoteric sense, and not in the sense used in physical science.)

As the favourite hymn of my childhood puts it: "Jesus bids us shine, with a pure clear light, like a little candle burning in the night; In this world is darkness, so we must shine, you in your small corner and I in mine."

Jesus said: "Ye are the light of the world . . . Let your light so shine before men . . ."
Matthew 5:14-16

THE SEVEN PLANES
or
THE PLANES OF CONSCIOUSNESS

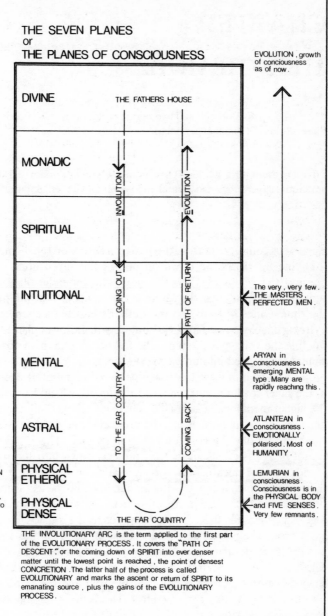

EVOLUTION , growth of conciousness as of now .

DIVINE — THE FATHERS HOUSE

MONADIC

SPIRITUAL

INTUITIONAL

The very , very few . THE MASTERS , PERFECTED MEN .

MENTAL

ARYAN in consciousness , emerging MENTAL type . Many are rapidly reaching this .

ASTRAL

ATLANTEAN in consciousness . EMOTIONALLY polarised . Most of HUMANITY .

PHYSICAL ETHERIC

PHYSICAL DENSE

LEMURIAN in consciousness . Consciousness is in the PHYSICAL BODY and FIVE SENSES . Very few remnants .

INVOLUTION

GOING OUT

TO THE FAR COUNTRY

EVOLUTION

PATH OF RETURN

COMING BACK

THE FAR COUNTRY

On the LEMURIAN continent man individualised 18 million years ago , and turned back to THE FATHER'S HOUSE .

THE INVOLUTIONARY ARC is the term applied to the first part of the EVOLUTIONARY PROCESS . It covers the "PATH OF DESCENT ", or the coming down of SPIRIT into ever denser matter until the lowest point is reached , the point of densest CONCRETION . The latter half of the process is called EVOLUTIONARY and marks the ascent or return of SPIRIT to its emanating source , plus the gains of the EVOLUTIONARY PROCESS .

CHART 4

CHAPTER 4
Incarnation

. . . the process whereby the Ego or soul draws to itself the form, utilising for
that purpose a mental unit and two permanent atoms, thus anchoring itself in
three worlds of human experience.
Esoteric Psychology Vol.II, page 313

What are these three worlds? They are the worlds of physical existence,
emotional experience, and mental endeavour and understanding.

Each of us comes forth from the Father's House on the divine plane, as
a Divine Spark, borne down on one of the seven great streams of
energy (the seven rays) to the next, the monadic plane, there to
remain, known to us as the Monad, for the aeons that will pass before
the time comes to return to the Father's House (see Chart 5 p. 42).

Being unable to come in direct contact with the lower planes – we could
say that the voltage is too high (the full power of a main power station
cannot be plugged into an electric kettle in the kitchen!) – the Monad
projects down into these lower worlds a cord of pulsating energy known
as the silver cord, the sutratma, or Life thread, which descends as far as
the higher mental or causal plane. There it anchors itself (in triple form)
and remains for millions of years in an envelope made of the matter of the
causal plane, like the yoke of an egg in its shell. This is *the soul in the
causal body*. The soul in its turn projects down into the three lower
worlds, at each incarnation, a continuation of the silver cord bearing
three focal points of energy – the mental unit and the astral and physical
permanent atoms, which are of sufficient power to attract and hold
together coherently the substance required by the soul to create a form of
expression. The mental unit attracts to itself the fire of the mental plane
and the astral permanent atom wraps around this the mists of the astral.
These are then encased in the etheric double, which is a golden web,
shaped according to the decision of the soul and the Lords of Karma
(small or large, weak or strong, etc.). This is the mould on to which the
physical body is later built in the mother's womb.

Geoffrey Hodson, clairvoyant and author, includes the following
fascinating description on pages 85 and 86 of his book *The Miracle of
Birth*:

Clairvoyantly examined, the prenatal etheric mould, which appears very soon after conception, resembles a baby body built of etheric matter, somewhat self-luminous, vibrating slightly, a living being, the etheric projection of the Archetype as modified by karma.

Within the etheric mould there is to be seen, in terms of flowing energy or lines of force, each on its own wave length, a sketch plan of the whole body. Every type of tissue-to-be is represented, differing from other types because the energy of which it is an end-product is itself on another frequency. Thus the bony structure, muscular, and vascular tissues, the nerves, the brain, and other substances are all represented in the etheric mould by currents of energy on specific frequencies.

Karmic deficiencies, which are to work out in terms of malformation, weakness, and disease, are presented in the mould by dissonances or even breaks in the particular lines of force along and according to which the tissues are built.

. . the whole body – as also the solar system – can be expressed in terms of frequency, each type of tissue and each organ having its own wave length, note, and color, these in their turn varying in states of health and disease. In perfect health, every part is in tune and the chord of the human body perfectly harmonized. In ill-health, the opposite exists; there is a dissonance at some part or other, the chord is out of tune.

There are two controlling factors in the formation of these bodies. The first is the matter of the planes which is impregnated with the energies of the seven rays. The second is karma which is carried over from previous incarnations.

The influences of the rays in the matter of the three bodies of the personality are different in each incarnation according to what is needed to enable an individual to experience and grow in consciousness.

For instance:

the mental body	could be 1st, 4th or 5th ray;
the astral body	could be 2nd or 6th ray;
the physical body	could be 3rd or 7th ray;
the personality	could be any of these.

The time of birth is also decided by the soul and the Lords of Karma, because anything born in a moment of time is part of the energies of that moment. A child is born when the rays flowing from the heavens are in harmony with his karmic pattern. Hence the interest in the astrological chart . . . In other words, it is the energies of the rays transmitted by the constellations of the zodiac and by the planets in our horoscopes, plus the particular ray energies impregnating the atoms gathered from each plane (in order to compose our "bodies"), that determine and qualify our "equipment" in each incarnation.

D.K. points out that if we are to understand an individual's Path of Life by studying his astrological indications:

It is necessary . . . to regard the sun sign into which a man is born, as indicative of his personality trends, and as embodying the characteristics which he has inherited from the past, but to regard the rising sign as holding within it the indications of the way that a man's soul would have him go. *Glamour: A World Problem*, pages 119/120

Do not allow the seeds of past negative tendencies to sprout by fertilizing them with evil actions now. The horoscope reveals the unalterable past and the challenge of the probable future. However, although we are influenced by the rays flowing from the heavens, we need not be *ruled* by them. Each of us instigated the causes of the effects now prevalent in our lives, and, if we created any limitations by our own past actions we can overcome them by our own present use of the spiritual resources available to us. The Zen Buddhists have a saying, "The time is *now*, the place is *here*". The present is the vital time to wipe out past negative karma and build for future positive karma. The indications of the stars at our birth do not mean that we are prisoners of our past but seek to arouse us to be free from limitation. A man can be free if he so wills, but the freedom depends not on outer but on inner victories.

It is a great pity that astrology, which, according to the Ageless Wisdom, was a great science, and will again be great in the future, has been brought into disrepute by some foolish people and some outright charlatans.

When, at the end of each incarnation, the soul "sounds the note" that recalls its expression (the personality), the mental unit and the two permanent atoms are withdrawn (wrapped in the incredibly beautiful life web) into the causal body, there to remain until needed again at the next descent into incarnation. (For more details about the "life web", read *A Treatise on Cosmic Fire*, page 98) The mental unit and the two permanent atoms contain the tendencies of the lower personality. The gains made by way of spiritual growth during each incarnation are returned to the soul itself in the form of light. One could call this interest returned on investment. This is symbolised for us in the masonic ritual as the "bricks for the Temple in Heaven" – the Temple not built by hands.

Thus the matter of each plane is scattered and regathered again and again, life after life. So what we call birth is simply the taking on of temporary mental, astral and physical bodies. What we call death is simply the discarding of these bodies.

The *sutratma* is the eastern name for the *silver cord* of the Bible. A third name is the *life line*. This is a current of pulsating energy that enters the body at birth and leaves it at death, through the centre at the top of the head.

It is a dual current of life and consciousness threads, which anchors the life thread in the heart and the consciousness thread in the head.

This sutratma is the current or cord that, no matter how far he travels, keeps an astral traveller attached to his physical body.

The consciousness thread can be withdrawn for longer or shorter periods and yet the body can still function. This is the cause of senility, of some forms of epilepsy, and of fainting. When the body is dying, the life thread leaves the heart, travels up the sushumna (the subjective channel in the spine), joins the consciousness thread in the head and together they leave via the sutratma or silver cord, which is then "cut" behind them. This is equivalent to "switching off the main electrical circuit". The physical body, without this energising current, falls apart – disintegrates into its component parts. "Ashes to ashes and dust to dust."

As the Bible says, "Or ever the silver cord be loosed, or the golden bowl be broken . . ." (*Ecclesiastes* 12:6) (The golden bowl being the etheric double.)

After the death of the physical body, the etheric body is still "alive" with the slow-life of its own plane matter and tries to stay "alive" by drawing energy from any available source – particularly from the disintegrating physical body. It also draws energy from the mourners and that is why flowers and candles are placed around a bier. They supply etheric energy. This explains too the "wraith" of the church-yard, which is the slowly disintegrating etheric double. Cremation, therefore, is desirable for two reasons. Firstly, it returns the matter of the physical and etheric bodies at once to their own spheres and leaves a person free on the astral plane. Secondly, burying a diseased body in the earth pollutes the earth with that disease.

So, as incarnation succeeds incarnation, the evolution of conscious-ness proceeds, until, at the fourth initiation, the crucifixion (better described as the renunciation because, at that moment all ties with the lower planes are renounced), the new spiritualised person discards the causal envelope or body and rises to the next plane, the buddhic or intuitional, there to begin the next stage in the return to the Father's House. This is all so far ahead in our future that it will not be considered here. At our present stage of evolution (of our consciousness) the soul is our goal: first, alignment, and then integration with the soul in the causal body on the causal plane. (See Chart 1, page 25)

The discarding of the causal body and withdrawal of the Spirit is described in the Jewish religion as "the destruction of the Temple of Solomon through the withdrawal of the Shekinah."

Each person in the human family, while in physical plane "incarnation", has a Guardian Angel or deva. Deva is the eastern word for angel.

It is interesting to note here that, as the soul grows in brightness through our efforts, so too does the brightness of the Guardian Angel. Angels (devas) are of varied colours. From amongst the white ones ". . are gathered the guardian angels of the race when in physical plane incarnation." (*A Treatise on Cosmic Fire*, page 913).

. . .the Guardian Angel . . . which walks with each human being from the moment of birth until death, embodying as much of the available light as the man – at any given moment upon the path of evolution – can use and express.
Esoteric Psychology, Vol II, page 357.

We also have with us the Dweller on the Threshold:

The dweller can be defined as the sum total of the forces of the lower nature as expressed in the personality . . .
Esoteric Psychology Vol II, page 312.

The Dweller on the Threshold is oft regarded as a disaster, as a horror to be avoided, and as a final and culminating evil. I would here remind you, nevertheless, that the Dweller is "one who stands before the gate of God", who dwells in the shadow of the portal of initiation, and who faces the Angel of the Presence open-eyed, as the ancient Scriptures call it. The Dweller can be defined as the sum total of the forces of the lower nature as expressed in the personality, prior to illumination, to inspiration and to initiation. The personality *per se*, is, at this stage, exceedingly potent, and the Dweller embodies all the psychic and mental forces which, down the ages, have been unfolded in a man and nurtured with care. It can be looked upon as the potency of the threefold material form, prior to its conscious cooperation and dedication to the life of the soul and to the service of the Hierarchy, of God, and of humanity.
Esoteric Psychology, Vol.II, page 312

Isn't this beautifully neat and just? Within ourselves and in our own space is everything we need in order to deal with life and to grow in spirit. A wonderfully constructed infrastructure of electrical frequencies/energies/bodies. On our right, to guide us, is a reflection of all the light we have managed to gather through the ages, and on our left – to be dealt with and transmuted – are the personality tendencies (transmutation is the raising of energy from a lower to a higher level). So we do indeed control our own destiny. Each of us is indeed the captain of our own ship!

But, of course, in this game of life the joker in the pack is *Free Will!* How are we going to use our free will to steer our ship? Into the personality traits of the Dweller, or upwards to the soul, guided by our Guardian Angel?

Two excellent books are recommended here. The first, *The Miracle of Birth*, by Geoffrey Hodson, is an account of the growth of the human foetus from the fourth month of pregnancy as seen by a trained clairvoyant. The second, *Testimony of Light*, by Helen Greaves, is an account of life on the astral plane after "death", received telepathically by the author. (See also Chapter 6, "The Subtle Bodies of Man").

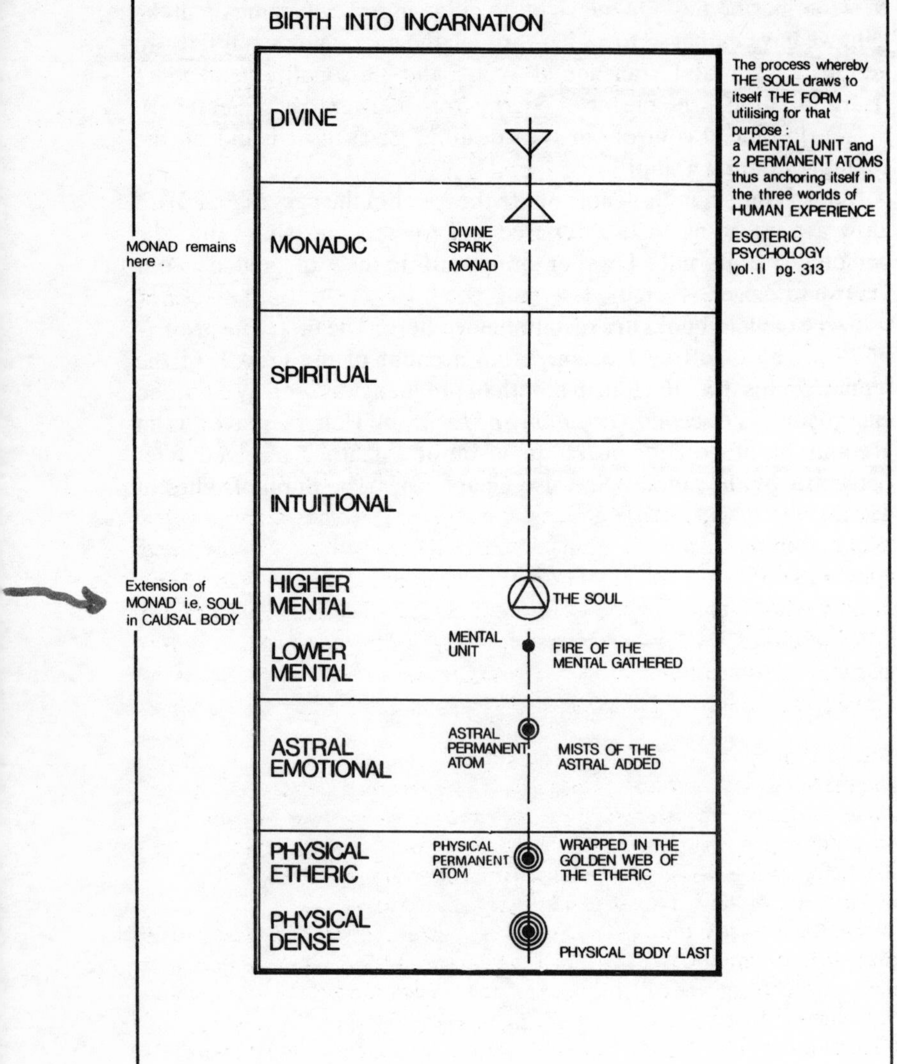

BIRTH INTO INCARNATION

The process whereby
THE SOUL draws to
itself THE FORM ,
utilising for that
purpose :
a MENTAL UNIT and
2 PERMANENT ATOMS
thus anchoring itself in
the three worlds of
HUMAN EXPERIENCE

ESOTERIC
PSYCHOLOGY
vol. II pg. 313

MONAD remains
here .

Extension of
MONAD i.e. SOUL
in CAUSAL BODY

DIVINE

MONADIC   DIVINE
                   SPARK
                   MONAD

SPIRITUAL

INTUITIONAL

**HIGHER
MENTAL**   THE SOUL

**LOWER
MENTAL**   MENTAL   FIRE OF THE
                   UNIT   MENTAL GATHERED

**ASTRAL
EMOTIONAL**   ASTRAL   MISTS OF THE
                   PERMANENT ASTRAL ADDED
                   ATOM

**PHYSICAL
ETHERIC**   PHYSICAL WRAPPED IN THE
                   PERMANENT GOLDEN WEB OF
                   ATOM   THE ETHERIC

**PHYSICAL
DENSE**   PHYSICAL BODY LAST

CHART 5

CHAPTER 5
Evolutionary Sequence and the Chakras

". . . Christ in you, the hope of Glory." (*Colossians 1:27*)

"Till we all come in the unity of the faith, and of the knowledge of the Son of God, unto a perfect man, unto the measure of the stature of the fulness of Christ."
(*Ephesians 4:13*)

A chakra or force centre, is a junction on the surface of the etheric double where many strands of energy meet and pass one another – like major railway junctions. They receive and transmit energy, and appear as dull, scarcely moving discs in the undeveloped person, but as rapidly whirling suns in the developed person. These centres are not *physical things*. They are whirlpools of force that swirl etheric, astral and mental matter into activity. The action being rotary, the result, as seen clairvoyantly, is a circular effect, like a fiery wheel.

The Science of the Centres is yet in its infancy, as is the Science of the Rays and the Science of Astrology. But much is being learned and developed along these three lines and when the present barriers are down and true scientific investigation is instituted along these lines, a new era will begin for the human being. These three sciences will constitute the three major departments of the Science of Psychology in the New Age. . . .
Where the lines of force cross and recross, . . . there are formed five areas up the spinal column and two in the head where the energies are more potent than elsewhere, because more concentrated. Thus you have the appearance of the major centres. Throughout the entire body, these crossings and recrossings occur and so the equipment of energy centres is brought into being:
1. Where the lines of force cross 21 times, a major centre is found. Of these there are seven.
2. Where they cross 14 times, you have the appearance of the minor centres.
3. Where they cross 7 times, you have tiny centres and of these minute centres there are many hundreds.
Esoteric Psychology, Vol II, pages 479, 592

Thus there are seven major chakras: five in the spine and two in the head (see Chart 6, page 53). The many smaller ones located all over the body, probably correspond to the acupuncture points of Chinese medicine.

The chakras are duplicated in the astral and mental bodies and are externalised in the endocrine glands of the physical body. Eventually, when we are all perfect, as we are meant to become, all these chakras and glands will be in perfect alignment and thus present clear channels for energies sent down from the soul. In other words, "the soul in perfect control".

D.K. tells us in *Esoteric Healing*, page 621 that The Christ is the first one of the human race ever to have reached this stage of perfect alignment which produced a "perfect man" – physically perfect, emotionally stable and mentally controlled. By this alignment He demonstrated how the spiritual man can live perfectly in a perfect human body in the physical world. This is the promise and example held out to us: that we too can perfectly express divine purpose.

These centres vary in activity according to the evolutionary status of the individual. In some people certain centres are "awake" and in others the same centres may be relatively quiescent. In some people, the solar plexus centre will be active or dominant, in others the heart, in still others the throat. In very few, as yet, is the head centre active. Speaking generally, in less evolved people the three centres below the diaphragm are dominant, but the centres above the diaphragm are "asleep".

In the average person the throat centre is beginning to make itself felt with the head and heart centres still asleep. In the highly evolved human being both the heart and the head centres are making their vibration felt, heart or head depending on the specific ray type, and quality of the emotional and mental consciousness.

In direct proportion, then, to the development of the person, these force centres become alive and dominant and, according to their aliveness, various types of activity make their presence felt. The centres below the diaphragm govern both the physical life of the material form and the lower psychic life found in both humans and in animals. Those above the diaphragm relate to the intellectual and spiritual life.

In *Esoteric Healing*, page 138, D.K. encourages his readers as follows: "The objective before the initiate is to have every centre in the etheric body responsive to the ray energy of the soul and with all the other ray energies subsidiary to it."

The eminent physician, Dr Brugh Joy, in his book *Joy's Way*, explains how he located chakras clairvoyantly and worked with them before ever reading about them or hearing them named. He had observed that the emanations from the chakras of a normal healthy person feel cylindrical, those of a more spiritual person cone shaped, and that the crown chakra of a very highly spiritual person changed from being cone shaped to be like a plume. This last is particularly interesting, because in some ancient South American cultures the initiates or spiritual leaders were known as the "plumed serpents".

Dr. Joy started this research while doing routine examinations as a practising physician. He would tell the patient to close his or her eyes, close his own, and proceed to pass his hands backwards and forwards some distance above the patient. One of them opened her eyes and asked him if he was one of those doctors who practised magic! He said it was very embarrassing when a medical colleague walked in and found him working at this "magic" with his eyes closed, out in space, and his hands moving several feet above the body on the examination table.

He found the names of these energy centres when looking through some books in a bookshop and was so delighted that he shattered the normal quiet of the shop by shouting out aloud, "My God, I have located the chakras!"

As a scientist he was particularly pleased that he had detected these before having any information on them, and therefore no preconceived ideas, and because later he found literature confusing, because the sources contradicted one another.

As these "sources" must have been clairvoyants, then their accounts could very well seem contradictory, because there are many different kinds and grades of clairvoyance, all leading eventually in the evolutionary sequence to the inclusive spiritual telepathy of the Adept. In other words, their accounts are different because they are seeing with different eyes – for instance some with etheric and some with astral sight, as explained in chapter 6. To further complicate the matter, in the etheric body the chakras are placed on the surface along the spinal column as in chart 6, page 53, but the astral force centres extend in quite a different direction and are frequently inside the body although one part is always coincident with its corresponding etheric centre.

The well known theosophical writer, Bishop Leadbeater, published many illustrated books on esoteric subjects at the beginning of this century. Being an astral clairvoyant, in his charts he always placed the chakras in the front of the body as in chart 7, page 54, and, omitting the sacral centre, replaced it with the spleen. There is no question about Bishop Leadbeater's high attainment on the Path or the value of his many books, but it is difficult for us to understand why he made this substitution. The role of the spleen centre is to supply vital prana and is not directly related to those energies which sweep man into spirituality by way of the seven major chakras as seen in chart 6. These include the sacral centre. Another clairvoyant theosophist, Phoebe Bendit, used to help her husband, the psychiatrist Dr Lawrence J Bendit, with his difficult cases by describing to him the condition of the chakras as looking like open and healthy convolvulus flowers or droopy, unhealthy ones. This husband and wife team wrote some very good books.

The highly gifted Diane, in chapter IV of *Breakthrough to Creativity* by Shafica Karagulla, describes the chakras themselves as "major vortices of force", made up of "spiral cones of these energies". (At the time of going to press an important sequel to this book was published by Shafica Karagulla and Dora van Gelder Kunz, *The Chakras and the Human Energy Fields*, in which it is stated that Mrs. Kunz was the sensitive called "Diane" and "DVG" in *Breakthrough to Creativity*. She was born with exceptional clairvoyant abilities, and can see not only the etheric or vital body and the major chakras in it, but also the astral body and the mental body as well as their corresponding chakras. Apart from her remarkable work with Dr. Karagulla on correlating her observations with medical case histories, she collaborated with other physicians in diagnosing difficult or ambiguous medical cases. We recommend this book highly to any student interested in the constitution of man, and to all interested in healing.)

The apparent effect of the movement of the energies emitted from the centres, like the spokes of a wheel, divides them into segments like the petals of a flower. In Hindu literature these are referred to as petals and the numbers in chart 7 denote the numbers of these petals in each centre.

Dr. Carl Jung commented that the chakras are gateways to consciousness in man.

The fiery strands of the etheric body underlie all the nerves in the physical body, and the centres, although of subtle matter, are directly related to the endocrine glands in the physical body. Knowledge of the etheric body is very important in healing and, for anyone interested in healing, David V. Tansley's books contain much useful information.

There are protective etheric webs between the centres in the etheric spine which permit the movement of energies from one "plane" or frequency to another only through the two top levels. They serve as filters and act as a barrier to the entry of any lower astral forces. The flow of energies up the subjective centre of the spinal column is depicted for us in the medical caduceus (the intertwined snakes around a central pole) and in the Kabbala, or Tree of Life, by the roots, crown and trunk with branches on either side.

The Cosmic Law of Dual Manifestation

Etheric energies exist in two polarities. These are known

in the West	as	*integration* *receptive and magnetic*	*self-assertion* *expressive and dynamic*
in China	as	*Yin*	*Yang*
in the East	as	*Pingala*	*Ida*
generally	as	*female*	*male*
by scientists	as acting on	*the right side of the brain*	*the left side of the brain.*

There is currently much interest in the development of the right side of the brain because of a growing feeling that there is a need, in our civilisation, for the better balancing of these elements yin and yang. For example, Esme Wynne-Tyson in *The Philosophy of Compassion* makes a plea for "the return of the goddess"; Carl Jung, in his *Answer To Job*, warns man that everything depends on whether he can temper his will with the spirit of love and wisdom.

Many prominent women of our time have written about this imbalance of the dual elements yin and yang:

"Women hold up half the sky", says a Chinese proverb. Women represent the greatest single force for political renewal in a civilization thoroughly out of balance. Just as individuals are enriched by developing both the masculine and feminine sides of the self (independence and nurturance, intellect and intuition), so the society is benefiting from a change in the balance of power between the sexes.

The power of women is the powder keg of our time. As women enlarge their influence in policymaking and government, their yin perspective will push out the boundaries of the old yang paradigm. Women are neurologically more flexible than men, and they have had cultural permission to be more intuitive, sensitive, feeling. Their natural milieu has been complexity, change, nurturance, affiliation, a more fluid sense of time. *The Aquarian Conspiracy*, page 226. Marilyn Ferguson

Man is no better than the woman, nor woman than the man. Yet many thousands regard women as embodying that which is evil and that which is the basis of temptation. But God has from the beginning ordained that men

and women should meet each other's needs and act as complements to each other.
Esoteric Psychology, Vol I, page 304.

The New Epoch requires spiritual cognition. The New Epoch must manifest due respect to the Mother of the World, to the Feminine Element. "The bird of the spirit of Humanity cannot fly with only one wing" – these are the words of Vivekananda, who meant to affirm the great significance of the Feminine Principle.
Helena Roerich

On the higher planes of Being everything is created by thought. But for the fulfilment of these thoughtforms, there must be the two Elements united by Cosmic Love. There is a great deal of misunderstanding surrounding the fundamental concept of the dual Element. Religions are to blame for this, and especially Christianity. The church profaned the greatest Cosmic Mystery by demeaning marriage and degrading the woman, by its contempt of love and its vows of celibacy and monasticism, and by declaring this spiritual impoverishment to be the highest achievement of the human spirit. This frightful fanaticism brought about terrible consequences, among which the mortification of the flesh was and is not the worst. Let us recall the criminal hypocrisy, the dreadful sexual perversions and crimes that resulted from these prohibitions and condemnations, which are completely against Cosmic Law.
Helena Roerich

In the future reconstruction of the World, on the higher spheres there will not be access for those who do not understand equilibrium. Long incarnations will be necessary to study how to create cosmic equilibrium. Indeed, empires have fallen, nations have fallen, countries have been destroyed, all because the greatest question, that of equilibrium, has been reduced to nothing. Therefore it is so important to affirm the significance of the feminine principle. Precisely, not in the household measuring scale, but in that of the state. If the planet is retained, then future countries will flourish only through equilibrium. We will even admit a preponderance on the side of the feminine principle, because the conflict will be very intense. Indeed, Councils of Ministers will have to include women. Woman, who gives life to a people, must also have a voice in the making of its destiny. Woman must have the right of voice. If woman were accepted, as was ordained, the World would be quite differently impregnated. Thus, only affirmation of the law of Existence can restore the order of man.
Helena Roerich

In the growth of the women's movement and the current interest shown in the development of the right side of the brain, we have hope for a better understanding of this law of cosmic equilibrium, the balance of the two elements, yin and yang.

Professor Raymond Dart, the eminent palaeontologist, carried a small object in his left pocket with which he exercised his left hand with a view to developing the right side of his brain.

In each of us these opposites veer from one side to the other through successive incarnations. Even the polarity of our planet Earth shifts from time to time.

The ultimate aim of evolution is to bring these opposites into a position of polarity – a state that may only be achieved in millions of years of growth; although there is the potential to be in polarity, we are a long, long way from that ideal state, which is depicted for us symbolically as the *crowned* hermaphrodite. This is in no way connected with the modern "gay" movement as is explained on page 16 of *A Compilation on Sex* published by the Lucis Press, and by Dion Fortune in *The Esoteric Philosophy of Love and Marriage*. I strongly recommend these books to any reader confused by the sexual problems of our times.

Sex is a radiating (positive), magnetising (negative) electrical activity, divine in origin and nature and is to be revered as sacred. It is a God-given function, an expression of the Law of Attraction and connected to the balancing of the forces in all departments of nature: the Cosmic Law of Dual Manifestation.

In the human kingdom this balancing is between the male stimulating force (positive) and the female latent energy (negative) functioning in polarity. Life must flow in a circuit and for so doing the positive and negative poles of manifestations are necessary.

In homosexuality, male or female, two streams of the same force are called forth, and naturally find no channels of return as the vehicles are both of the same polarity, and this is against the Cosmic Law of Dual Manifestation. These forces *could* then be available for dubious magical purposes and have so been used in the mysteries of all races and ages in periods of decay, as the records of ethnologists and historians show. This explains the tragic abuse of young boys foully made use of in black occultism.

It disturbs me to read, in newspapers and magazines, the invitations to classes, workshops and seminars involving kundalini, or kundalini and sexual energies. Probably the advertisers are as innocently ignorant and as eager for enlightenment as the pupils they hope to attract. However, and this is a serious warning (see KUNDALINI in glossary), these fires can only safely be approached, alas, *after* enlightenment. Before that they can be very dangerous and are best left severely alone.

D.K., on page 699 of *The Externalisation of the Hierarchy*, and page 49 of *A Compilation on Sex* explains the importance and the divinity of sex in our lives:

(When the Masters incarnate,) they will take modern life and what it means and will proceed to demonstrate how that life (the normal product of the evolutionary process) can be lived divinely; They will express the highest ideal of marriage (I would here remind you that many of the Masters are married and have raised families). . . .

However, he is explicit in *A Treatise on Cosmic Fire* page 135, under the heading "Kundalini and the Three Triangles", that the sexual energies have *no place in the magical work of transmutation and enlightenment of the white occultist or white magician:*

It is not my intention to lay any stress on the sex side of this subject, for these are organs with which the occultist has nothing to do. I will not therefore enumerate them in detail. I would only point out that in the transference of the fire at the base of the spine and the turning of the attention to the two higher triangles comes the redemption of man.

The triangle omitted consists of the three lower centres:
i) a point at the base of the spine; ii) and iii) the two major sex organs in the male, or the two major sex organs in the female.

In spiritual development, the energies of the chakras below the diaphragm are raised to the chakras above the diaphragm:

from	the solar plexus (feeling, emotion: "gut level"),	to	the heart (love);
from	the sacral (creation of physical bodies),	to	the throat (creative action);
from	the base of the spine (Mother Earth: matter),	to	the ajna centre between the eyebrows (symbolizing the work of at-one-ing soul and body).

Nevertheless, it remains a fact that when the energies, latent at the base of the spine, are carried to the head and are brought (via the solar plexus, that clearing house of energy, and the medulla oblongata) to the centre between the eyebrows, then the personality, the matter aspect, reaches its apotheosis . . . *A Treatise on White Magic*, page 192

Apart from this, the powerful Mother-Earth-force, the kundalini fire, lies coiled at the base of the spine chakra and only after a very advanced stage of spiritual development has been reached, becomes at one ". . . with the fire of Spirit at the point where these two united fires of matter and of mind issue from the top of the head" (*A Treatise on Cosmic Fire*, page 183).

Kundalini, as it is called in connection with the human form, is the force latent in matter itself; it is the integral life of the atom. It is the force of matter and its work is only *with* matter. (This, of course, includes the etheric, which is matter at its finest.) The kundalini does not work with the spiritual energies at all. Once it has been awakened and raised, its work is to destroy the enfolding, protective etheric webs which lie between the force centres or chakras along the etheric spine, thus allowing the freer flow of energies between the chakras.

The dangerous practice of using meditation or mantras for the specific purpose of stimulating or opening the chakras, or raising the kundalini before the channels are cleared, can burn away the protective etheric webs up the spine and open the chakras to astral forces which the individual may not be able to handle. The abuse of alcohol or drugs has the same effect: causing the delirium tremens of the alcoholic or the "bad trips" of the drug addict. (Read page 139 of *A Treatise on Cosmic Fire*).

In *Esoteric Healing* page 212, D.K. explains the following:

Another school of thought, branding themselves untruthfully as occultists, are equally in error. They work, or rather profess to work, with the centres, only fortunately for them nature protects them often from themselves. They endeavour consciously to vitalise the centres, to burn away the protective web, and *to raise the fires of matter before the fire of spirit has combined with the fire of the soul. They then fall victims to premature stimulation of the fires of substance before the balancing of the forces can take place.* Disease, insanities, and many neurotic conditions, plus serious pathological conditions, then occur. Some of the glands become overactive; others are overlooked, and the entire glandular system and the dependent nervous system are in a state of complete imbalance. (Author's italics)

The premature raising of the kundalini is equivalent to the irresponsible use of the atom bomb. Aroused prematurely, this tremendous force can rise up the etheric spinal column, burning everything in its path and may even cause insanity or death.

It is best to ignore short cuts – there *are* none anyway. Aspire, study, meditate, serve and purify the character, thereby clearing all the energy channels. The kundalini will then rise of its own accord and in its own time, it will rise geometrically, using the cleared channels according to the stage of development and the ray type of the person.

Using drugs for a "high" only raises the user's consciousness as far as a low point on the astral plane of glamour and illusion and never to the mental or spiritual plane. Thus drugs, alcohol (and wicked thoughts and habits) damage the aura and it is only through a damaged aura that evil possessing entities from the lower astral plane can gain entry to, and influence, a person. In extreme cases this can even lead to possession, with disastrous results.

In the use of drugs for the purpose of gaining altered states of consciousness, only the mind and emotions (personality will and desire) are involved. This drug induced state, as Dr. Carl Jung emphasised, is not *earned*.

The true higher state of altered consciousness (and this is glorious beyond belief when compared with that obtained through the use of drugs) can only be achieved when spiritual energy is involved. This is reached only in the higher mental body through the antahkarana (that bridge between the higher Spiritual Self and the lower personality self), built and paid for by the true gold of spiritual endeavour and development. The fake gold of drugs is not acceptable here. As Jesus said, "Verily I say unto thee, Thou shalt by no means come out thence, till thou hast paid the uttermost farthing" *Matthew* 5:26.

The rule of learning is that all experience has to be bought. "There is no birth of consciousness without pain" (Carl Jung).

THE FORCES CENTRES

The Seven Major Spinal Chakras

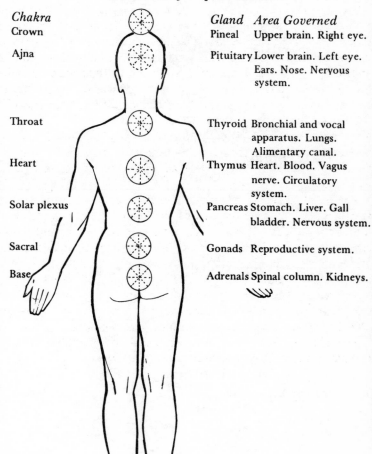

Chakra	*Gland*	*Area Governed*
Crown	Pineal	Upper brain. Right eye.
Ajna	Pituitary	Lower brain. Left eye. Ears. Nose. Nervous system.
Throat	Thyroid	Bronchial and vocal apparatus. Lungs. Alimentary canal.
Heart	Thymus	Heart. Blood. Vagus nerve. Circulatory system.
Solar plexus	Pancreas	Stomach. Liver. Gall bladder. Nervous system.
Sacral	Gonads	Reproductive system.
Base	Adrenals	Spinal column. Kidneys.

CHART 6

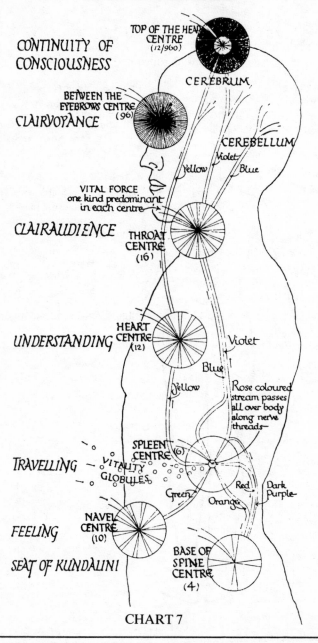

THE ETHERIC DOUBLE

MAN AND HIS ETHERIC CENTRES

CONTINUITY OF
CONSCIOUSNESS

TOP OF THE HEAD
CENTRE
(12/960)

CEREBRUM

BETWEEN THE
EYEBROWS CENTRE
(96)

CLAIRVOYANCE

CEREBELLUM

Yellow   Violet   Blue

VITAL FORCE
one kind predominant
in each centre

CLAIRAUDIENCE

THROAT
CENTRE
(16)

UNDERSTANDING

HEART
CENTRE
(12)

Violet

Blue

Yellow

Rose coloured
stream passes
all over body
along nerve
threads

TRAVELLING

SPLEEN
CENTRE (6)

VITALITY
GLOBULES

Green

Red   Dark
Purple

Orange

FEELING

NAVEL
CENTRE
(10)

SEAT OF KUNDALINI

BASE OF
SPINE
CENTRE
(4)

CHART 7

CHAPTER 6
The Subtle Bodies of Man

"You are the candles of God holding the eternal flame. Know this."
(*Through the Curtain*, page 314)

Subtle bodies are qualified energy centres of the mind and emotions. They are not like the physical bodies but are composed of particular types of force and are collections of atoms vibrating at high rates, each having both a form and defined functions.

It is difficult at first to realise that we are not in our bodies, but that our bodies are in us. The Italian psychiatrist Dr Roberto Assagioli taught an excercise that helps with this: to repeat several times daily these words, "I have a thinking body, but it is not me. I have a feeling body, but it is not me. I have a physical-etheric body, but it is not me. I *use* these. I am the soul".

These force bodies vibrate at different rates or frequencies and all interpenetrate the physical body without displacing either it or one another.They extend beyond the physical: the etheric by about one quarter of an inch, the astral further and the mental and causal further still. These extensions form what is known as the aura, the extent of which is dependent upon spiritual development. Buckminster Fuller speaks of man as a "multi-concentric Halo system", and Vera Stanley Alder, in her book *From the Mundane to the Magnificent*, gives a very clear and helpful description of these subtle bodies as seen by a clairvoyant.

The soul, when functioning through a personality on the mental, astral and physical planes, uses these vehicles or bodies which are made of the matter of these planes. Interpenetrating and interacting, they vary according to the level of consciousness acting through them. The more evolved the person, the more his pattern of consciousness includes the higher and finer frequencies. We should bear in mind that each of the planes (the mental, astral and physical) is divided into seven sub-planes, the "top" being the finest (See Chart 1).

The energies passing through these bodies should flow harmoniously through the force centres or chakras, which are duplicated in each of the subtle bodies and externalised in the physical body as the major glands of the endocrine system. Usually however, there is disharmony, coming mostly from emotions in the astral body and sometimes from the thoughts produced in the mental body. These cause what healers refer to as "blockages" in the flow of energies, which hinder or divert this flow. This leads to disease (dis-ease) in the physical body.

Emotionally or mentally disturbed people, such as alcoholics or drug addicts, often act unconsciously as parasites, draining away the energies from the aura – the subtle bodies – of anyone near them. This is the cause of the feeling of exhaustion often experienced by those working with such disturbed people.

There is also a constant exchange – a coming and going of thoughts and feelings as energies – in the energy field of groups of people during ordinary social intercourse. This can sometimes result in the diminishing or depletion of some individual auras.

There are methods of protecting the aura from this depletion and the well known scientist, Marcel Vogel, has dramatically demonstrated this in his work with dowsing rods and the human aura. He has produced many papers, cassettes and videos describing these methods.

The power of love – unconditional love – consciously felt and projected, is the most powerful protection, and harmlessly deflects from the aura any ill-natured or even malevolent energies directed towards it.

The following beautiful method for using this stupendous power of unconditional love is given by D.K. in *Discipleship in the New Age, Vol I*, page 156:

I would ask you to carry forward this insulation along the line of love, using the ancient method which has been called "the wheel of living fire which burns not but ever heals". This method is occult and safe and constitutes no barrier to relationships as does the building of a separative wall. The method is as follows:

See before you a wheel of fire with seven spokes. See it immediately before your eyes. Then, by an act of the creative imagination, see yourself standing in the centre at the hub of the wheel; there regard yourself as if you were that hub. From that central position, send out the seven streams of living love, radiating upon the world. When you do this you serve and are, at the same time, completely protected. This exercise can become instantaneous and effective. It generates a protective force and at the same time makes you a living centre of light and love.

The Etheric Body

The dense physical body is an automaton held together by, and expressive of, the energies which comprise the etheric body. The etheric body is not a body of consciousness; it is a body of activity and is the means of contact with the ocean of energies in which we live.

This body is the vehicle of life force which substands and energises and vivifies the dense physical body, giving it warmth, motion and sensitivity. Every form has its etheric counterpart. Because the etheric is the finer substance of the physical plane, it is sometimes referred to as the physical-etheric body. All communications, all energies, all "messages" from the inner planes reach the physical body and brain via the etheric body. (See Chart 7, page 54).

Medical science has for ages been concerned with the dense physical body, but is now researching the finer etheric layers underlying and vitalising it. It terms these the "Human energy field".

The etheric body has been described as a network permeated by fire, or as a web, animated by golden light. It is spoken of in the Bible as "the golden bowl" (*Ecclesiastes* 12:6), and is a composition of that matter of the physical plane which we call etheric. Its shape is brought about by the fine interlacing strands of this etheric matter being built into the form, or mould, upon which the dense physical body can later, in the womb, be built. (See Chart 5, page 42) Under the Law of Attraction, the denser matter of the physical plane is made to cohere to this vitalised form, and is gradually built up around and within it, until the interpenetration is so complete that the two forms meld into a single unit. It is this integral unit that will be the real field of healing in the future. Science in general is rapidly coming to an understanding of what the Ageless Wisdom has long taught: that there is nothing in the manifested universe which does not possess an energy form, a form subtle and intangible yet substantial, which controls, governs and conditions the outer physical body.

The whole human race is rapidly coming to recognise etheric matter. Some people are able to demonstrate etheric vision, as Dr. Shafica Karagulla has described in her book *Breakthrough to Creativity*. The sensitive named Diane, on page 124, was surely seeing the etheric body when she described a

vital or energy body or field which sub-stands the dense physical body, interpenetrating it like a sparkling web of light beams. This web of light frequencies is in constant movement and apparently looks somewhat like the lines of light on a television screen when a picture is not in focus. This energy body extends in and through the dense physical body and for an inch or two beyond the body and is a replica of the physical body.

Etheric vision is the power to see the next grade of matter, i.e. that which is the vital or the etheric. From this matter the inner structure, or etheric double, of all outer forms is made, whether it be a stone or man himself. Etheric vision is a capacity of the strictly human physical eye and is in no way connected to what we at present call clairvoyance.

Although etheric vision is not yet the norm, it soon will be. Research in such areas as Kirlian photography and quantum physics are clearly preparing the way. Today the idea of the underlying unity of life and interconnectedness of everything is fast growing in acceptance, thanks, in part, to the work of physicists like Fritjof Capra, one of the many scientists who are helping to spread this recognition amongst the general public. In the revised edition of his book *The Tao of Physics*, page 142, he has this to say: "The basic oneness of the universe is not only the central characteristic of the mystical experience, but is also one of the most important revelations of modern physics."

Through etheric vision, these realisations will ultimately become the universal experience of humanity. The energy body will be revealed for what it is as it encompasses people, animals, plants and the planet. The focus of attention will shift from the outer physical form to the etheric form or level.

D.K. gives us an indication that etheric vision will come about from the present scientific investigations into light and colour, and he suggests what some of the stupendous consequences will be:

The effect of colour on people, animals and units in the vegetable kingdom will be studied and the result of those studies will be the development of etheric vision or the power to see the next grade of matter with the strictly physical eye. Increasingly will people think and talk in terms of light, and the effect of the coming developments in this department of human thought will be triple.
a. People will possess etheric vision.
b. The vital or etheric body, lying as the inner structure of the outer forms, will be seen and noted and studied in all kingdoms of nature.
c. This will break down all barriers of race and all distinctions of colour; the essential brotherhood of man will be established. We shall see each other and all forms of divine manifestation as light units of varying degrees of brightness and shall talk and think increasingly in terms of electricity, of voltage, of intensity and of power. The age and status of men, in regard to the ladder of evolution, will be noted and become objectively apparent, the relative capacities of old souls, and young souls will be recognized, thereby re-establishing on earth the rule of the enlightened.

Note here, that these developments will be the work of the scientists of the next two generations and the result of their efforts. Their work with the atom of substance, and their investigations in the realm of electricity, of light and of power, must inevitably demonstrate the relation between forms, which is another term for brotherhood, and the fact of the soul, the inner light and radiance of all forms.
A Treatise on White Magic, pages 334, 335

Another kingdom of nature, the deva kingdom, will be seen and recognised for what it is. Devas exist on all levels. They are the builders of all forms, including man (read Geoffrey Hodson's *The Miracle of Birth*). They exist in a variety of forms and at all stages of evolution; some are known to humanity through fable and fairy story. The origins of these tales must have come from people with etheric vision. Examples are fairies, gnomes, elves and nature spirits which some children and adults see.

In due course, therefore, the devas will be studied and their work in connection with the animal and vegetable kingdoms recognised. Schools of medicine will be founded on new lines: their purpose will be to study the etheric body, its relation to the dense physical body and its functions as the receiver, storer and transmitter of the vital energies of the system. When The Christ comes he will bring with Him some of the great angels, or devas, and especially the group of violet devas who work on the four etheric levels (see Chart 1, p 25). They have much knowledge to impart regarding colour and sound and their effect, on the etheric levels, on people, animals and plants. In due time, this knowledge will help offset physical ills and sickness. They will assist in teaching humanity to see etherically and will train human beings in superhuman physics. A new church will be founded that will have for its basis the scientific recognition of what was formerly an unseen world and the application of new laws and ceremonies. For further information about this church read page 454 of *A Treatise on Cosmic Fire*. (See also Chapter 9, "The Reappearance of the Christ", pages 88–91)

So many people will have personal knowledge of the presence and the powers of the deva kingdom that scepticism will fade away. Indeed, in the coming centuries a person's normal habitat, because of etheric sight, will extend from the physical plane – as we know it with our physical eye sight – to include the two lowest etheric subdivisions; these will then become as familiar to us as is the usual physical world to which we are now accustomed. With the coming in, in the Aquarian Age, of the seventh ray, the ceremonial ray of violet, there will be great opportunity for contact between the human and deva kingdoms –

particularly those devas of the etheric levels who are coloured violet, because the etheric body responds strongly to the colour violet and because the study of the etheric is the next step in our evolution.

The Astral (Emotional) Body

Although knowledge of the etheric double is the next step ahead for humanity as a whole, the student of the Ancient Wisdom is aware of it as a body of activity, not of consciousness: that it is a transmitter of thoughts and emotions from the astral and mental bodies in the form of personality force. Later, when a man is on the path of initiation, the etheric body becomes a transmitter of soul energy. Therefore his next subject of study will be the astral and mental bodies – the realm of causes.

The astral and mental bodies, which exist on the emotional and mental planes, (see Chart 1) are part of the equipment of the personality (mental, emotional and physical-etheric). They are composed of the elemental life of those planes and the whole struggle of the evolutionary process, which is the growth of consciousness, is between these elemental energies (which wish to follow their own tendencies) and the soul in its effort to control them. By steady purification of the mind and emotions, using dispassion, discrimination and detachment, these vehicles can be brought under control, and matter of a finer and more responsive quality to soul energy, can be built in.

The astral body is the vehicle through which all emotions, passions, desires and appetites act on the physicial body and find their expression in the physical world. This body must be understood, controlled and trained to function under the domination of the soul.

Starting with the astral, the person on the path of initiation first learns to understand it, then to stand free *from* it and then to work *on* it. He learns to distinguish between the unreal and the real; to distinguish between the vibrations, impulses and desires of the personality and those vibrations coming from the soul. They impact differently on the astral body. The soul impact on the emotional body results in the person acting in a way that helps those with whom he comes in contact, but the personality impact can lead to hurtful actions, which can harm those with whom he comes in contact. He will become aware that he constructs his own astral body of astral matter which is attracted to him by his emotions, desires and fears.

The astral body is usually in a constant state of restless movement, and is sometimes stormy. In appearance it is not unlike the physical body, but it is finer and of flashing colours that change as feelings and desires change. The desire aspect of this body is what brought humanity forward in the earlier stages of evolution. But now, as we are more evolved, it is to be used to respond to vibrations from the soul, and thus to develop the higher astral heart-love aspect. This can only be done when the chaotic movement is controlled, and it is for this reason that students of meditation are taught to visualise a still pool or a mirror as a vehicle for the reflection of soul purpose. Soul impression cannot be registered by astral matter when it is in violent motion!

During sleep the undeveloped person leads a very vague existence in the astral world, floating usually only a short distance from the physical body, but remembering nothing of it when he awakens in the physical world. For the more developed person the astral life is active and interesting. The ability to remember these astral journeys, even though only partially, depends on the development of the *etheric* spleen centre. The ability to astral travel *consciously*, depends on the development of the *astral* spleen centre. The astral body can move with great rapidity and to great distances beyond the physical body, but still remain attached to it by the life thread (named in the Bible "the silver cord", and in the East the Sutratma). In the undeveloped person this cord is attached at the solar plexus and in the more developed person, either between the shoulder blades (the heart centre) or at the top of the head. It is a vibrating, connecting flow of energy, and should it be cut, then the person in his subtle bodies cannot return to the physical body and death ensues. "Or ever the silver cord be loosed . . ." (*Ecclesiastes* 12:6).

Physical sight enables one to see dense physical objects. Etheric sight enables one to see *into* and *through* physical objects. People with this gift are very useful in healing groups. They are able to see *into* bodies and report on the condition of the organs in these bodies. (This is illustrated very well in Dr. Shafica Karagulla's excellent book, *Breakthrough to Creativity*.)

With astral sight, every object is seen from all sides at once. No astral sense is confined to any particular part, but belongs to all the particles of the astral body. This explains the ability some psychics have of "seeing through the back of their heads", reading sealed letters, or, in a darkened room, blindfolded, "seeing" colours through their feet or hands. There is an interesting chapter entitled "Dermo-Optical Perception: The Science – and art – of Sight by Touch" in the book *The New Soviet Psychic Discoveries* by Henry Gris and William Dick. I was interested, when reading this book, to note that the touching hands were held a short distance from the physical body under observation. This means the touching hands were touching the subtle bodies and not the physical body. This same chapter refers to a report from the Popov Group, Moscow's parapsychology centre, which reads, "Investigations of optical sensitivity of the human skin to record images, both by direct contact and at a distance". Dr. Shafica Karagulla writes about this as "para-optical" sense in her book *Breakthrough to Creativity*, pages 225 – 227.

I have witnessed Ronald Beesley, the well-known English psychic, and later on an African witchdoctor, demonstrate their ability to "see", and describe accurately, what was going on behind their backs. And once, in a packed London hall, I watched a psychic "read" and answer sealed questions sent to him by members of the audience, while holding them unopened in his hands, after which the letters were opened by someone else on the platform and the questions contained therein read out to the audience. These instances cannot be questioned; however, magicians often perform tricks which appear similar. Also, this field is very open to outright fraud.

Paramahansa Yogananda, in his book *Autobiography of a Yogi*, tells of how, when his guru heightened his consciousness, his ordinary frontal vision changed to spherical sight and he watched through the back of his head some men strolling down the road behind him. He also watched the leisurely approach of a white cow and *continued* to see her clearly *after* she had passed behind a brick wall. The roots of plants and trees appeared to him through what was now the "dim transparency of the soil" and he discerned the inward flow of their sap.

There are on the astral and mental planes, particularly the astral – because strong emotion is usually involved – myriads of very clear and more or less permanent thoughtforms of historical or religious characters, built up by the thoughts and feelings of generations of people. This explains the genuine accounts by untrained seers of seeing historical figures and beloved religious figures such as the Christ, the Buddha, the Masters and the Saints; a trained seer, however, can distinguish between a thoughtform and an entity. (Note that the great entities do not use these thoughtforms. See the section "Thoughtforms", page 66, in this chapter.)

The Mental Body

To those with clairvoyant sight, the mental body appears as dense mist in the shape of the physical body, surrounded by an ovoid of much finer mist. For this reason, in the mental world, an acquaintance is just as instantly recognisable as in the physical or astral world.

Unlike the physical body – which has remained substantially the same size since Atlantean days – the mental body grows in size as the man himself develops. It is more or less refined according to the stage of intellectual development. It is of a delicate iridescent beauty, and every passing thought gives rise to vibrations of delicate changing colours.

Waking or sleeping, our mental bodies are ever changing. Every thought brings into this body particles of mental matter. If it is vibrating to spiritual thoughts, the rapidity of this vibration causes heavy atoms to be thrown out and finer ones built in. (These are the heavy and light atoms of esoteric science, not physical science.) In this way the mental body can be made finer and purer until it no longer responds to coarse or evil thoughts.

For most people the centre of consciousness is embedded in kama-manas. (kama: desire; manas: mind, intermingled, working together and acting as one). But the more cultured and developed are beginning to govern desire by reason, i.e. the centre of consciousness is gradually transferring itself from the higher astral to the lower mental. As men progress it will move further up still.

On the mental plane feelings and thoughts are no longer hidden and language is not necessary. Thought pictures are read as they are formed and their interchange is instantaneous.

The vibrations of a thought in the mental body can produce either a thought *wave*, or a thought*form*. A thought wave radiates the character of the thought, which could influence other people in the vicinity.

Particularly in big cities, we all walk in a world of these thought and feeling waves created by the crowds around us. We are affected by these, unless there are no latent tendencies in our frequencies which respond and act as magnets. Thus a pure heart and mind are the best protection against anything idle or evil in these impacts.

Our scientists are busy proving, under strictly controlled conditions in their laboratories, that thoughts and feelings are *very* infectious. People continually affect each other by their thoughts, sent out mostly without definite intent. It was in 1939 that a radio microscope (a radio frequency spectroscope) revealed a new world of hitherto unknown rays. This instrument "sees" the rays constantly being emitted by human beings, and provided the first scientific proof that rays really travel from one person to another, and between all living things.

So the mental body is a perfect human radio and thoughts are no more than subtle vibrations in the ether. Just as a radio can be correctly tuned to pick up a certain programme from thousands of others, so can our human mental radios be tuned. This is the basis of thought reading and how spiritual leaders and gurus so easily read the thoughts of the pupils they so lovingly direct.

What seems like magic at present, may turn out to be the normal working of unknown scientific laws.

The life and light of the Deity flood the whole of His system, the force at each plane being normally strictly limited to it. If however, a special channel is prepared for it, it can descend to, and illuminate, a lower level. Such a channel is always provided when any thought or feeling is entirely unselfish. Selfish thoughts and feelings move in a closed curve and so bring response at their own level. Utterly unselfish thoughts and emotions cause an outrush of energy which does not return but in its upward movement provides a channel for a downpouring of divine power from the level next above. This is the reality behind the belief in the answer to prayer.

We are all of us familiar with those people, apparently incapable of thinking badly of others: by just being what they are, they change and lighten the home, office, or wherever they happen to be: "By the strength of his silent thought, he can bring light and peace to all" (*A Treatise on White Magic*, page 603).

The mental body is subject to the laws of habit, as are all of our vehicles.

A violent dislike, a gnawing worry, a jealousy, a constant anxiety or a longing for something or someone, may act so potently as an irritant or poison that the entire life is spoilt, . . . embittered and devitalised . . . All relationships with other people are rendered equally futile or even definitely harmful, for the worried or suspicious aspirant spoils the home circle or his group of friends by his inner poisonous attitude . . . His relation to his own soul and the strength of the contact with the world of spiritual ideas is at a standstill, for he cannot progress onward and is held back by the poison in his mental system. His vision becomes distorted, his nature corroded, and all his relationships impeded by the wearing, nagging thoughts which he has himself embodied in form and which have a life so powerful that they can poison him.
A Treatise on White Magic, page 489

. . . the mind is the main creative factor and the utiliser of the energies of the cosmos. . . . The race is progressing into an era wherein men will function as minds; when intelligence will be stronger than desire, and when thought powers will be used for appeal and for the guidance of the world, as now physical and emotional means are employed.
A Treatise on White Magic, page 125

Everyone uses the mental body when thinking, but very few, apart from trained occultists, consciously use it to fully *express consciousness*, which is something very different. This ability enables a man to move about freely on the mental plane and observe all that exists there, and is developed only after a very long period of practice in meditation, purification, discipline and special effort.

Madame Blavatsky (Helena Petrovna Blavatsky, usually referred to by the initials H.P.B.) was a highly trained occultist of this calibre. D.K. has this to say of her:

> . . . as in the case of H.P.B. you have deep knowledge, ability to be inspired and mental clairaudience combined.
>
> Inspiration originates on the higher levels; it presupposes a very high point in evolution, for it involves the egoic consciousness and necessitates the use of atomic matter, thus opening up a wide range of communicators. It spells safety.

A Treatise on White Magic, page 180
(Note here the reference to Egoic consciousness, i.e. that of the higher mental plane.)

A great deal of nonsense has been written about Madame Blavatsky. For those readers wishing to find out about her as she truly was, a dedicated and tireless worker for humanity under the Hierarchy, I recommend *Reminiscences of H.P. Blavatsky and The Secret Doctrine*, by Countess Constance Wachtmeister, et al., and the numerous references to this "great Initiate" in the Alice Bailey books. For this the *Master Index* could be used. (See page 170)

Meditation

All religions recommend meditation, and its desirability has been recognised by every school of philosophy. Just as a man who wishes to be strong uses prescribed exercises to develop his muscles, so the student of occultism uses definite and prescribed exercises to develop his astral and mental bodies.

Meditation is the readiest and safest method of developing the higher consciousness. It serves as a kind of astral and mental gymnastics, to preserve these higher bodies in health and to keep the stream of divine life flowing through them. For these purposes it should be remembered that the *regularity* of the exercises is of the first importance.

By meditation a man's astral and mental bodies gradually come out of chaos into order, slowly expand and gradually learn to respond to higher and higher vibrations. Each effort helps to thin the veil that divides him from the higher world, from direct knowledge. His thoughtforms grow more definite day by day, so that the life poured into them from above becomes fuller and fuller.

Real meditation means strenuous effort; it is not the sensation of happiness which arises from a state of semi-somnolence and bodily luxury!

One of the first things a student of meditation learns is how to consciously construct thoughtforms and to vivify them. He learns that thought control is a prerequisite to the development of the powers of the soul.

The student should also be aware of "at-one-ment", or "at-one-ness", which is to be conscious of oneself as a whole (Spirit, soul and body), the mind and soul functioning as a unit to express the will of the indwelling soul. That state is achieved when, through the ordered stages of meditation, the physical body is brought under the control of the soul, the emotional body reflects the Love nature, and the mental body expresses perfectly the Will or purpose of God. (See also Chapter 21, "The Science of Meditation", page 40).

THOUGHTFORMS

Every thoughtform comes under the law of karma through the effect it produces. Energy flows as the result of thought.

The mental elemental essence is a strange semi-intelligent life which surrounds us, vivifying matter of the mental plane. It responds very readily to the influence of human thought, so much so that every impulse sent out from the mental body of a man immediately clothes itself in a temporary vehicle of this essence, and becomes a thoughtform: a brilliantly coloured and vital, temporary living entity of intense activity animated by the one idea that generated it. If made of the finer kinds of matter it will be of great power and energy, and may be used as a most potent agency when directed by a strong and steady will. A thought then becomes, for a time, a kind of living creature, called an elemental, or sometimes an artificial elemental.

The principles underlying the production of all thoughtforms are:
1. Quality of thought determines colour. 2. Nature of thought determines form. 3. Definiteness of thought determines clearness of outline.

As the thoughts of most people are indefinite, thoughtforms are usually indefinite and vague, but where a thought is definite, a definite form is created, and a clearcut – and often beautiful – shape is assumed. Such shapes, while of infinite variety, are often in some way typical of the kind of thought which they express. Abstract ideas usually represent themselves by all kinds of perfect and most beautiful geometrical forms. It should be remembered in this connection that the merest abstractions to us on the earth plane become definite facts/ shapes on the mental plane. A thoughform's duration depends also upon the nutriment supplied to it after its generation by the repetition of the thought – either by its originator or by others.

Some of these thoughtforms are collective, from history, drama and religion, such as the Christ, the Buddha and the Masters. They have coalesced from the imagination of countless individuals through the ages and are very often mistaken for real entities by untrained sensitives. There are numerous strong thoughtforms of the Lord Jesus, usually with golden hair and wearing a long, white robe.

In the book *Krishnamurti. The Years of Awakening* by Mary Lutyens, Krishnamurti gives a very interesting account on page 37, of how, at one of his initiations, he was taught to distinguish between a real Master and an imitation:

Then He (the Lord Maitreya) showed me many astral objects and I had to tell him what they were. I had to distinguish between the astral bodies of a living man and a dead man, between a real person and a thought-image of a person, and between an imitation Master and a real one.

At the present stage of evolution, the majority of the thoughts of people are usually self-centred. Such thoughts hang about the thinkers. Most people, in fact, surround their mental bodies with a cage of such thoughts, which hover ceaselessly about them, like bees around a honeypot, and constantly react on them. The tendency of these thoughts is to reproduce themselves, i.e. to stir up in the person a repetition of these thoughts. Many a person feels this pressure upon him from within, this constant suggestion of certain thoughts, especially when he is resting. If the thoughts are evil he frequently thinks of them as tempting demons goading him into sin. Yet they are none the less entirely of his own creation; he is his own tempter.

Our mental bodies, like our other bodies, are subject to the laws of habit, and a person in the habit of thinking of evil actions may find himself performing them before he realises what he is doing.

We are continually peopling our own space with a world of our own creation: with the offspring of our fancies, desires, images and passions. These thoughtforms remain in our space (auras), and increase in intensity until certain kinds of them so dominate our mental and emotional life, that we answer to their impulse. In this way habits are created and character is built.

If the thought be intellectual and impersonal, e.g. if the thinker is attempting to solve a problem in algebra or geometry, then his thoughtforms (as well as his thought-waves) will be confined to the mental plane.

If his thought be of a spiritual nature, e.g. if it be tinged with love and aspiration of deep, unselfish feeling, then it will rise upwards from the mental plane and will borrow some of the splendour and glory of the buddhic levels above. In such a case its influence is most powerful and every such thought is a mighty force for good, as it radiates outwards.

If, on the other hand, the thought has in it something of self or of personal desire, its vibrations will at once turn downwards, and draw around itself a body of astral matter, in addition to its clothing of mental matter. Such a thoughtform – which could be termed more accurately a thought-emotion-form – is, of course, capable of affecting both the mental and the astral bodies of other men. This type of thoughtform is by far the most common, as few thoughts of ordinary men and women are untinged with desire, passion, or emotion. We may consider this class of thoughtform as generated by the activity of kama-manas, i.e. by mind dominated by desire.

When a person thinks of any concrete object – a book, a house, a landscape – he builds a tiny image of the object in the matter of his mental body. These images float around his head. Most people move through life encased within a cage of their own building, occupied by masses of these forms created by their habitual thoughts and feelings. Each person looks at the world *through* these and thus sees everything tinged by them. As my wise Scottish grandmother told me: "You can't see a clean street through dirty windows."

Hypnotism provides examples of the objectivity of thoughtforms. It is well known that the thoughtform of an idea may be projected on to a blank paper, and there become visible to a hypnotised person. Or it may be made so objective that the hypnotised person will see and feel it as though it were an actual physical object.

Recently Dr. Marcel Vogel, by concentrating for one hour, succeeded in projecting into liquid crystal a thoughtform of the Mother Mary. This was later photographed. An account and print of this appears in *Psychic Research Newsletter*, Vol 5, no 4, July/Aug 1988, published by Marcel's research institute.

The "clever men" of the Australian Aborigines are said to be able to create powerful thought *forms* that can be seen by others and are able to exist for a time independent of their creator. These they describe as "power animals".

Similarly, a jewel which has been the cause of many crimes may, with unimpaired clearness, retain the impression of the passions which prompted the crimes, and continue to radiate them for thousands of years. Marcel Vogel has described in his lectures and newsletters how these ancient energies can be dispelled by a scientific method of breath expulsion. (At the time of writing, Marcel Vogel's long-awaited book, *Marcel Vogel: On Crystals*, was in press. Expected publishing date: sometime in 1989)

Thoughts coloured by desires of a low or evil nature attract evil forces and thereby become active on their own account, hanging about in the neighbourhood where they were generated and so influencing the atmosphere that persons coming into it are tempted by the same low or evil desires. These thoughtforms are the incubi and succubi of mediaeval legend.

Strong thoughtforms of love, or of the desire to protect, remain as a protection in the aura of the person thought of, strengthening friendly energies and weakening unfriendly ones impinging on the aura. A mother's prayers for a distant child come under this category. Distance is no object and these loving thoughtforms may sometimes be seen by clairvoyants.

Apparitions at the time of death are very often the astral form of the dying person, but they can also be a thoughtform created by a dying person's earnest wish to see a loved one before passing on.

Daily, usually about 5 a.m., I use an occult form of "absent healing", not for those with physical ills but for those with mental and emotional problems. Often those whom I seek thus to help subjectively are far away, and mostly unaware of my efforts on their behalf, yet on a number of occasions I have subsequently received telephone calls telling me that I had been seen by them "in the middle of the night, when it was dark, in a frame of light". These were surely thoughtforms, as I do not astral travel consciously and always work fully awake, aware of my surroundings and of the work I am doing.

Annie Besant and Bishop Leadbeater together wrote an excellent book entitled *Thoughtforms*, in which they describe and illustrate the various shapes and colours which can be seen in these thoughtforms.

About the correct building and directing of thoughts, D.K. has this to say:

Students would do well to study these cycles of creative building, of performance and of subsequent disintegration. They are true of a solar system, of a human being, and of the thought-forms of a creative thinker. The secret of all beauty lies in the right functioning of these cycles. The secret of all success on the physical plane lies in right understanding of law and of order. For the aspirant the goal of his endeavour is the correct building of forms in mental matter remembering that "as a man thinketh so is he"; that for him the control of mental substance and its use in clear thinking is an essential to progress.

This will demonstrate in organization of the outer life, in creative work of some kind – a book written, a picture painted, a home functioning rhythmically, a business run along sound and true lines, a life salvaged, and the outer dharma carried out with precision, whilst the inner adjustments proceed in the silence of the heart.

A Treatise on White Magic, pages 279, 280

Most of us are conditioned and controlled by the thoughts and feelings of the groups in which we live: family circles, business associates, fellow club members, our race and nation. Very few of us break away even partly *from* or are even aware *of* these thought and feeling conditioning influences.

The occult student, however, should be fully aware of this and should refuse to be dominated by these crowd feelings, and particularly by persuasive crowd leaders. He should only accept ideas of his own will, with all his faculties alert. He must be his own master, in control of his own emotional and intellectual life and not become immersed in, and controlled by, collective emotions and thoughtforms.

The Causal Body

On the causal plane, as on all planes, there are subplanes. On the third subplane, counting downwards (see Chart 5, page 42), there is a triple point of brilliant light enclosed in an envelope of higher mental matter – like the yolk of an egg in its shell. This is the soul (or Ego) in the causal body, known in masonic ritual as the Temple of Solomon – the "temple not built by hands". At inception it is a colourless ovoid, but when developed is of rare brilliant beauty, radiating the finer shades of all the colours of the rainbow.

The wider and inclusive consciousness of the Ego includes the faculty of abstract thought and contemplation and the power to transcend the limitations of time and space. Genius, too, is of the soul or Ego, and true intuition is one of its faculties. Lower mind uses methods of induction and deduction, but intuition is insight, a process as direct and swift as physical sight.

The lower bodies are new for each incarnation, but the causal body remains the same throughout the ages and is the divine storehouse into which is withdrawn and accumulated the essence from the personality experiences of each successive incarnation. It is the final repository of all that is good experience, and it seems logical, therefore, that this is the lowest level at which reliable information can be obtained about past incarnations.

Only good is stored in the causal body, evil finding no means of expression at this level. Vices, even though continued life after life, cannot affect it, except insofar as their opposite virtues will not be "available for storage".

This causal body owes its name to the fact that in it resides the *causes* which manifest as *effects* on the lower planes. For it is these stored experiences which are the *causes* of the attitudes and actions manifested in the life of the personality in incarnation. (Refer here to Chapter 11, "Karma and Karmic Bonds", page 99)

This body is dissipated after the fourth initiation when the need for rebirth down into the lower planes no longer exists. The soul then rises to the Buddhic plane, the fifth Kingdom, the Kingdom of God. (Refer also to Chapter 4, "Incarnation", page 39)

Considering All This Together

We may, for purposes of study and understanding, divide man into Monad, Ego and Personality; we may divide his bodies into physical, etheric, astral, mental, and causal: yet the man himself *is no one of these things, nor even all of them together*. These are all but means through which he expresses portions, aspects, or functions of himself: but he himself "remains" an entity, a mystery, if the truth be told, different from, and greater than, all of these categories into which we divide him.

Bishop Leadbeater gives an analogy which may be useful here:.

If an electric current be made to flow round a bar of soft iron, through a coil of German-silver wire, and within a tube filled with mercury vapour, it will give rise repectively to magnetism, heat, and light. The current is the same, but its manifestations vary according to the nature of the matter through which it is acting. So with man: the current of life flowing in him is split up into different varieties of manifestation, according to the bodies through which it expresses itself. We study the bodies in turn, and their methods of functioning: but the man himself, that which results in consciousness of various kinds in the various bodies, is the noumenon behind all these external phenomena: and, be it noted, just as the true nature of electricity still eludes our scientists, so does man himself, in his true nature, still elude us.

The poets refer to the "Orchard of the Rose" or the "Garden of Eros" as being *within*. Shakespeare wrote (*Othello* Act I, Sc. 3):

Our bodies are gardens; to the which our wills are gardeners; so that, if we will plant nettles, or sow lettuce, set hyssop and weed up thyme, supply it with one gender of herbs or distract it with many; either to have it sterile with idleness or manured with industry; why, the power and corrigible authority of this *lies within our wills*.

While physically asleep many students have become aware of being in another dimension, attending lectures. The following is an account of one of these "night classes", and is taken from the book *Through the Curtain*, pages 319 – 320: (see also Chapter 16, "Dreams", page 117).

In the Fifth Kingdom, man is referred to as the Mason or builder. By his emotions and feelings he sets up frequencies which draw to him the substances on the physical, etheric, astral and mental planes with which he builds a structure which is the human personality vehicle, the physical etheric, astral and mental bodies.

The quality of substance is determined by the frequency of his thoughts and emotions. A thoughtform was shown to the students in which the frequencies that a person sends out may be likened to a conveyor belt which brings in the building blocks. This could be presented in slides to the students with the analogy of building a house of adobe, bricks or alabaster. The kind of substance built into the structure also, in turn, determines the kind of frequency to which the vehicle is responsive. However, man, the thinker, the dweller in the house, has the power to change his thoughts and emotions and, therefore, to change the substance and structure. Because the etheric, astral and mental substances are much more fluidic types than dense physical, this is easier than building an actual physical structure. Man often takes a long time to do this, because he is slow in changing his mental and emotional frequency.

The energies which flow automatically into the centers are made up of all the ranges of frequencies, but the vehicles respond only to those ranges of frequencies to which they resonate. A good analogy is the string of the violin. The tension and thickness of the string determine the tone and frequency. The thicker the string the lower the note.

Although all frequencies of energies are available at all times, the individual has access to those frequencies to which the substance of his vehicles is resonant. This goes back to the quality of his thinking and emotions. Man, the thinker, the dweller in the house.

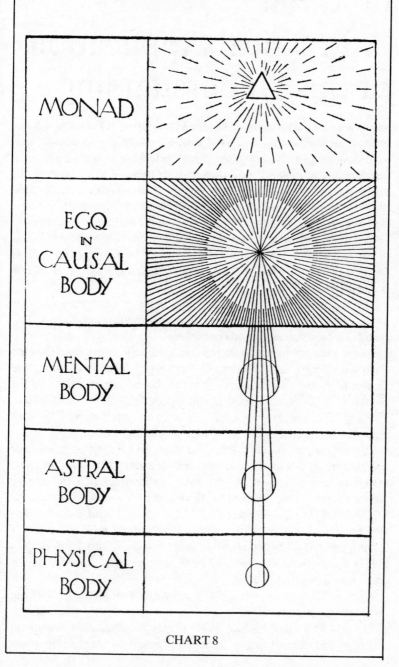

MONAD	
EGO IN CAUSAL BODY	
MENTAL BODY	
ASTRAL BODY	
PHYSICAL BODY	

CHART 8

CHAPTER 7
A Practical Application of this Understanding

We now know that the human energy field consists of the subtle energy bodies: mental, astral, and vital etheric, which interpenetrate and surround the physical body. As these bodies are in reality electrical frequencies, we should train ourselves to think of them as such. In other words we are, each of us, equipped as a highly sophisticated radio station, potentially capable of receiving and transmitting a vast range of energies on different planes, from the highest on the spiritual planes, to the lowest on the astral plane. We are "tuned in" according to the frequencies inherent within ourselves, and contact is made at any given time according to the quality of the frequencies received and transmitted.

The I Ching and Tarot cards are highly condensed codes for perceiving this energy flow. The same flow is imprinted on our physical bodies – hence palmistry and phrenology.

So the Path about which there is so much talk, is the Path through our own energy field. We weave our own habitation, as does the spider, from our own substance. And in this energy field the goal for us, at this stage of our evolution, is unimpeded alignment with the soul. The way of steady progress towards alignment with the soul is through study, meditation and service. With this achievement comes joy.

This alignment process needs clear channels for the transmission of spiritual energies. However, in the removing of the blocking obstacles, comes suffering. The old forms must die in order that the energy contained therein be released for the use of new and better forms. As St. Paul said, in *I Corinthians* 15:31: "I die daily". And in Carl Jung's words, "There is no birth of consciousness without pain". The rule of learning is that all experience has to be bought. Every step forward means the sacrifice of something held dear: new relationships, ideals and beliefs take the place of old formerly cherished ones now outgrown. The Zen Buddhists have a saying: "Our altars of today are our firewood of tomorrow".

We now know that each of us is in reality a wonderfully equipped receiving and transmitting set, constantly sending and receiving waves of energy in the form of thoughts and feelings. These thoughts and feelings are factual on their own plane and have effects for which we are responsible. (As we went to press, a book by a distinguished medical practitioner was published in which this point, and many others, are developed in a most convincing and captivating manner. Dr Deepak Chopra's *Quantum Healing. Exploring the Frontiers of Mind/ Body Medicine* should have considerable impact on the scientific community.)

Spiritual power should not be used for material gain. This law is for our protection because opening the door to such a temptation can lead to the darkened path.

Madame Blavatsky was a very great initiate and powerful white magician. (A White magician is one who uses energies unselfishly for the Light on the right-hand path. A black magician is one who uses the same energies selfishly on the darkened or left-hand path.) In New York, when founding the Theosophical Society, she demonstrated evidence of supernormal powers by producing material objects apparently from nowhere. But at the end of her life, when she was very ill and struggling to finish *The Secret Doctrine* in Europe, she wrote to Colonel Olcott in India asking him to please send her money to buy a carpet for her feet because she felt the cold so acutely. She knew better than to use her powers to produce anything for her own material gain. It is against the danger of black magic that the student of occultism is guided by the law which forbids him to use his occult powers for himself. It is best to check evil at its beginnings.

One cannot help others unless they wish to help themselves. Occultly this means that if there is no thread of light in their frequencies to act as a magnet for the help being offered, all efforts are wasted. Knowing this we should not, *unasked*, try to change either the character or beliefs of others. Workers in the modern medical field are only now beginning to understand this law. In a Medical Briefing Special Address entitled "Freedom from the Needle", in the London *Times* of Friday, July 4th 1986, one of the headings from Jennifer Beasdale, of the Standing Conference on Drug Abuse, an authority on the subject, reads: "Whatever the drug in question, an addict has to make the firm decision to stop before any help will be useful".

Even when those we wish to serve are dearly loved by us, we must still detach ourselves when we find no response from them and recognise that only the Law of Karma is applicable in such a case, and that they, and only they, must work out their own salvation. No service should be enforced no matter how sure we are that we are right and that they can only bring suffering and sorrow to themselves by their line of action. Maybe that suffering is necessary for their growth and they should not be deprived of it. It is a common experience to see parents shielding their children in this manner, often thus inflicting undue pain and denial upon themselves, while the child has learnt nothing. This is a particularly hard teaching.

Over many years and in different parts of the world I have contacted many groups and churches but found only one group that *to me* truly understands, and works correctly with, basic laws – God's Laws, not man-made laws – and that is Alcoholics Anonymous. I once heard a wife pleading with them to come and stop her husband's drinking only to be told that they could only help when he himself asked. "But," she cried, "he will land in the gutter!" Their reply was, "Then madam, when he is there and decides he wants to get out and sends for us, *then* we can help."

They know the law – that nothing helps from without unless it receives recognition from within.

I take my shoes off on any man's holy ground even if I do not share his beliefs because what he feels for them makes them holy. But in an Alcoholics Anonymous open meeting I bend the knee as well. Observing their ravaged faces and having witnessed how they suffer in conquering their demons I feel truly humble and frequently ask myself, "Have I dealt with mine as successfully?"

I was with a leading member of this wonderful group when he explained to a weeping wife that he could not help her husband because he (the husband) was a dry drunk and he himself had never *been* one, but that he would send someone who *had* been a dry drunk and therefore was appropriately qualified to give assistance. (A dry drunk is a person who has been a drinking alcoholic, who has given up drinking but still shows all the unpleasant aggressive behavioural patterns of a drunk.)

This same member explained to me once that he had not been able, when visiting a farmer, to help him because he had not stayed long enough on the farm. His explanation was: "If I had stayed longer he might have opened his mind to me and I could then have helped. On my way back I will stay longer."

His work was based on the following three rules from *A Treatise on White Magic*, page 320, without his ever having heard of them:

Rule 1: Enter thy brother's heart and see his woe. Then speak. Let the words spoken convey to him the potent force he needs to loose his chains. Yet loose them not thyself. Thine is the work to speak with understanding. The force received by him will aid him in his work.

Rule 2: Enter thy brother's mind and read his thoughts, but only when thy thoughts are pure. Then think. Let the thoughts thus created enter thy brother's mind and blend with his. Yet keep detached thyself, for none have the right to sway a brother's mind. The only right there is, will make him say: "He loves. He standeth by. He knows. He thinks with me and I am strong to do the right." Learn thus to speak. Learn thus to think.

Rule 3: Blend with thy brother's soul and know him as he is. Only upon the plane of the soul can this be done. Elsewhere the blending feeds the fuel of his lower life. Then focus on the plan. Thus will he see the part that he and you and all men play. Thus will he enter into life and know the work accomplished.

A note, appended to these three rules says:

"These three energies of speech, of thought, and of purpose – when wielded with understanding by the chela and blended with the awakening forces of his brother whom he seeks to aid, are the three energies with which all adepts work."

We should endeavour to tune in to the second ray of love-wisdom, the Ray of the Christ and of the Buddha, which is the magnetic, cohering agent in any form whether an atom, a man or a solar system. We must remember that the Christ Ray is in ourselves; anchored in our hearts. "Christ in you the hope of glory" (*Colossians* 1:27). This Christ light in our hearts, together with all that is sentient in the three lower Kingdoms: animal, vegetable and mineral (sentience in the mineral kingdom manifests as chemical attraction) are one with, and entirely within, the great Christ Ray.(See Chapter 17, "The Law of Attraction", page 122)

I have not come so far with these rules as I would like, but, through the trials and tribulations of life and through the example of that wonderful doctor Elizabeth Kubler-Ross, I have tried to practice what she terms "unconditional love", and not to be judgemental. My own experience might help the reader here: I find that when I try to *understand* people and that which, in them, "conditions" them to behave in a certain way (remembering that the life force is the same in all, although manifested differently in each of us), I find myself not only ceasing to judge, but, sometimes to my great surprise, *feeling* love for them, "warts and all". There is no sentiment about this. Dr. Kubler-Ross is no milk and water lady!

I have thus, through experience, learned that love is not sentiment, but a real feeling of relationship: a feeling of being neither inferior nor superior, but *akin*. I have found that the ones I feel most akin to and for whom I feel the most empathy, are those who are making the same mistakes that I have made! The American Indians have a saying, "Don't judge a man until you have walked in his moccasins for a mile".

We know that our "bodies" are, in reality, frequency garments and we need to train ourselves to think of them as such. We need to become aware that that which we perceive all around us with our physical senses, is only the crust covering the astounding life, light, colour, sound and movement which lies beneath. Everything is interconnected in one dynamic network of relationships. Everything is a part of one single whole.

One can find a deep esoteric significance in one's daily routine and formal occupations because all fields of human endeavour offer legitimate opportunities for occult creative service activity, and one should not in any way create a dichotomy between what one may tend to consider 'spiritual' work on the one hand, and 'ordinary' work and domestic duties on the other. It is all a continuum in which incoming life energies and outgoing, qualified life forces are involved, all contributing to the pattern.

We, by now, should be aware that brotherhood is a fact and is not just an impractical, unattainable ideal, because all in Creation is indeed One by way of the inter-connecting threads or frequencies. This is what St. Francis fully understood: he referred to all – the sun, moon, wind, rivers, animals, stones and birds as his brothers and sisters.

Heaven is not *up* there and hell *down* there and our physical world somewhere in between, as I was taught in my childhood. All "layers" or frequencies of our world occupy one space. It is an accepted fact, for instance, that a ghost can walk through a wall without in any way displacing it. Similarly, several entities could occupy one chair without being aware of one another if on different planes or frequencies. I remember reading about a little Victorian boy who was banished from the parlour as a punishment for telling lies. He had asked a guest to please vacate the chair he was using because "you are sitting on Grandpa". Grandpa had been dead for several years!

Often, apparently by coincidence, just the experience, the book or teacher we need "happens" to appear, proving that old saying that "When the pupil is ready the teacher will appear". As Dr. Kubler Ross says, ". . .there is no such thing as coincidence."

Dr. C.G. Jung explains all this – brings it all beautifully together – in his fascinating book *Synchronicity, An Acausal Connecting Principle*. He describes synchronicity as "meaningful coincidence" and implies that, whenever an outer event takes place, it reflects some inner movement of the soul.

Many people find it very difficult to start meditation. They have great difficulty in concentrating – the mind keeps wandering.

As concentration is a necessary first step in meditation, a good idea is to practice concentration in daily life: to pay one-pointed attention to whatever we happen to be doing, be it baking a cake, writing a letter or talking to a friend.

My careful Scottish grandmother taught me that if I took care of the pennies, the pounds would take care of themselves, and the same principle applies here. If we take care of every thought and word, our spiritual growth will take care of itself.

Ugly thoughts accompanied by similarly ugly feelings can, when constantly indulged in, reach saturation point. They then inevitably spill over into ugly words, leading to equally ugly actions and consequences. If we "tune in" our thoughts to the "good" frequency in any situation, a balance can be achieved. This is not easy, but it works! As St. Paul said:

. . . whatsoever things are true, whatsoever things are honest, whatsoever things are just, whatsoever things are pure, whatsoever things are lovely, whatsoever things are of good report; if there be any virtue, and if there be any praise, think on these things.
Philippians 4:8.

What is meant by SERVICE IN THE NEW AGE? To give and not to count the cost; to work without thought of regard or result or acknowledgement. Service is the immediate response of the personality to soul contact; the outflow of a loving heart and an intelligent mind.

The motive for service must be towards the general and the universal; the response of the group in answer to human need. The qualities of discrimination, keen analysis of motive, and the understanding of the nature and methods of right service, are of supreme importance.

The *body temple* is to be kept clean and healthy by rhythmic working of the atoms of which it is composed. The *emotional body* aids the physical body by keeping rhythmic and stable and serving the soul as a channel of force, and not as a waster of energy. The *mental body* serves by building in knowledge, in preparation for receiving the wisdom of the soul. The personality serves the soul by self-discipline and sacrifice.

We must also become aware of the existence of consciousness magnetism. As our consciousness changes, our new frequencies magnetically attract new friends "on the same wavelength" and we find that we have outgrown, or no longer have anything in common with some former friends.

We find around ourselves those who are at a similar point "on the Path", reinforcing one another with radiations similar in quality, frequency and voltage.

Above all, let us remember that we are responsible for our own consciousness magnetism. Our free will chooses the channels to which we "tune in" our "sets". In more modern terminology, it is our free will that programmes our personality computers.

And that brings us again to St. Paul, who said: "Wherefore, my beloved, . . . work out your own salvation . ." *Philippians* 2:12.

Conclusion to Part I

Annie Besant has said:

The value of knowledge is tested by its power to purify and ennoble life, and all earnest students desire to apply the theoretical knowledge acquired in their study of theosophy to the evolution of their own character and to the helping of their fellow men. The emotion which impels to righteous living is half wasted if the clear light of the intellect does not illuminate the path of conduct, for as the blind man strays from the way unknowing till he falls into the ditch, so does the man blinded by ignorance, turn aside from the road of right living till he falls into the pit of evil action.

From Confucius we have the stimulating thought:

Reading without reflection is a waste of time.
Reflection without reading is dangerous.

The eminent historian, Toynbee, said that the future of mankind depends on each single person withdrawing into himself and finding his own depths, then coming forth to serve his fellow men.

The Bible tells us in Genesis 18 : verses 23 to 32, that it took ten such men to save a city; how many will it take to save a planet?

Part 2
SOME NEW AGE TOPICS

Thoughts from the Teachings
on subjects of topical
"New Age" interest.

CHAPTER 8
The Reappearance of The Christ

There has been, down through the ages, a great continuity of Avatars who have come in the times of humanity's need and given to men ideas and concepts of truth suited to their state of consciousness at the time, thus bringing about a better civilisation. An Avatar is a Being who is capable of reflecting some cosmic Principle or divine quality which will produce the desired effect upon humanity, evoking a reaction and producing a needed stimulation.

The Egyptians spoke of the "Ever Coming One", and in the *Bhagavad Gita*, Book IV Sutras 7,8, Krishna says:

Whenever there is a withering of the law and an uprising of lawlessness on all sides, *then* I manifest Myself.

For the salvation of the righteous and the destruction of such as do evil, for the firm establishing of the law, I come to birth age after age.

In the past these teachings have been given to a chosen few, because only these few had awakening minds ready to accept the newly presented divine truths and to teach and spread them.

The first Avatar we know of, way back in the mists of time, was the hero teacher Hercules. He presented a goal towards which men must make their way despite obstacles. The obstacles that have to be overcome were depicted in dramatic form as the Twelve Labours of Hercules. For those who could understand them, these labours depicted the crises and opportunities confronting all who were treading the evolutionary path back to God.

Next was Hermes who proclaimed himself the Light of the World. Then came Vyasa, who taught that death is not the end. Other teachers followed in this dim and distant period of our history, when man's intelligence had been growing, and an increasing number of questions were being asked. Then the Buddha came and responded to these questions with the Four Noble Truths. He brought great light to humanity and paved the way for the Christ, whom He prophesied would come after Him.

Between the times of Buddha and the Christ came Shankaracharya, who taught the nature of the Self, and Shri Krishna of the *Bhagavad Gita*, who many believe to have been a previous incarnation of the Christ.

The Christ, when He came, gave to the world the truth of the existence of the human soul and the system of service to God and to one's fellowmen. He taught, loved, lived a life of spiritual livingness and service, asking nothing for His separated self, and thus carried forward the great continuity of revelation. He left us an example that we should follow His steps (*I Peter* 2:21).

The world now awaits another great Approach and spiritual revelation.

Today (1947), humanity stands at a peculiar and unique middle point, between an unhappy past and a future which is full of promise if the reappearance of the Christ is recognised and preparation for His coming is undertaken. The present is full of promise and also full of difficulty; in the hands of human beings today and in the immediate present, lies the destiny of the world and – if it may be reverently said – the immediate activity of the Christ. The agony of the war, and the distress of the entire human family led Christ, in the year 1945, to come to a great decision – a decision which found expression in two most important statements. He announced to the assembled spiritual Hierarchy and to all His servants and disciples on Earth that He had decided to emerge again into physical contact with humanity, *if* they would bring about the initial stages of establishing right human relations; secondly, He gave to the world (for use of the "man in the street") one of the oldest prayers ever known, but one which hitherto had not been permitted to be used except by the most exalted, spiritual Beings. (See "The Great Invocation", page 135).
The Reappearance of the Christ, pages 30, 31

The early signs of His approach with His disciples can already be discerned by those who note and rightly interpret the signs of the times. There is (among these signs) the coming together spiritually of those who love their fellowmen. This is in reality the organising of the outer physical army of the Lord – an army which has no weapons but those of love, of right speech and right human relations. This unknown organisation has proceeded with phenomenal speed during the aftermath of war, because humanity is sick of hate and controversy.
The Reappearance of the Christ, page 44

The development of spiritual recognition is the great need today in preparation for His reappearance; no one knows in what nation He will come; He may appear as an Englishman, a Russian, a Negro, a Latin, a Turk, a Hindu, or any other nationality. Who can say which? He may be a

Christian or a Hindu by faith, a Buddhist or of no particular faith at all; He
will not come as the restorer of any of the ancient religions, including
Christianity, but He will come to restore man's faith in the Father's love, in
the fact of the livingness of the Christ and in the close, subjective and
unbreakable relationship of all men everywhere. The facilities of the entire
world of contact and relation will be at His disposal.
The Reappearance of the Christ, page 19

It is to the whole world that Christ comes and not just to the Christian world.
He comes to the East and to the West, and has foreseen this "time of the
end", with its planetary catastrophes, phenomenal disasters, despair and
invocation – arising from both the East and West. He knew that in the time
of final crisis and tension, humanity itself would force His emergence. *The
New Testament* story is true and correct; it is only the man-made
interpretations which have misled humanity.
The Reappearance of the Christ, page 100

(Written in 1947 by D.K.) Many years ago I indicated that the Christ would
come in three ways, or rather, that the fact of His Presence could be proved
in three distinctive phases.

I said then that the first move which the Hierarchy would make would be
the stimulation of the spiritual consciousness in man, the evocation of
humanity's spiritual demands on a large scale, and *the nurturing – on a
worldwide scale – of the Christ consciousness in the human heart* (italics by
author) This has already been done, and with most effective results. Of the
factual nature of this process, the vociferous demands of men of goodwill, of
welfare workers and of those pledged to international cooperation, to the
relief of world distress and to the establishment of right human relations are
the undeniable expression. That phase of the preparatory work which is
indicative of His coming has now reached a stage where nothing can arrest
its progress or slow down its momentum. In spite of appearances, this
uprising of the Christ consciousness has been successful, and what may
appear as reverse activity is of no importance in the long run, and only of a
temporary nature.

The second move of the Hierarchy, I told you, would be the impressing of
the minds of enlightened men everywhere by spiritual ideas embodying the
new truths, by the "descent" (if I may so call it) of the new concepts which
will govern human living, and by the over-shadowing of all world disciples
and the new group of world servers by the Christ Himself. . . . This planned
move of the Hierarchy is also progressing well; men and women everywhere
and in every department of life are enunciating those new truths which
should in the future guide human living; they are building those new
organisations, movements and groups – large or small – which will
familiarise the mass of men with the reality of the need and the mode of
meeting it. This they are doing because they are driven thereto by the

warmth of their hearts and their loving response to human distress; without formulating it thus to themselves, they are nevertheless working to bring into visibility the Kingdom of God on earth. No denial of these facts is possible, in view of the multiplicity of this type of organisations, books and speeches.

Thirdly, I told you that Christ might come in person, and walk among men as He did before.

(When this statement was made in 1936 it appears to have been the ashramic view that the status of humanity would not permit more than an overshadowing by the Christ. When *The Reappearance of the Christ*, dictated by the Tibetan, appeared in 1948, the discipline of the war, the destruction of material values, the suffering and the mental growth of humanity had produced an effect which we are told exceeded the expectations of the Hierarchy. In the book on the reappearance the following statements are found: "The point of decision, as it is called in all hierarchical circles, was reached during the period between the Full Moon of June 1936 and the Full Moon of June 1945. The point of decision covered, therefore, nine years, a relatively brief time; it resulted in the decision arrived at by the Christ to reappear or return to visible presence on Earth as soon as possible and considerably earlier than had been planned."

It is indeed a momentous thing to realise that humanity could so notably affect the time and manner of the reappearance of the Christ by a change in its receptivity. We have repeatedly been told that only humanity could condition these points. Here is a dramatic instance of humanity's potential and responsibility in speeding up the evolutionary process.)
(Editor's note from *The Labours of Hercules*, page 202)

Belief in His coming is basic in the human consciousness. How He will come, in what manner, I may not and should not say. The exact moment has not yet arrived, nor has the method of His appearance been determined. The factual nature of the two earlier and preparatory moves, already made by the Hierarchy under His direction, are the guarantee that He *will* come and that – when He does – mankind will be ready.
The Externalisation of the Hierarchy, pages 600 – 602

What this divine purpose may be the Christ Himself will reveal upon His arrival; the focal point of His activity will be dependent upon the medium used by Him to implement that purpose – known only to Him and to the senior members of the Hierarchy. Should politics be the medium through which He best can serve, that then will determine the locality of the focal point; if it should be the religious organisations of the world, it may prove to be elsewhere; if the field of economics or of the social sciences, then still another locality may prove appropriate. The determining factor in all cases, and that which will indicate to Him the appropriate place for this focal point, *will be the number and the ability and status of the disciples found active in the chosen field*. More, I may not suggest. . . . (*Italics by author*)

The *over-shadowing* of all disciples and initiates, and the consequent stimulation of their natures and of their environment, must inevitably produce conflict; the outpouring of the stimulating love of God into the hearts of men must equally and inevitably produce conflict; the line of cleavage between men of goodwill and the unresponsive natures of those uninfluenced by this quality will be made abundantly, usefully and constructively clear. It will be obvious also that when Christ establishes the "centre or focal point of the divine Purpose" in some definite place on Earth, its radiation and implementary potency will also produce the needed conflict which precedes the clarification and the renunciation of obstructions.

. . . As far as humanity as a sum total is concerned, the conflict of ideas and of emotional desire is today so acute that it will finally exhaust itself, and men will turn, with relief and with a longing to escape from further turmoil, towards right human relations; this will constitute the first major human decision leading to the longed-for harmony. The attitude of the masses will then be soundly tending towards harmony, owing to the work of the men and women of goodwill as they implement the "streaming forth of the Love of God into the hearts of men".

The Rays and the Initiations, pages 617 – 618

The Son of God is on His way and He cometh not alone. His advance guard is already here and the Plan which they must follow is already made and clear. Let recognition be the aim.

The Externalisation of the Hierarchy, page 612.

THE NEW WORLD RELIGION

The religious spirit of humanity is more alive and more definitely focused on reality than ever before in our history, particularly in those countries devastated by the world war, notably Russia.

The network of modern communication, particularly via television, is having a stupendous effect on the awakening minds of men. Our modern scientists are proving the truths that the Ageless Wisdom has taught for centuries, and, above all, as D.K. says, the heart of humanity is sound. The walls of separation are breaking down and there is a growing sense of the need for a global outlook, particularly in religion, as the fundamentals of all faiths are the same.

When the Christ reappears, the non-essentials will surely disappear; the fundamentals of faith will remain, upon which He can build that new world religion for which all men wait. That new world religion *must* be based upon those truths which have stood the test of ages and which have brought assurance and comfort to men everywhere. These surely are:

1. **The Fact of God.**

First and foremost, there must be recognition of the fact of God. That central Reality can be called by any name that man may choose according to his mental or emotional bent, racial tradition and heritage, for it cannot be defined or conditioned by names.

2. **Man's Relationship to God.**

The second truth to which all give allegiance – no matter what the faith – is that of man's essential relationship to God. Inherent in the human consciousness – inchoate often and undefined – is a sense of divinity. "We are all the children of God" (*Galatians* 3:26); "One is our Father, even God," says the Christ and so say all the world Teachers and Avatars down the ages. "As He is, so are we in this world" (*I John* 4:17) is another biblical statement. "Closer is He than breathing, nearer than hands and feet," chants the Hindu. "Christ in us, the hope of glory" is the triumphant affirmation of St. Paul.

3. **The Fact of Immortality and of Eternal Persistence.**

Third, is the sense of persistence, of eternal life or of immortality. From this recognition, there seems to be no escape; it is as much a part of humanity's reaction as is the instinct of self-preservation.

4. **The Continuity of Revelation and the Divine Approaches.**

A fourth essential truth and one which clarifies all the planned work of the Christ is tied in with spiritual revelation and the need of man for God and of God for man. Never has Deity left Itself at any time without witness. Never has man demanded light that the light has not been forthcoming. Never has there been a time, cycle or world period when there was not the giving out of the teaching and spiritual help which human need demanded. Never did the hearts and minds of men go out towards God, but that divinity itself came nearer to man.

The Reappearance of the Christ, pages 144 – 148

These are the foundational truths upon which the world religion of the future will rest. Its keynote will be *Divine Approach*. "Draw near to Him and He will draw near to you" (*James* 4:8) is the great injunction, emanating in new and clear tones from Christ and the spiritual Hierarchy at this time.

The great *theme* of the new world religion will be the recognition of the many divine approaches and the continuity of revelation which each of them conveyed; the *task* ahead of the spiritually minded people of the world today is to prepare humanity for the imminent and (perhaps) the greatest of all the Approaches. The *method* employed will be the scientific and intelligent use of Invocation and Evocation and the recognition of their tremendous potency. . .

The science of invocation and evocation will take the place of what we now call "prayer" and "worship". Be not disturbed by the use of the word "science". It is not the cold and heartless intellectual thing so oft depicted. It is in reality the intelligent organisation of spiritual energy and of the forces of love, and these, when effective, will evoke the response of spiritual Beings Who can again walk openly among men, and thus establish a close relation and a constant communication between humanity and the spiritual Hierarchy.

In order to clarify, it might be said that Invocation is of three kinds: there is, as stated above, the massed demand, unconsciously voiced, and the crying appeal, wrung from the hearts of men in all times of crisis such as the present. This invocative cry rises ceaselessly from all men living in the midst of disaster; it is addressed to that power outside themselves which they feel can and should come to their help in their moment of extremity. This great and wordless invocation is rising everywhere today. Then there is the invocational spirit, evidenced by sincere men as they participate in the rites of their religion and take advantage of the opportunity of united worship and prayer to lay their demands for help before God. This group, added to the mass of men, creates a huge body of invocative applicants and at this time, their massed intent is in great evidence and their invocation is rising to the Most High. Then, lastly there are the trained disciples and aspirants of the world who use certain forms of words, certain carefully defined invocations and who – as they do this – focus the invocative cry and the invocative appeal of the other two groups, giving it right direction and power. All these three groups are, consciously or unconsciously, swinging into activity at this time and their united effort guarantees a resultant evocation.

This new invocative work will be the keynote of the coming world religion and will fall into two parts. There will be the invocative work of the masses of the people, everywhere, trained by the spiritually minded people of the world (working in the churches whenever possible under an enlightened clergy) to accept the fact of the approaching spiritual energies, focussed through Christ and His spiritual Hierarchy, and trained also to voice their demand for light, liberation and understanding. There will also be the skilled work of invocation as practised by those who have trained their minds through right meditation, who know the potency of formulas, mantrams and invocations and who work consciously. They will increasingly use certain great formulas of words which will later be given to the race, just as the Lord's Prayer was given by the Christ, and as the New Invocation has been given out for use at this time by the Hierarchy.

This new religious science for which prayer, meditation and ritual have prepared humanity, will train its people to present – at stated periods throughout the year – the voiced demand of the people of the world for relationship with God and for a closer spiritual relation to each other. This work, when rightly carried forward, will evoke response from the waiting Hierarchy and from its Head, the Christ. Through this response, the belief of the masses will gradually be changed into the conviction of the knowers. In this way, the mass of men will be transformed and spiritualised, and the two great divine centres of energy or groups – the Hierarchy and Humanity itself – will begin to work in complete at-one-ment and unity. Then the Kingdom

of God will indeed and in truth be functioning on earth.
The Reappearance of the Christ pages 150 – 153

CHAPTER 9
Reincarnation

REINCARNATION or REBIRTH means repeated earth experiences through
birth in a physical body. This planet is a school of experiences through which
we journey at intervals to undergo further unfoldment of the divine powers
latent within us.

Always, when I am asked if I believe in reincarnation, I am reminded
of a television interview in which Dr. Carl Jung was asked if he
believed in God. He looked surprised, hesitated a moment and then
said, "I don't *have* to believe, I know."

I feel the same way about reincarnation. I don't *have* to believe, I
know. How else can the many apparent injustices we meet with every
day be explained? In my own family two members were born cursed
with alcoholism whilst I, with the same parents, was born allergic to
alcohol! Where is the justice in that if we are to be judged on this one
life, or one incarnation?

Some of our scientists are looking for acceptable answers to the
question of reincarnation and will, I am sure, find them. Meanwhile, I
think that anyone who does not believe in reincarnation must find it
extremely difficult to reconcile the inequalities of life with the image of
God as a loving Father.

The attitude of the Western world towards the question of life after
death, has changed dramatically. The belief that life ends with the
dissolution of the physical body is no longer popular. The belief that
immortality and the entry into God's heaven is only for those who
accept specified religious beliefs is losing ground. The threat of eternal
damnation for those who do not share these specified beliefs is,
thankfully, not acceptable to the basically kind-hearted majority of
mankind.

The general public has been very interested in the testimony of such
eminent scientists as Elizabeth Kubler-Ross, Raymond Moody,
Margot Grey, David Lorimer and Konstamm Raudive about the near
death experiences of hundreds of people who were resuscitated after
having been pronounced clinically dead. Moody and Grey indicate
that, in the flashback to the past life immediately after death, the
assessment is *totally unjudgemental*.

Included in this change has been the attitude to reincarnation. Until the advent of Madame Blavatsky and the Theosophical Society towards the end of the last century, the response in the Western World to the word reincarnation would probably have been a blank "What's that?". Until the second world war it might have sometimes been "Ah yes, I have heard about that strange belief."

Now, at the end of this 20th century, speculation is rife. There is a flood of books on the subject, including exciting novels and auto-biographies. It is now quite acceptable, at all levels of society, to discuss reincarnation, and speculate about past lives and what effect they might be having on this present incarnation.

I include here some very interesting passages from Roland Peterson's book, *Everyone is Right. A New Look at Comparative Religion and its Relation to Science.*

In Matthew (17:10-13), we find the following:
His disciples asked him, saying, "Why then say the scribes that Elias must first come?" And Jesus answered and said unto them, "Elias truly shall first come, and restore all things. But I say unto you, that Elias is come already, and they knew him not, but have done unto him whatsoever they listed. Likewise shall also the Son of man suffer of them." (The prediction of the return of Elijah is found in Malachi 4:5 in the Old Testament.)
Then the disciples understood that he spake unto them of John the Baptist (p.117).

Leonardo Da Vinci's notebooks clearly indicate that he accepted the pre-existence of the soul, and in one entry he writes, "Read me, O Reader, if you find delight in me, because very seldom shall I come back into this world". That someone as advanced as Leonardo would require few additional earth lives is, of course, consistent with the reincarnationists' view of evolutionary development (p.124).

General Patton's case is especially interesting because he not only claimed to recall past lives but was able while in France for the first time at the ancient Roman town of Langres to correctly direct his driver to, and identify, the old Roman amphitheater, the drill ground, the forum, and the temples of Mars and Apollo. He accomplished this even though some of the structures had been torn down or built over. He also correctly identified the site where Caesar had pitched his tent. Patton was convinced that he had been in Langres in a past life. In response to his nephew Fred Ayer, who asked if he really believed in reincarnation, he replied, "I don't know about other people, but for myself there has never been any question. I just don't think it, I damn well know" (pp. 130, 131).

Some of D.K.'s teachings on reincarnation and the problems we have in accepting it at present, and even some suggestions on how science might come to recognise it, are given below in a selection from *Death the Great Adventure*, (compiled from his writings by two students) pages 4 to 7:

Within the next few years the fact of persistence and of the eternity of existence will have advanced out of the realm of questioning into the realm of certainty . . . There will be no question in anyone's mind that the discarding of the physical body will leave a man still a conscious living entity. He will be known to be perpetuating his existence in a realm lying behind the physical. He will be known to be still alive, awake and aware. This will be brought about by:

a. The development of a power within the physical eye of a human being will reveal the etheric body . . . men will be seen occupying that body.

b. The growth of the number of people who have the power to use the "reawakened third eye" will demonstrate immortality, for they will with facility see the man who has discarded his etheric body as well as the physical body.

c. A discovery in the field of photography will prove survival.

d. Through the use of the radio by those who have passed over will communication eventually be set up and reduced to a true science. (This was published in *Esoteric Healing*, in 1953. In 1985, John G. Fuller published *The Ghost of 29 Megacycles*, an account of a successful series of experiments by a group of American scientists to communicate with the dead by radio.)

e. Man will eventually be keyed up to a perception and to a contact which will enable him to *see through*, which will reveal the nature of the fourth dimension, and will blend the subjective and objective worlds together into a new world. Death will lose its terrors and that particular fear will come to an end.

And about reincarnation, D.K. writes:

The Christian interpretation as given by the orthodox and the fundamentalist schools proves untenable when submitted to clear reasoning; among the arguments which negate its accuracy lies the fact that Christianity posits a long future but no past; it is likewise a future entirely dependent upon the activities of this present life episode and accounts in no way for the distinctions and differences which distinguish humanity. It is only tenable upon the theory of an anthropomorphic Deity Whose will – as it works out in practice – gives a present that has no past but only a future; the injustice of this is widely recognised, but the inscrutable will of God must not be questioned. Millions still hold this belief, but it is not so strongly held as it was one hundred years ago.

The theory of reincarnation, so familiar to all my readers, is becoming increasingly popular in the Occident; it has always been accepted (though with many foolish additions and interpretations) in the Orient. This teaching has been as much distorted as have the teachings of the Christ or the Buddha or Shri Krishna by their narrow-minded and mentally limited theologians. The basic facts of a spiritual origin, of a descent into matter, of an ascent through the medium of constant incarnations in form until those forms are perfect expressions of the indwelling spiritual consciousness, and of a series of initiations at the close of the cycle of incarnation, are being more readily accepted and acknowledged than ever before.

Such are the major solutions of the problems of immortality and of the persistence of the human soul; they aim to answer the eternal questioning of the human heart as to Whence, Why, Whither and Where?
Esoteric Healing page 402

From *Through the Curtain* by Viola Petitt Neal and Shafica Karagulla, pages 295 and 296: (In this "night class", Viola attended a lecture on "Reincarnation" on 11 September 1960. As described earlier, she had total recall, the next morning, of the teaching she was subjected to the previous night while she was asleep.)

There is very little technical information on reincarnation. Asia is familiar with the idea, but often does not understand its implications. The Western world is ready for the knowledge. More must be given out and written.

Each personality is a mathematical equation of energies which makes up that personality pattern for the Soul for the given incarnation. Sometimes certain soul qualities already developed are inhibited and others used in order to achieve what is needed. More can be understood about what the individual is doing and working out in a given lifetime and what activities will assist him. This could help greatly in assisting mankind. It is the only basis for the teaching of the moral law, energies, and cause and effect in a universe that works according to law and order.

So far man on this planet has made progress slowly with much pain and suffering. It does not need to be this way. Man should grow as the tree grows – in rhythmic cycles with order and beauty, and with far less suffering. But because he does not understand the cosmic laws of cause and effect, or how and why we grow, or for what end or reason, he stumbles blindly. He thinks he must be here to amass possessions. Often he knows no other goal. Or he struggles to be clothed and fed and sheltered, and barely does so. He does not know his divine destiny or the why or wherefore of existence in a physical body.

For many Christian readers who are still uncertain about the issue, the bottom line in the question of whether they should accept the idea of reincarnation or not, will be to find irrefutable evidence that reincarnation has had a place in the history of Christianity, and that it is today accepted by leading Christians who have studied the matter. To that end, the following two quotations may help:

Firstly, from Roland Peterson's scholarly and most readable work, *Everyone is Right*, mentioned earlier, pages 118 and 119:

Researchers have concluded that although reincarnation is not generally taught in the Christian churches today, it was much more widespread in the early Church. The early Church fathers Origen (A.D. 185? – ?254) and St. Clement of Alexandria (A.D. *ca* 150-213) are cited as supporting reincarnation. Origen writes:

"Is it not rational that souls should be introduced into bodies in accordance with their merits and previous deeds, and that those who have used their bodies in doing the utmost possible good should have a right to bodies endowed with qualities superior to the bodies of others?

"The soul . . . at one time puts off one body, which was necessary before, but which is no longer adequate in its changed state, and it exchanges it for a second."

St. Gregory (A.D. *ca* 335-*ca* 394), Bishop of Nyssa, wrote, "It is absolutely necessary that the soul should be healed and purified, and if this does not take place during its life on earth it must be accomplished in future lives."

In his book *Reincarnation, the Cycle of Necessity* Manly P. Hall indicates that "Arnobius, a Numidian apologist of Christianity . . . has left a record that Clement of Alexandria had written a most important account of metempsychosis ((reincarnation)). Clement of Alexandria declared that reincarnation was a truth transmitted by St. Paul himself." He also references St. Jerome as declaring "that the doctrine of transmigration was taught as an esoteric mystery in the early Church, being communicated only to a few specially selected members of the congregation." Mr. Hall also provides a reference citing advocates of reincarnation in the Middle Ages to include St. Francis of Assisi (1182-1276); Johannes Scotus Erigena (*ca* 810-*ca* 877), the learned Irish monk; St. Bonaventura (1221-1274), cardinal and general of the Franciscan order; and Thomas Campanella (1568-1639), a Dominican monk who was exiled for this belief.

Regarding the question of the doctrinal compatability of reincarnation with modern Christianity, Manly P. Hall quotes William R. Inge, late Dean of St. Paul's Cathedral, London, as a Protestant authority who finds no conflict between this, "the oldest creed," and modern Anglicanism. For the Catholic faith Hall cites Cardinal Mercier, the Belgian prelate and scholastic philosopher, who stated that the doctrine does not in any way conflict with Catholic dogma.

A factor that seems to have prevented dialogue concerning reincarnation in orthodox Christianity for many centuries was the generally held belief that the Second Council of Constantinople, opened in 553 (the Fifth Ecumenical Council), anathematized (cursed) the doctrine of the pre-existence of the soul before physical birth. (This despite the references to pre-existence in Jeremiah 1:5, Proverbs 8:22-31, Wisdom 8:19-20 (The Book of Wisdom appears only in the Catholic version of the Old Testament), Ephesians 1:4, and John 17:5.) A denial of pre-existence, of course, precludes reincarnation.

Recent research by Catholic scholars who now have access to original Council records shows that this anathema was not approved by the Council (which was called for another purpose) or by the pope (who refused to attend the Council), but was issued at the direction of Emperor Justinian for political reasons in an attempt to condemn a sect of which he disapproved. Justinian not only convened the Council over the pope's objection but actually held the pope captive for a time. The facts concerning this episode are very thoroughly reviewed by Head and Cranston in their comprehensive book on the subject of reincarnation. (*Reincarnation: The Phoenix Fire Mystery*, by Joseph Head and S.L. Cranston. New York: Julian Press/Crown Publishers. 1977)

In his recent book *Reincarnation in Christianity*, Dr. Geddes MacGregor, Emeritus Distinguished Professor of Philosophy at the University of Southern California, provides a detailed study of the subject of his title, including the proceedings of the Fifth Ecumenical Council, and concludes his book with the following paragraph:

"We can conclude that there is nothing in biblical thought or Christian tradition that necessarily excludes all forms of reincarnationism. We have seen many historical reasons why it has been suppressed both officially and at the popular level, in the history of the Christian Church. We have seen no reason why it must be in conflict with the historic teachings that have come to us through the Bible and the Church. We have seen, above all, that some form of reincarnationism could much enhance the spirituality of the West, not least at the present time when it stands so much in need of fresh avenues of development and new means of illumination."

The second quotation comes from *Testimony of Light* by Helen Greaves. The author shares a series of communications with the reader, sent from beyond the grave by her close friend and colleague, Frances Banks, who was a Sister in the Anglican Community of the Resurrection in South Africa, and Principal of the Teachers' Training College in Grahamstown. The preface to this remarkable book about a remarkable person, was written by Canon J.D. Pearce-Higgins, Vice-Provost of Southwark Cathedral, who pays tribute to the work, and continues:

I have been asked to comment on the fact that Frances occasionally refers to Reincarnation, since such references may be a stumbling-block to Christian readers, few of whom, unless they are scholars, probably are aware that there was a 500-year tradition of such belief within the early Church itself; mainly in the Alexandrian school, including such names as Clement, Justin Martyr, St. Gregory of Nyssa, and most notable of all, Origen, who had a well worked out reincarnational system of belief, which certainly makes sense, and avoids many of the objectionable features of oriental versions. Further, it is far from clear that the Church ever officially rejected such belief, however little the medieval mind was able to contain it. The Council of Constantinople in A.D. 553, at which it seems that a corrupt form of Origen's teaching was anathematised, is held by many historians to have been imperfectly constituted – the Pope himself refused to be present – and even Roman Catholics contest its validity as a General Council.

The Church today has got to face the fact that in our shrunken world, with the eastern cultures on our doorstep, Reincarnation is again a life issue, since according to Geoffrey Gorer's sociological study ('In search of English character' 1955) some 12 per cent of our population believe in it, as against 10 per cent who accept traditional Christian and biblical eschatology, and the spread of the belief continues . . . .

And finally, from the first page of the same book: An Interview with the late Sir Malcolm Sargent on the B.B.C. April 19th 1968 *(Transcribed from a recording by Radio Direction Telediphone Unit):*

Sir Malcolm Sargent: I feel death, which I've never been afraid of, which I look forward to . . .
Interviewer: You look forward to death?
Sir Malcolm Sargent: Oh, very much. Er . . . Obviously. I mean this life has been wonderful and because I've loved this life so much, I know I shall love death more. Don't you remember, He said, 'When I came into this world, I do not remember a moment but I was not a stranger' . . . So shall it be when one passes from life to death, from life to life . . .

CHAPTER 10
Karma and Karmic Bonds

In your literature the mention of the words incarnation and karma has
become common. Nevertheless, this reality enters little into consciousness
otherwise it would transform the whole of life.
Agni Yoga, paragraph 553

Karma, or the Law of Cause and Effect, is a law which governs "action and
its coming into effect". In the mental, emotional and material worlds no
good deed can escape its reward and no evil deed its fit penalty. "As a man
soweth, so shall he reap." Perfect justice thus rules. By this Law, *our
characters* are the consequences of our past evolution; therefore the future is
now in our hands.

There is no place for "accident" in the common meaning of something
"fortuitous" or "untimely", in the events which come to us. Everything is determined by our own state of mind, completely fitting this
state from moment to moment. Jung describes this as synchronicity, a
word which he uses to imply that whenever an outer event takes place,
it reflects some inner movement of the soul. Thus, life is a constantly
moving pattern which adjusts itself to individual need at every instant
of our existence.

Our surroundings and companions react to us in a way that responds
to what and where we are at any given moment. In other words, they
"tune in" to us and respond, consciously or unconsciously, to our
frequencies just as they are at that particular moment in time. If we or
they fail to understand and adjust to these frequencies but react to
them instead, a further chain of reaction is set up. Action, reaction;
this in brief is the Law of Karma. We have all heard tales of the *"I* said,
then *she* said, then *I* said – I wasn't going to let her get away with *that"*,
variety. Sometimes one has to say, "This must stop, now, with me."

Karma is not a punishing and rewarding moralistic law, nor is it a
fixed process of bookkeeping with entries of debit and credit on
opposite pages, but is instead a constant balancing of forces between
ourselves and the world in which we live. It is a dynamic self-adjusting

system in which there is constant feedback according to the manner in which we accept or refuse experience from moment to moment.

An incarnation is a definitely determined period (from the angle of the soul) wherein *Experiment, Experience* and *Expression* are the keynotes in each incarnation. Each successive incarnation continues the experiment, deepens the experience and relates the expression more closely to the latent unfolding divinity.
The Rays and the Initiations, page 337

Our reaction and attitude in the face of experience is more important than the experience itself. That which we know through ourselves, our own conscious experience, teaches us more than does any experience of others which we may have observed or read about. These experiences can lead to success or failure, but in a certain sense that is not important. What *is* important is that the experiencing continues. In other words, that the balancing of karma continues – karma conditioning, not determining.

In each successive incarnation the equipment needed to continue the experiment, experience and expression is necessarily different. The decisions about this equipment and about circumstances are made, as we know, by the Lords of Karma in conjunction with the soul. Some of the resulting handicaps are what our medical friends would term "irreversible", and must be lived with through a specific incarnation. This would seem rather a drastic way of balancing karma, but we are told that we are never given more than we are capable of handling. (See Chapter 4, "Incarnation", page 36)

Some people find it difficult to accept that sometimes equipment such as a severe physical handicap is necessary. Consider Helen Keller and Douglas Bader. Both faced this challenge and became shining examples of how the human spirit can triumph over adversity.

Handicaps are not always physical. All social workers are familiar with the enigma of the different reactions of children from the same family, to identical challenges under the same unsatisfactory conditions. One will fight back, one will somehow seem unaffected by it and get on with life, the third will give in, "drop out" and look for anyone and anything to blame except his own failure to cope. The juvenile courts are full of such cases.

We could say that each of us is given, in each incarnation, some kind of mountain to climb and it is up to us as to how we do this: just doggedly getting on with it because it has to be done, or, we are darn well not going to be beaten by any old mountain, or getting to the top hoping that there will be something better on the other side. There is always someone who will grumble and stay put at the bottom, because, "My feet hurt", "I am tired", "It's too hot", "I don't want to climb any old mountain and why should I anyway?", "None of my neighbours has to", "*Why should this happen to me?*" One thing is for sure: for those with that attitude, the same old mountain will be looming up next time around.

I find it very helpful, when faced with some of the tiresome, boring and difficult aspects of daily living in a material world, to speculate about karma in relation to character, because, after all, karmic changes manifest as character changes at the level of everyday living. What would my character have been at the end of my last incarnation? What were the strengths, weaknesses, talents and ignorances to be considered by the soul, in consultation with the Lords of Karma, when deciding what to provide in the way of bodies and ray energies that would lead to growth in this, my present incarnation?

I then make a list of my character traits and any talents – or lack therof – and then another list of the important blessings or trials met with in this lifetime and consider how I have reacted to them, or dealt with them.

Have I become more intelligent, useful, understanding and loving? Have I changed at all for the better? Have I accepted gracefully, as did Helen Keller and Douglas Bader, what could not be changed and made of it a plus factor? Am I stuck at the bottom of my mountain or am I climbing it, and how?

It is interesting to speculate how the world karma might change if we were all to deal with the causes of our problems instead of reacting to the effects, if we considered life as a laboratory of the soul, and the experiences to which we are submitted, as karma.

KARMIC BONDS

The *action* of one person sending thoughts and feelings to another does not link them together. There must be a *reaction* of acceptance or rejection of these from the person thought or felt *about* before that fine subjective thread that forms the link between them comes into being. Only indifference prevents this link being formed. Any reaction sets up a rapport.

This thread cannot be formed by physical proximity alone. There must be *action* and *reaction* on the planes of emotion and mind before any karmic bond can be established.

The influence of these bonds of love and empathy or hate and resentment, on the lives of those concerned, depends on their intensity.

If these subjective threads are strong enough in the consciousness of a dying person, at the time of death they are "carried over" and "stored up", so to speak, for longer or shorter periods until in some later incarnation those concerned react in the same way to the same conditions when those conditions again become available, and continue the connection. This explains instant attraction or repulsion and also the sense of intimacy and understanding that "twin souls" experience.

Twin souls are not created *as* twin souls. Such unions are built in the course of many incarnations, as each renewal of karmic bonds increases their strength.

The rapport between:
– friends, family and
lovers   is usually on the emotional plane;
– teachers and pupils
and fellow students   is usually on the mental plane;
– spiritual guides and
fellow worshippers   is usually on the mental and causal planes.

However, the many degrees of feeling on the emotional plane and thoughts on the lower mental plane are so closely intertwined that the Theosophists have given this area a separate name – kama manasic: kama for emotional, and manasic for mind. Therefore the above neat classification does not always apply as here the bonds range freely and co-exist over the wide number of possibilities available.

Nothing in relation to our contacts or affiliations happens by mere chance, nor are there any accidents, but only cause and effect. As we grow in awareness we inevitably develop a magnetic centre as it were, which by its auric sphere of radiation attracts to it those individuals and circumstances resonant with it. This is why all the situations we become involved in, and all the associations which come into our lives are exactly right for us, offering the best means to spiritual growth, progress and constructive ability. Many of our familiar contacts and close associates will have, in previous life cycles, formed karmic links with us. One can in time learn to recognise something of the pattern of these contacts, and it seems most likely that the New Age type of spiritual progress will take place in formation on a group basis of this kind, with individuals at different stages of evolutionary growth contributing to the welfare of each other and of the Whole.

Some thoughts and feelings, very necessary and therefore being right in the earlier stage of our evolution when these bonds are first formed, are discarded as we move onward. However, all of us do not move onward at the same pace. Should one of a pair or of a group develop on the higher planes before the others, he could find no reaction from them at this higher level but still feel for them the strong "pull" of the lower bonds in his lower bodies. This imbalance can lead to unhappiness, suffering and sometimes tragedy. How often we find ourselves saying "how *could* that fine person become so involved with that coarse person (or group)!"

Strong karmic bonds can hold souls together, incarnation after incarnation, until, in the course of evolution, they reach the higher planes. If they are both of the same ray type they will come together there in perfect sympathy and understanding. However, if they are of different ray types they will then be drawn apart there by different ideals.

D.K. tells us that the personality ray and soul ray in both people concerned must be the same before there can be that *perfect* friendship or marriage. But this is very very rare.

CHAPTER 11
The Akashic Records

In the excerpt below D.K. explains the nature of these records of the
past and gives us some clues as to the qualities that need to be
developed before a person becomes able to read the akashic records.
He gives some of the reasons that make it so difficult to locate and
isolate specific incidents.

From *The Light of the Soul*, pages 275, 276:

KNOWLEDGE OF PREVIOUS INCARNATIONS BECOMES AVAILABLE WHEN THE
POWER TO SEE THOUGHT-IMAGES IS ACQUIRED.

The significance of this sutra is very great, for it gives the basis for the
regaining of a knowledge of past experience. This basis is strictly mental, and
only those mentally polarised and with the mind under control can regain
this knowledge if they so wish. The power to see thought-images only comes
through mind control, and the mind can only be controlled by the real or
spiritual man. Therefore only egoically centred people can truly acquire this
knowledge. It might be asked here what therefore do those people see who
are emotional and *not* mental, when they claim to know who they are, and to
relate the past lives of their friends? They are reading the akashic records
and because their mental control and equipment are not adequate, they
cannot discriminate nor ascertain accurately what they see.

The akashic record is like an immense photographic film, registering all
the desires and earth experiences of our planet. Those who perceive it will
see pictured thereon:

1. The life experiences of every human being since time began,

2. The reactions to experience of the entire animal kingdom,

3. The aggregation of the thought-forms of a kamic nature (based on desire)
of every human unit throughout time. Herein lies the great deception of the
records. Only a trained occultist can distinguish between actual experience
and those astral pictures created by imagination and keen desire.

4. The planetary "Dweller on the Threshold" with all that appertains to that
term and all the aggregations of forms which are to be found in its
environment.

The trained seer has learnt to dissociate that which pertains to his own
aura and the aura of the planet (which is in actuality the akashic record).

From the above you will gather that the rare qualifications of an

Egoically centred person, i.e. a purified, highly intelligent, dedicated, properly trained occultist (white magician), are needed for conscious work on the causal plane (or higher mental plane: see chart 5, page 35) where the akashic records are to be found. Only one with these qualifications can clearly distinguish between these records and their reflection to be found amid the confusing glamour of the astral plane.

People of this calibre, such as Madame Blavatsky, are, however, very few and far between.

There is an interesting account on pages 17 and 18 of *Through the Curtain* by Viola Petitt Neal and Shafica Karagulla, of the method whereby Edgar Cayce and the band of discarnate healers-helpers, who were disciples working on the higher mental plane, contacted the akashic records to obtain the information which Cayce passed on with such wonderful results.

Like everyone else, I would find it very interesting to learn about my previous lives; but I suppose because I was born a Scot (and we Scots do not easily fall prey to glamour) and also because I am well aware of how open this field of study is to conscious and unconscious glamour and fraud, I have never been motivated to find out, through others, about my past lives.

As I am not a trained occultist and am therefore unable to read the akashic records for myself at will, I have had to be content to be like Abraham Lincoln when he said that he was not so much interested in what his ancestors *had been* as in what he, their descendant, *could become!*

However, on four widely separated occasions in my life, and at the most unlikely times, I have been given glimpses into past incarnations through my own inner eye. These were distinctly different from the usual visions in that, instead of being a spectator, I was a participant in the pictured events.

Within a few weeks of each of these occasions I was confronted by a major crisis, and what was interesting, was that on each of these occasions the karmic link with the events in the akashic "flashback" was clearly evident. This helped me greatly to deal with each crisis as it arose, without hurting anyone and without making any waves that would perpetuate past negative karma.

I do not know the mechanics of how these events came about; whether through my own higher Self or through some other incarnate or discarnate entity. I do know however, and these experiences provide the confirmation that, when we commit ourselves and walk the razor edged path sincerely and to the best of our ability, we are often "pointed" in the right direction: *pointed*, not helped – please note the difference. We have to do the work ourselves. If, for instance, we fall, we are shown how to get up; we are not picked up!

On these occasions I am so grateful, I give heartfelt thanks!

CHAPTER 12
The Occultist

An occultist is a practical mystic, adding to the heart approach the intelligent use of the mind.

The average man in the street has been conditioned, on hearing the word "occult", to shudder and conjure up visions of black magicians in black cloaks, "satanism", and devils wearing tails and brandishing forks! This misconception is wholly due to ignorance, but, unfortunately and regrettably, is being loudly and vigorously supported by some religious groups.

This is very confusing for students on the Path, because they will find that this word is given a very different connotation in all the classic and worthwhile literature in this field. For instance, Our Lord The Christ, and those Masters and initiates working with Him are referred to as "The Occult Hierarchy". (See page 454 in *A Treatise on Cosmic Fire*)

The words "occult" and "occultist" are found, correctly used, in all of Alice Bailey's books and in many of the Theosophical Society's publications, such as *The Kingdom of the Gods*, by Geoffrey Hodson. Cyril Scott entitled one of his books *An Outline of Modern Occultism*.

When speaking of the books he dictated to Alice Bailey, the Master Djwhal Khul said: "These (books) will serve . . . to lead humanity forward and nearer to the time when present day occultism will be the theme of world education in some modified form." *The Externalisation of the Hierarchy*, page 322.

The following excerpts from some of these books should clear up any misunderstanding about the meaning of the word "occult".

From *A Treatise on White Magic*, page 120:

The path of knowledge is that of the occultist and the sage; that of love is that of the mystic and the saint. The head or the heart approach is not dependent upon the ray, for both ways must be known; the mystic must become the occultist; the white occultist has been the saintly mystic. True knowledge is intelligent love, for it is the blending of the intellect and the devotion. Unity is sensed in the heart; its intelligent application to life has to be worked out through knowledge.

So occultism is the science of energy flow and energy relationships.

Energy *per se* is impersonal; the *motivation* of the occultist is the
determining factor. If unselfish and helpful, he is a white magician; if
selfish or harmful, he is on the darkened path.

It is a central idea of occultism that even the tiniest atom of
substance contains within it a germ that can respond to the Christ
Spirit. Madame Blavatsky, that great occultist, was once asked why
she, so able to read people's thoughts and character, should have
employed a couple who later slandered and abused her. She replied
that she could also see the light in everyone and that her task was to
give that light an opportunity to grow.

An occultist is a practical mystic, adding to the heart approach the
intelligent use of the mind. We are entering the age of the development
of the mind, and scientists – coming into their own – are exploring the
subtle world of energies underlying form. This is the world of the
occultist. The true occultist, however, adds aspiration to this, and
consciously uses these energies for the carrying out of soul purpose.

From *A Treatise on White Magic*, page 638:

Where, however, there is steady growth, an application to occult principles
so that definite changes are produced in the bodies used, and an increasing
radiatory light, it is known and recorded, and the aspirant is rewarded by
increased opportunity to serve his fellowmen.

From *A Treatise on White Magic*, pages 348 to 350:

Everything depends upon the pupil's ability to grasp the inner meaning of all
events. His entire progress upon the Path rests upon his attitude in making
the teaching his own. It is only as we transmute the lessons on the inner
planes into practical knowledge that they become part of our own experience
and are no longer theoretical. Expansion of consciousness should be an ever
increasing practical experience. Theories are of no value until we have
changed them into fact. Hence the value of meditating on an ideal. In the
meditation our thoughts vibrate temporarily to the measure of the
conception, and in time that vibration becomes permanent.

Those who, with open eyes, enter on occult training need indeed to count
the cost. The reward at the end is great, but the path is rough and the true
occultist walks it alone. The capacity to stand alone, to assume
responsibility, and then to carry all through single-handed, and to brave evil
for the sake of the good achieved is the mark of a White Brother. Be
prepared then for loneliness, for dangers of a dim and obscure character,
and expect to see your life spent for no reward that touches the personality.
It is only as the consciousness expands, and one finds one's true position in
the cosmic whole that the reward becomes apparent; but cease from fear,

and know that the personality is only temporary, and what matter if it suffer? Some good gained for the universal Brotherhood, some law explained and demonstrated in the life of every day, may make the Master say eventually (yes, eventually, after all is over) well done! Let your eyes therefore look straight on. Turn not to the right hand nor to the left. The path leads upward and on to greater rapidity of vibration and to greater sensitiveness. Seek the point of balance in your work and keep that balance, for the years hold much work, much pressure and much suffering.

Are you strong enough to see the world's woe, to see disaster and yet keep joyful? Can you be a partner in the work of furthering the evolution of the race and see the necessity for trouble and for discipline and yet not move to stem the tide of sorrow? Picked and tried souls are being trained all over the world at the present time. The Masters are overwhelmed with the work and Their time is over-occupied. They give what They can but on the individual aspirant depends the use made of that which is given.

Those of us who watch and guide on the inner side of life realize more than perhaps you who bear the burden and heat of physical plane existence know. We know your physical disabilities and some day may be able to help definitely in the building up of strong bodies for world service. Now – such is the astral miasma – it is well nigh impossible for you, our struggling brethren, to have good health; the karma of the world prohibits it. The astral corruption and the foul cesspools of the lower levels of the mental plane infect all, and lucky is he who escapes. We watch with tenderness all of you, who, with weak and sensitive bodies, struggle, work, fight, fail, continue and serve. Not one hour of service, given in pain and tension, not one day's labor followed with racked nerves, with head tired and with heart sick, is allowed to pass unnoticed. *We know and we care, yet, we may do naught that you, struggling in the field of the world, can do of that which is needed. The world's karma engulfs each of you at this epoch. If you could but realize it, the time is short, and rest, joy and peace are on their way.* (Author's italics)

CHAPTER 13
Channelling

There is available today a bewildering amount of literature containing "inspired" or "channelled" messages. It behoves us to realise that, even if these do come from discarnate entities, they should not necessarily be accepted without question.

Upon the discarding of the physical body a man does not automaticaly become all knowing and all wise. The non-physical planes "there" have just the same mixture of wise and ignorant, good and mischievous, as has the physical plane "here".

I would remind the earnest student that, in the Aryan race in the Aquarian age, the mind is to be developed as well as the heart. Therefore do not be carried away by claim making and when reading messages purporting to be from the Masters or even the Christ Himself, use the discriminating mind. Ask yourself, "Is this the quality to be expected from our Lord the Christ – the Master of all the Masters and teacher alike of angels and of men, or from the Masters of the Wisdom?"

D.K. has written a good deal on this interesting subject. The following are some extracts which may prove useful to the reader:

So much is said and written these days which purports to come from the Great Ones and which is stated to embody Their will and Their intention. It is based on astral sensitivity and astral reaction to the many thoughtforms found upon the astral plane; these include among their number many thought forms of the Great Ones. These thoughtforms necessarily exist, and are built by the devotion of the aspirants of the world, and by the selfish spiritual ambition of those aspirants. They are not constructed by the disciples of the world, for no man is admitted to the status of accepted discipleship until he has at least overcome the worst aspects of personal ambition. This freedom from ambition is proved or expressed by personal reticence and by freedom from the publicity-making activities of the aspirants of the world, and also by freedom from the making of statements as to relationship or status. It might be well for us to ponder on these words. *Esoteric Psychology, Vol.II*, pages 713, 714

There are the writings of those sensitive souls who can tune in – again on psychic levels – with the mass of aspirations, longings and ideas of the mystics of all times, or, equally, they can tune in on the fears of the ages, the racial and hereditary fears, or the fears engendered by world conditions prevailing at this time. These they record and write down and hand around to their friends. Under this category come the writings of those who are sensitive in a more mental manner, and can tune in telepathically with the mental world; they are responsive to the mind of some powerful thinker, or to the massed concepts of the religious world; they register, on mental levels, the fear and hatred and separativeness of the masses. Whether the material they record is good or bad, whether it is happy, which it seldom is, or unhappy in nature, and whether it carries a vibration of fear and foreboding, it is all psychic stuff, and it in no way indicates the revealing quality of the soul. . . .

The writer may be tapping the wealth of the subconscious knowledge which is his, and which he has accumulated through his reading, thinking and contacts. His mind has recorded and stored up much of which he remains for years totally unaware. Then he begins to meditate and suddenly taps the depths of his own nature and penetrates to the resources of his own subconsciousness and to information which has dropped below the threshold of his ordinary consciousness. He begins to write assiduously. Why he should regard these thoughts as emanating from the Christ, or from some great Teacher is a puzzle. . . .

How, it might be pertinently asked, can one distinguish between the truly inspired writings of the true knower, and this mass of literature which is flooding the minds of the public at this time? First, I should say that the true inspirational writing will be entirely without self-reference; it will sound a note of love and will be free from hatreds and racial barriers; it will convey definite knowledge and carry a note of authority by its appeal to the intuition; it will respond to the law of correspondences, and fit into the world picture; above all, it will carry the impress of Divine Wisdom and lead the race on a little further. *As to its mechanics; the writers of such a type of teaching will have a real understanding of the methods they employ. They will have mastered the technique of the process; they will be able to guard themselves from illusion, and from the intrusion of personalities, and will have a working knowledge of the apparatus with which they are working. If they are receiving teachings from discarnate entities, and from great Masters, they will know how to receive it, and will then know all about the agent transmitting the teaching.* (Italics by author)
From Intellect to Intuition, pages 248 to 252

Guidance can come, therefore, from all kinds and types of incarnate or discarnate men, ranging in character from very good to very bad.
Esoteric Psychology Vol II, page 490

Apart from the many mediocre channeled messages flooding book-shops today, there are those that bring help and inspiration to many; for instance, the teachings of Lazaris through Jach Purcel, Seth through Jane Roberts, *The Star Seed Transmissions* through Ken Carey and *A Course in Miracles*. All the teachings that answer my needs and which I have chosen to follow, have been channelled. These are:

the Teachings of the Master Djwhal Khul channelled through Alice A. Bailey;

the Teachings of the Master Djwhal Khul and other Masters channelled through Madame Blavatsky;

the White Eagle Teachings channelled through Mrs Grace Cooke;

the Agni Yoga Books channelled through Helena Roerich.

This is an era where much discernment is needed. When evaluating the quality and source of these messages, it is well to remember that no true Initiate or disciple ever gives a direct order or attempts to control anyone.

In a "night class" in September 1960 that dealt with "New Developments in Consciousness", Viola Petitt Neal recalled the following, quoted from *Through the Curtain* written jointly with Shafica Karagulla, page 299:

The world is flooded today with literature written by "contactees" – by
people "in touch with other worlds". Much of this data is distorted; much of
it is clothed in trailing garments of astral glamour. This is a part of moving up
to new states of consciousness. They feel the impact of a new era in
consciousness and of necessity, if undisciplined and untrained, it produces
this type. Look for all the grains of wheat in all the chaff of this
phenomenon.

CHAPTER 14
Yoga

An important result of correct meditation is correct alignment, at-one-ment, which is to be conscious of oneself as a whole (Spirit, soul and body), the mind and soul functioning as a unit to express the will of the Indwelling soul. That state is achieved when, through the ordered stages of meditation, the physical body reflects the Love nature, and the mental body expresses perfectly the Will or purpose of God.

Most of my acquaintances who practice Yoga seem quite content with the asanas of Hatha Yoga, plus, maybe, a little philosophy and sometimes special breathing exercises added. These breathing exercises, unless taught by a really knowledgeable teacher, could be dangerous.

Raja Yoga, the Kingly Science of the soul, as laid down in the Yoga Sutras of Patanjali, has so much more to offer. To quote from Volume II of *Discipleship in the New Age*, pages 326, 327: "For the next seven thousand years his (Patanjali's) system will be used to train disciples in mind control. They will, through this system, achieve the stage of isolated unity . . ."

A man living the life of "isolated unity" works, lives and experiences in the world, but is not *of* the world. He is at one with the soul of all, but separated from everything that concerns the material nature. We can well imagine the skill needed to go through life, holding fast to the vertical alignment, yet remaining untouched by the glamour and the evils of the world. We are told that this will be the outstanding characteristic of the Western disciple of the future, and it is this which will in due course supersede the Eastern method of isolation from the pressures of daily living and constant contact with others.

The following excerpts from the introductory remarks in the book *The Light of the Soul*, a paraphrase of the Yoga Sutras of Patanjali by the Master Djwhal Khul and Alice Bailey, pages vii to xv, give some idea of the beauty and grandeur of this kingly science:

Hitherto the mind has either been prostituted to material ends or has been deified. Through the science of Raja Yoga, the mind will be known as the instrument of the soul and the means whereby the brain of the aspirant becomes illuminated and knowledge gained of those matters which concern the realm of the soul. . . . . .

All the various Yogas have had their place in the unfoldment of the human being. In the first purely physical race, which is called the Lemurian, the Yoga at that time imposed upon infant humanity was Hatha Yoga, the Yoga of the physical body, that Yoga which brings into conscious use and manipulation the various organs, muscles and parts of the physical frame. The problem before the adepts of that time was to teach human beings, who were then little more than animals, the purpose, significance and use of their various organs, so that they could consciously control them, and the meaning of the symbol of the human figure. Therefore, in those early days, through the practice of Hatha Yoga, the human being reached the portal of initiation. At that time the attainment of the third initiation, resulting in the transfiguration of the personality, was the highest initiation that man was capable of achieving.

In Atlantean days, the progress of the sons of men was procured through the imposition of two Yogas. First, the Yoga which is called by the name of Laya Yoga, the Yoga of the centres which produced a stabilizing of the etheric body and of the centres in man and the development of the astral and psychic nature. Later on, Bhakti Yoga, growing out of the development of the emotional or astral body, was incorporated with Laya Yoga and the foundation of that mysticism and devotion, which has been the underlying incentive during our particular Aryan root race, was laid. The fourth initiation was at that time the objective. The subject of these great initiations has been discussed more at length in my previous volume, "*Initiation, Human and Solar*".

Now, in the Aryan race, the subjugation of the mental body and the control of the mind is brought about through the practice of Raja Yoga, and the fifth initiation, that of adept, is the goal for evolving humanity. Thus, all the Yogas have had their place and served a useful purpose and it will become apparent that any return to Hatha Yoga practices or those practices which deal specifically with the development of the centres, brought about through various types of meditation practices and breathing exercises, is, from a certain aspect, a retrogression. It will be found that through the practice of Raja Yoga, and through assuming that point of directional control which is to be found by the man who centers his consciousness in the soul, the other forms of Yoga are unnecessary, for the greater Yoga automatically includes all the lesser in its results, though not in its practices.

When these are studied, it will become apparent why the day of opportunity has only just arrived. The East has preserved rules for us since time immemorial. Here and there orientals (with a few Western adepts) have availed themselves of those rules and have submitted to the discipline of this exacting science. Thus has been preserved for the race the continuity of the Secret Doctrine, of the Ageless Wisdom, and thus has been gathered together the personnel of the Hierarchy of our planet. In the time of the Buddha and through the stimulation He produced there was a great gathering in of Arhats. These were men who had achieved liberation through self-initiated effort. This period, in our Aryan race, marked a climax for the East. Since then the tide of spiritual life has steadily flowed westward, and we may now look for a corresponding climax in the West, which will reach its zenith between the years 1965 and 2025. Towards this end the adepts of the East and of the West are unitedly working, for they follow always the Law. . . . . . .

In the *Yoga Sutras* there are embodied for us the laws of that becoming, and the rules, methods, and means which – when followed – make a man "perfect even as your Father in Heaven is perfect." Step by step there is unfolded for us a graded system of development, leading a man from the stage of average good man, through those of aspirant, initiate and master on to that exalted point in evolution at which the Christ now stands. . . . . .

The date of the birth of Patanjali is unknown and there is a good deal of controversy upon this matter. Most of the occidental authorities ascribe a date between the years 820 B.C. to 300 B.C., though one or two place him after Christ. The Hindu authorities themselves, however, who may be supposed to know something about the matter, ascribe a very much earlier date, even as far back as 10,000 B.C.. Patanjali was a compiler of teaching which, up to the time of his advent, had been given orally for many centuries. He was the first to reduce the teaching to writing for the use of students and hence he is regarded as the founder of the Raja Yoga School. The system, however, has been in use since the very beginning of the Aryan race. The Yoga Sutras are the basic teaching of the Trans-Himalayan School to which many of the Masters of the Wisdom belong, and many students hold that the Essenes and other schools of mystical training and thought, closely connected with the founder of Christianity and the early Christians, are based upon the same system and that their teachers were trained in the great Trans-Himalayan School. . . . . . .

The following extract is from a pamphlet *The Science of Meditation* by the Arcane School (Lucis Trust):

Raja Yoga is for the spiritually awakened individual intent on the right application of all available energy and resources.

There are essentially two types of meditation – mystical and occult. And both of these differentiate into various meditation techniques.

Mystical forms of meditation depend largely upon an active *feeling* nature and an intense desire for spiritual union.

Occult meditation, on the other hand, builds upon whatever mystical experience may have occurred, taking the whole idea of meditation a step further.

Today, when so much nonsense and inaccuracies are attributed to the term "occult", it's useful to bear in mind one simple definition. *Occultism is the science of energy flow and energy relationships*. Occult meditation is a means of consciously and purposefully directing energy from a recognised source to the creation of some specific effect. Effective occult meditation depends on the quality, the motive, the state of consciousness, the spiritual status and the defined purpose of the meditator.

Occult meditation is a mental activity, requiring a condition of alignment, or at-one-ment, between the three aspects of the mind: the lower or concrete mind, the soul, and the higher or abstract mind. This alignment integrates all three aspects of the individual meditator, spirit, soul and body, making available to him the spiritual resources of life, consciousness and form.

By way of this alignment the meditator is also united with the *life principle* in all things within the planet, and with the *soul or consciousness* of all manifestation. Thus, alignnment is dual; vertical and horizontal. And this creates the basic form of all truly spiritual occult meditation.

Today, the most effective type of occult meditation is called Raja Yoga, the "kingly science of the soul." A yoga is a disciplined way of achieving union or alignment, and a measure of control on some plane of consciousness. Raja Yoga uses the creative imagination, the art of visualisation and the use of a seed thought to exercise and expand the mind into the world of meaning and significance. It is in becoming aware of life's meaning and significance that we train ourselves to function fully as souls in incarnation.

CHAPTER 15
Dreams

The study of dreams is helpful if we realise that they are remembrances, in our physical brain, of activities on the inner planes during the hours of sleep. For students of the ageless wisdom these dream remembrances are a helpful resource on the journey inwards, connecting the inner and the outer life and reflecting the inner situation of the dreamer.

To really understand, use and profit from dreams, a student should start by examining and accepting certain facts such as:

1. That he himself leads an active life on other planes during the hours when his physical body is asleep.

2. That dreams are not messages from "somewhere", but recollections, in the physical brain, on waking, of these activities. Sometimes the recollections come in sequence but occasionally that of a single dream comes immediately, clearly and powerfully. Dr. Carl Jung has named these latter "manna dreams".

3. The inner subjective life of humanity which includes ancient memories. (Dr. Carl Jung wrote a great deal about the – collective unconscious".)

4. The continuity of the soul.

5. Reincarnation.

When sleeping lightly and not fully withdrawn from the body, dreams could be just a jumbled continuation of the day's activities and are of no importance. When deeply asleep and fully withdrawn from the body, the memories brought back into the physical brain are of activities on the astral or mental planes in which the dreamer himself has been a participant, or the observer of the activities of others around him.

His own activities can be of various kinds, such as meeting with loved ones or hated enemies, or wish fulfilment. This fulfilment can be for the gratification of the physical senses, or the desire to meet an exalted being such as a special saint or Master of the Wisdom, or Jesus, Krishna, the Christ or the Buddha. Thoughtforms of these exalted Beings exist on the inner planes for all to see, created by the loving thoughts and wishes of millions of devotees over the centuries.

On awakening, these experiences reach us dramatised in dreams in which the dreamer is the actor *and* the spectator, and aspects of ourselves are brought to our attention, personalised in friends, relatives and others of whom we are dreaming. The meaning of names can be very important.

On whatever planes these are enacted, and whether with teachers or helpers, or on different levels of our own consciousness, they frequently convey knowledge not available to us in our everyday conscious minds.

There is the famous story of how the German chemist F.A. Kekulé was helped in a dream to solve the riddle of the chemical formula of benzene one night in 1865. He was writing a textbook, but the work did not progress. So he turned to stare at the fire and dozed off. He described how he saw atoms gambolling before his eyes. Then his mental eye distinguished larger structures, all twining and twisting in snake-like motion. But look! What was that? One of the snakes had seized hold of its own tail and the form whirled mockingly before his eyes. As if by a flash of lightning he awoke. He spent the rest of the night working out the consequences of a wonderful new theory because this was the clue he needed to think of a ring formula for benzene, which marked a great step forward in the understanding of chemistry. "Let us learn to dream, gentlemen," he advised his fellow scientists at a convention in 1890, "then perhaps we shall find the truth … but let us beware of publishing our dreams before they have been put to the proof by the waking understanding."

Students on the Path can add something to this advice by remembering that if any spiritual work is to be really successful, right motive and commitment are essential. Therefore it is suggested that, before falling asleep, a habit is formed of asking to be guided so that the hours spent out of the physical body be useful and instructive. By consciously and constantly "sending oneself up" in meditation, study, service or *in sleep,* we touch on higher dimensions. I very often go to sleep at night puzling over a problem and wake up in the morning with a clear solution.

Over the years we have found that powerful dreams and visions, helpful to the work of our group, generally come during the few days before the full moon, and on the day itself. We have learned to benefit from the energies available at these periods, particularly those of Aries (Easter), Taurus (Wesak), and Gemini (Christ Festival).

A dream can indicate how we *subjectively* regard an *objective* experience or show symbolically an awakening or inner growth, or how some behaviour affects us harmfully.

The memory of a dream is more likely to be retained if the whole is memorised in pictures before attempting to translate it into words. Then it is recommended that the whole dream, or clue words, be immediately written into a scrapbook, at whatever hour of the night, otherwise the whole or part may be forgotten. These notes could later be transferred to a dream journal which has on each page a margin for interpretations.

Ready-made interpretations are worthless. Dreams are highly individualised and a dream's meaning cannot be pigeonholed or given any fixed dogmatic or generalised meaning. The dream belongs to the dreamer, therefore he should, from his knowledge of himself, endeavour to interpret it himself before asking anyone else to help. Dreams can be *understood* but not always explained.

In my dreams, for instance:

A **doctor or priest** always means the Healer, the Higher Self.

A **tiger**, approaching death.

A **small black dog** always means my physical body, and over the years has usually appeared in dreams in which I am being warned that I am over-taxing it.

The **telephone** indicates my connection to my higher Self.

And when **thieves** are in my house I immediately know it means that "where your treasures are, there will thieves come to steal". In other words, some spiritual gain I have made is being stolen away by the "shadow" side of my personality. Sometimes I don't really dislike these intruders, and, in the dream, only half-heartedly chase them away with a rolled-up newspaper!

Perhaps because I am of Scottish Highland stock, I am given forewarnings of death. Always differently, always beautifully, and sometimes with the exact date! Of course, I never grieve over death, which I know is ruled by the Law of Liberation, but sometimes one misses the physical presence of loved relatives, friends or animal companions. If the death is going to leave a large gap in my life, the Lord Jesus is present in my dream.

If the reader is consciously "on the Path" (experiencing the journey inward), his dreams will include symbolic presentations of teachings received in the halls of learning on the highest level of the astral plane, or the halls of wisdom on the mental plane, or of group work. This is why the study of symbols is so important.

Signs and emblems are deliberately invented and designed by people. Symbols are not invented, they "happen". They are the outer signs of our inner spiritual reality carried out into expression on the physical plane by the force of the inner Life. Put to right use, they make possible the redirection of energy and the progressive transformation of anyone using them.

However, the transforming symbol, which is saying, "you must change", does not take over and do all the work, although it musters all the energies by which this may be done – mobilising the combined energies of the conscious and unconscious. The consciousness of the person perceiving it must recognise and use it if it is to have its effect.

A symbol is the outer and visible sign of an inner reality, and as a reflection of spiritual concepts into our dreams and visions, it is an indication that these ideas are percolating right through and are having a conditioning influence.

All communication between the inner planes and the physical brain is through the etheric double. The clear remembering of dreams depends on the development of the etheric spleen chakra.

Some dreams common to us all are of:

The wilderness or the desert: This might mean the beginning, the emptiness of the no man's land as described by Dante and Bunyan. A world of solitude and loneliness where the saving and destructive powers collide – where the work takes place; the generation of the spirit.

The Gate: This might mean commitment, like the little wicket gate at the beginning of Bunyan's journey.

Being naked: Those on the journey of the soul, like the rich man in the bible who was told to "sell all that thou hast . . . and follow me", *St Luke* 18:22, must resign all personality resources and face the ordeal stripped; and like the fool in the unnumbered card of the tarot, who sets out on his journey with all his worldly possessions tied up in a tiny handkerchief.

Being unready: Making ready for a journey (one is sometimes in a hotel – this might mean that the journey has started), but preparations do not go smoothly. The suitcase won't close, or an essential garment is missing, or one arrives at the station, bus stop or airport, to find that the train, bus or plane has left or is just pulling out. This might mean that one part of one wants to go but another part of one does not. There is a stalemate.

The Great Man. The soul; that which psychologists term "the totality of the psyche".

Blood. The sacrifice of the animal nature. The driving force behind the mechanism of sacrifice is the zodiacal sign of Libra, representing divine legality; the inner conscience of man with its ability to inflict terrible self chastisement.

I always advise those of our students who wish to make a serious study of their dreams, to start by reading *Memories, Dreams and Reflections* by Carl G. Jung. Then, since they are all "on the Path" and therefore bringing through – in their dreams – symbols from the upper astral and lower mental planes and the halls of learning and of wisdom, to include the following books in their dream library:

Dreams by C.G. Jung
Man and his Symbols by C.G. Jung
A Dictionary of Symbols by J.E. Cirlot
An Illustrated Encyclopaedia of Traditional Symbols by J.C. Cooper
The Lost Language of Symbolism by H. Bayley
Joy's Way by W. Brugh Joy, pages 74 to 82
Esoteric Psychology, Vol II pages 499 to 510
Journey Into Self by Esther M. Harding.
Any book of masonic symbolism. These symbols are of an occult, traditional and valid type.

Journey Into Self, unfortunately, is out of print but is included here because it is to be hoped it will be reprinted, and I have found it one of the most helpful, so much so that, as there is no index, I compiled my own. This is a modern Jungian psychiatrist's interpretation of Bunyan's *Pilgrim's Progress* – a discussion of the journey of the soul, and deals directly with the inner experiences.

Related to the dream world is the twilight world of hypnogogic images which flash before the closed eyes when on the verge of falling asleep and hypnopompic images when waking. They are quite different from dreams – just flashes: vivid, sudden, detailed, and not consciously formed or manipulated. They can, if studied, give the key to unconscious processes or provide creative inspiration.

CHAPTER 16
The Law of Attraction

Even the tiniest atom of substance has in it a germ that can respond, under the Law of Attraction, to the Christ Spirit of Love. Love is the great unifier, the prime attractive impulse in this system; the magnetic, attractive, cohering agent in any form, whether an atom, a man or a solar system.

The quality of love functions through the medium of the Law of Attraction with the aim of producing a synthesis in consciousness. The objective of our evolution is the unfoldment of consciousness.

They (the Masters of the Wisdom) embody and express the love aspect of the divine purpose: They wield, direct and control the Law of Attraction – the motivating energy which swings the Law of Evolution into activity in the three worlds, (physical, astral, mental). (See Chart 4, page 36) *Discipleship in the New Age, Vol II* page 211.

. . . (A) law is in reality the effect of the life of a greater entity as it encloses a lesser within its living processes. It embodies that formulated purpose or organised will of an enfolding life . . . *Esoteric Healing*, page 522.

Three of the basic cosmic laws which affect humanity are
1. The Law of Economy – of matter and substance – 3rd Ray.
2. The Law of Attraction – a major soul law – 2nd Ray.
3. The Law of Synthesis – the major law of the Spirit in the Universe - 1st Ray.

At first a disciple is ruled and conditioned by the Law of Economy, but after the first initiation he comes under the Law of Attraction which carries and wields the energy of love. After the fourth initiation – the cross, the renunciation – he comes under the Law of Synthesis.

The electric fire of will (1st Ray), and the solar fire of love (2nd Ray), in cooperation with fire by friction (3rd Ray), produce the world of created and creative forms. These proceed under the law of attractive magnetic love towards the evolutionary accomplishment of a purpose at present inscrutable." *Esoteric Psychology, Vol I*, page 43.

The Law of Attraction as the Law of Magnetisation, attractive and dynamic, is the expression of the Spiritual Will in the three worlds as far as humanity is concerned. All of our system works under this building law of magnetic attraction; therefore, according to our colour, vibration and tone we attract to ourselves what we need to build into our bodies. This Law of Attraction governs our birth into incarnation. The mental unit attracts the fire of the mental plane, the astral permanent atom attracts the mists of the astral and together they are wrapped in the vital etheric body.

Under the Law of Attraction, the denser matter of the physical plane is made to cohere to this vitalised form, and is gradually built up around it, and within it, until the interpenetration is so complete that the two forms make but one unit.
A Treatise on Cosmic Fire, page 80.

Sex and the Law of Attraction
The indwelling Consciousness, seeking its opposite, comes under the Law of Attraction, and this leads to atomic, human, planetary, spiritual, solar and cosmic marriage.
Extract from *A Compilation on Sex*, pages 24 to 30:

The drama of creation and the story of revelation are depicted for us, if we could but see truly and interpret our facts with spiritual exactitude, in the relation of the two sexes and in the fact of their intercourse with each other. When this relation is no longer purely physical but is a union of the two separated halves on all three planes, – physical, emotional and mental – then we shall see the solution of the sex problem and the restitution of the marriage relation to its intended position in the Mind of God. Today it is the marriage of two physical bodies. Sometimes it is the marriage also of the emotional natures of the two people concerned. Rarely indeed is it a marriage of minds as well. Sometimes it is the union of the physical body of one party, with the physical body of the other party left cold and uninterested and uninvolved, but with the emotional body attracted and participating. Sometimes the mental body is involved with the physical body, and the emotional nature left out. Seldom, very seldom, do we find the coordinated, cooperating fusion of all the three parts of the personality concerned in both parties to the union. When this is indeed found, then you have a true union, a real marriage, and a blending of the two in one.
It is here that some of the schools of esoteric teaching have gone sadly astray. The false idea has crept into their presentation of truth that marriage of this kind is essential for spiritual liberation and that without it the soul remains in prison. They teach that through the marriage act, at-one-ment with the soul is brought about, and that there is no spiritual deliverance

without this marriage. At-one-ment with the soul is an individual interior experience, resulting in an expansion of consciousness, so that the individual and specific becomes at-one with the general and universal. Behind the erroneous interpretation, however, lies truth.

Where this true marriage and these ideal sexual relations on all three planes are found, the right conditions exist in which souls can be provided with the needed forms in which to incarnate. Sons of God can find forms in which to manifest on earth. . . .

Under the symbol of sex, you have also the reality of love itself expressing itself. Love in reality connotes a relation, but the word "love" (like the word "sex") is used with little thought and with no attention to its true meaning. Basically, love and sex are one and the same thing, for both express the meaning of the Law of Attraction. Love is sex, and sex is love, for in those two words the relation, the interplay and the union between God and His universe, between man and God, between a man and his own soul, and between men and women are equally depicted. The motive and the relation are emphasized. But the impelling result of that relation is creation and the manifestation of form through which divinity can express itself and come to be. Spirit and matter met together, and the manifested universe came into being. Love is ever productive, and the Law of Attraction is fruitful in results. Man and God came together under the same great Law, and the Christ was born, – the guarantee of the divinity of humanity and the demonstration of the fact. Individual man and his soul are also attempting to come together, and when that event is consummated the Christ is born in the cave of the heart, and Christ is seen in the daily life with increasing power. . .

Again, in man himself the great drama of sex is enacted, and twice over in his body, within his personality, the process of union and fusion takes place. Let me briefly refer here to these two symbolic happenings, for the use of esoteric students, so that the great story of sex may be comprehended in its spiritual sense.

Man, as you know, is the expression of energies. These energies galvanise the physical man into activity through the medium of certain force centres in the etheric body. These, for our immediate purposes, can be divided into three centres below the diaphragm and four above.
These are:
I. Below the diaphragm:
1. The base of the spine.
2. The sacral centre.
3. The solar plexus.
II. Above the diaphragm:
1. The heart centre.
2. The throat centre.
3. The centre between the eyebrows.
4. The head centre.

We know that two fusions have to take place and, in these two we have two enactments of the symbolic sex process, and two symbolic events that externalise a spiritual happening and picture forth to man his spiritual goal and God's great objective in the evolutionary process.

First, the energies below the diaphragm have to be lifted up and blended with those above the diaphragm. With the process and rules for so doing we cannot here deal, except in one case, – the raising of the sacral energy to the throat centre, or the transmutation of the process of physical reproduction and of physical creation into that of the creativeness of the artist in some field of creative expression. Through the union of the energies of these two centres we shall come to that stage in our development wherein we shall produce the children of our skill and minds. Where, in other words, there is a true union of the higher and the lower energies, you will have the emergence of beauty in form, the enshrining of some aspect of truth in appropriate expression, and thus the enriching of the world. Where there is this synthesis, the true creative artist begins to function. The throat, the organ of the Word, expresses the life and manifests the glory and the reality behind. Such is the symbolism lying behind the teaching of the fusion of the lower energies with the higher, and of this, physical plane sex is a symbol. Mankind today is rapidly becoming more creative, for the transfusion of the energies is going on under the new impulses. As we develop the sense of purity in man, as the growth of the sense of responsibility is fostered, and as his love of beauty, of colour and of ideas proceeds, we shall have a rapid increase in the raising of the lower into union with the higher, and thereby the beautifying of the Temple of the Lord will be tremendously accelerated.

In the coming Aquarian age this will go rapidly forward. The majority of people today live below the diaphragm, and their energies are turned outward into the material world and prostituted to material ends. In the coming centuries this will be corrected; their energies will be transmuted and purified, and men will begin to live above the diaphragm. They will then express the potencies of the loving heart, of the creative throat, and of the divinely ordered will of the head. Of this relation between the lower and the higher, physical plane sex is the symbol.

But in the head of man himself is also to be found a marvellous symbolic happening. In that living organism is enacted that drama whereby the purely human being merges himself in divinity. The great final drama of the mystical union between God and man, and between the soul and the personality is there enacted. According to the Eastern philosophy, there are in the head of man two great energy centres. One of them, the centre between the eyebrows, blends and fuses the five types of energy which are transmitted to it and blended with it, – the energy of the three centres below the diaphragm and of the throat and heart centres. The other, the head centre, is awakened through meditation, service and aspiration, and it is through this centre that the soul makes its contact with the personality. This head centre is the symbol of the spirit or positive masculine aspect, just as the centre between the eyebrows is the symbol of matter, of the negative feminine aspect. Connected with these force vortices are two physical plane organs, the pituitary body and the pineal gland. The first is negative and the second is positive. These two organs are the higher correspondences of the male and female organs of physical reproduction. As the soul becomes increasingly potent in the mental and emotional life of the aspirant, it pours in with greater power into the head centre. As the man works with his personality, purifying it and bending it to the service of the spiritual will, he automatically raises the energies of the centres in the body up to the centre between the eyebrows. Eventually the influence of each of the two centres increases and becomes wider and wider, until they make a contact with each other's vibratory or magnetic field, and instantly the light flashes out. Father-spirit and mother-matter unite and are at-one and the Christ is born. "Except a man be born again, he cannot see the kingdom of God," said the Christ. This is the second birth, and from that moment vision comes with increasing power.

This is again the great drama of sex, re-enacted in man. Thus in his personal life he three times knows the meaning of union, of sex:
1. In the physical plane sex, or his relation to his opposite, the woman, resulting in the reproduction of the species.
2. In the union of the lower energies with the higher, resulting in the creative work.
3. In the union within the head of the energies of the personality with those of the soul, resulting in the birth of the Christ.

Great is the glory of man and wonderful are the divine functions which he embodies. Through the passage of time, the race has been brought to the point where man is beginning to raise the lower energies into the higher centres, and it is this transition which is causing much of the trouble in the world today. Many men everywhere are becoming politically, religiously, scientifically, or artistically creative, and the impact of their mental energy and of their plans and ideas is making itself felt competitively. Until the idea of brotherhood dominates the race, we shall see these powers prostituted to personal ends and ambitions, and to consequent disaster, just as we have seen the power of sex prostituted to personal satisfaction and selfishness and consequent disaster. Some few, however, are raising their energies higher still and translating them into terms of the heavenly world. The Christ is being born today in many a human being, and increasingly will the sons of God appear in their true nature to take over the guidance of humanity in the New Age.

CHAPTER 17
Inner Groups, the Separated Self, and the Path

When a probationer on the Path becomes a disciple and therefore more under soul control, his *attention* becomes fixed more on his work and less on his "separated self" (which is another name for his personality). Still, as an individual personality, his individual gifts are given as an offering to the group work.

Esoterically, at soul level, all work is groupwork, because at that level all workers are connected *by*, are aware *of*, and communicate *on*, the electric frequency bands on which they operate. These groups are known as "Inner Groups" and the *attention* is on the work to be done.

Exoterically, a disciple in one of these groups, while working on the physical plane, may have no communication – at this level – with his fellow workers in the group; they could be scattered all over the physical world. This is so because the real links in a group are subjective.

(Note: The word "esoteric", from the Greek esoterikos, meaning "inner or "within", is not used here to mean that knowledge only intended for, and understood by, initiates, but: "That which exists in the inner subtle worlds and so cannot be cognised by the physical senses". Its opposite, "exoteric", is used to mean: "That which is of the outer world and so can be cognised by the physical senses".)

Paradoxically, as the attention of the disciple switches more and more away from his separated self (the personality), and he continues to study, to meditate and above all to serve, this personality becomes purified and strengthened and therefore a better instrument for soul purposes. Once the commitment is made to walk the Lighted Way, the momentum is set for spiritual growth.

The Masters and Initiates of the spiritual Hierarchy form the One Ashram, working for the Plan – God's Plan for the planet Earth – but they too, differentiate into subsidiary ashrams for specific work. At the same time, each member is preparing for the next higher initiation because *all in the Universe is in the process of becoming.*

THE PATH
The Path is the way of discipline and enlightenment which everyone eventually treads on their way back to God. Man himself becomes the Path. (See Chart 4, page 35)

The Path of Discipleship is the path of self-discipline to be followed in order to achieve union of the personality with the soul. It is the conscious following of the Christ, the Way of Service. As the Masters of the Wisdom and their initiates are very knowledgeable occultists, they make no attempt to guide an aspirant until they see, by the growth of the Light in him, that he is ready to respond, and make use of any guidance given.

The stages on the path are:
1. **Aspirant.**
2. **Probationer.**
3. **Disciple.**
4. **Initiate.**
5. **Master or Adept.**

In *A Treatise on White Magic*, pp 396,397, D.K., when addressing disciples, describes the early stages of this path in the following words:

The outstanding characteristics of those personalities who are not as yet soul-centered or controlled, are dominance, ambition, pride and a lack of love to the whole, though they frequently possess love for those who are necessary to them or to their comfort.

You have therefore in the sequential development of humanity the following stages:
1. That of the animal consciousness.
2. The emotionally polarised individual, selfish and governed by desire.
3. The two above stages, plus a growing intellectual grasp of environing conditions.
4. The stage of responsibility to family or friends.
5. The stage of ambition and of longing for influence and power in some field of human expression. This leads to fresh endeavor.
6. The coordinating of the personality equipment under the above stimulus.
7. The stage of influence, selfishly used and frequently destructive, because the higher issues are not registered as yet.
8. The stage of a steadily growing group awareness.
This is viewed:
a. As a field of opportunity.
b. As a sphere of service.

c. As a place wherein sacrifice for the good of all becomes gloriously possible.

This latter stage puts a man upon the path of discipleship, which includes, needless to say, that of the earlier phase, probation or testing.

The problem consists in ascertaining upon which step of the ladder and in which phase one finds oneself at any particular time. Behind each human being stretches a long series of lives and some are now headed towards the stage of dominant selfish personality expression and are making themselves individuals in full conscious awareness. This is, for them, as much a step forward as is discipleship for all of you.

Every religion in the world which emphasises the need for treading the Path, or Way, lays down the same rules, is divided into similar divisions and stages, and holds out the same goal – reunion with the Divine. All roads lead to the centre.

The moves from stage to stage are, of course, through our own energy fields, because all those changes are *within* – are changes of consciousness. Then our frequencies resonate to increasingly finer and more spiritual notes.

CHAPTER 18
Networking or United Effort in Prayer and Meditation

If thought itself contains creative energy, then how useful it would be to direct good thoughts into one's space, even a few times daily; not just about oneself, but about the world. It need not be a long and tiring effort; just a few moments of forgetting of oneself in invoking good for the world – God's Good – "Thy Will be done."

In the sublime words of Francis Bacon: "God forbid that we should give out a dream of our own imagination for a pattern of the world; rather may He graciously grant us to write an apocalypse or true vision of The Footsteps of the Creator imprinted on His Creatures."

This wonderful prayer ends: "Therefore do Thou, O Father, who gavest the visible Light as the first fruits of creation, and didst breathe into the face of man the Intellectual Light as the Crown and Consummation thereof, guard and protect this work, which coming from Thy goodness returneth to Thy glory."

Is prayer the same thing as invocation? All invocation is prayer but not all prayer is effective invocation! The power of united invocation is stupendous, and if the work is done with *knowledge* and *intent*, it can become so much more effective.

Invocation means "calling down" or "calling into" and is an inner action which includes and combines the use of all our inner functions. It is simultaneously of the mind, of feeling, of the imagination and of the will.

Readers of this book, now knowing something about thoughtforms, will, I am sure, find the following excerpts of interest:

A Thoughtform for Peace:
. . . when a thoughtform has been constructed of sufficient potency and has been built over a long period of time by the people of the world, a further and final stage becomes ever possible. The form can be rendered so magnetic that it can attract an Energy which will inform it and give it active potency; it

can then become a vital link between the subjective world of energy and the objective world of forces and a thing of power, of impelling and guiding activity, and therefore the expression of a Life. This thoughtform, duly informed, becomes a mediating factor, constructed by humanity but animated by the will-to-good of some great and spiritual Entity. . . .

A great and vital thoughtform is in process of construction upon our planet and within our planetary aura. It is being built by the power of sound, by the magnetic pull of invocation leading to eventual evocation, and by the force of desire-substance, animated by the power of thought. It is being constructed by the united efforts of the Hierarchy, of the world disciples and aspirants, of the men and women of goodwill in all nations, and also through the inchoate longings of men everywhere, of all religious beliefs, political views and group loyalties. It is safely anchored upon the physical plane, is of vast proportions upon the astral or emotional plane, but lacks vitality and power upon the mental plane. It is here, within the realm of thought substance, that the weakness of the structure of this thoughtform becomes apparent. It is already potent spiritually, owing to the scientific work of the occult Hierarchy and Their trained helpers. . . . It is potent physically and emotionally through the work of the lovers of humanity . . .

There is, however, a gap or hiatus upon the mental plane, for the minds of men are not functioning correctly. The disciples and world aspirants are not thinking with clarity, nor are they working in unity. They are evading issues or are thinking separatively or nationally or fanatically; they are not convinced of the potency of invocation or of prayer . . . they fail to love all men without exception in their longing to see their own loyalties emerge triumphant; they work doubtingly, hoping for the best but believing in the worst. . . .

It is this negative and lukewarm attitude, this mental uncertainty and this failure to link up the spiritual and the physical worlds in a positive relationship which is holding back the Forces of Light and the actual presence of the Spirit of Peace, and thus negativing a possible divine intervention. It is the test of group work.
The Externalisation of the Hierarchy, pages 222–224

There is an encouraging growth of that which might be termed planetary spirituality. Much of this comes from modern scientists, especially physicists, who are revealing a universe of unbroken wholeness. This in turn is leading to what Frithjof Schoun calls "the transcendent unity of all religions" and to what Aldous Huxley named "a perennial philosophy of insights": wisdom found in every culture.

There has been an outburst of appeals for united effort in prayer and meditation for peace and goodwill, because peace would not be enduring unless based upon goodwill. Goodwill must come first.

Humanity is becoming aware, in these times of stress, of the power of subjective work, of service through group prayer or meditation, and of the immense power of constructive thought. Good news is the reprinting of a very special book which is an excellent introduction to meditation in general: *The Silent Path*, by Michal J. Eastcott, published by Ryder, London, in 1969, reprinted in 1979 and 1989. We recommend it highly.

Full Moon Meditation Meetings:
According to the Ancient Wisdom Teachings, the moon is now a dead shell. It is slowly disintegrating physically, but not yet astrally.

Although people who are emotionally polarised may be overstimulated and upset at the time of the full moon, those on the path of discipleship, or mental in their attitudes, can benefit by the lunar cycles. At the time of the full moon, over a period of five days there is an unimpeded alignment between the earth and the sun so that our planet receives more reflected light from the sun than at other times.

For some, the results of this are in hallucination, astral vision, and psychic urges. For others, working on the plane of the mind and using occult meditation techniques, higher contacts become easier than at other times and receptivity to impressions from soul levels is increased. Vera Stanley Alder's teacher, Raphael, always took her on inner jouneys at the time of the full moon.

This offers to humanity as a whole – regardless of nationality or creed – an opportunity to co-operate with one another in this subjective group work. The higher spiritual energies that are available can be used for world service. We are told that the New World Religion will be based on a science of invocation that is in tune with the rhythms of the lunar cycle. It will be a science of absorbing, sharing, circulating and then distributing energy.(See 'Group Meditation' and 'Meditation at the Full Moon' in Chapter 20, "The Science of Meditation", page 140)

Expressing this concept in terms of electrical energy, desire forms the cable and invocation is the switch that turns the current on.

CHAPTER 19
The Triangles Network

This is a service activity for men and women of goodwill who, by working in groups of 3, establish right human relations by creating a worldwide network of light and goodwill. This is carried out by recognising the immense power of constructive thought and the fact that energy follows thought.

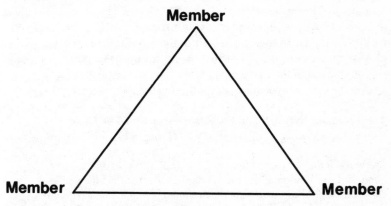

What exactly does this activity involve?

1. A triangle is a group of three people who link each day in thought for a few minutes. They need not live in the same area (many international triangles exist), nor is it necessary for members to synchronise the time at which they do their triangles work each day. Once the triangle is built, it can be brought to life by any one of its members.

2. Each day, members of the triangle sit quietly for a few minutes, linking mentally with each other. They call forth the energies of light and goodwill and by means of the creative imagination, see these energies flowing through the network into the hearts and minds of men and women everywhere. They then link their triangle with all the other triangles which exist throughout the world and visualise a lighted network of triangles surrounding the planet.

3. While doing this, they repeat the Great Invocation, thereby acting as a channel between the world of spiritual realities and humanity for the downpouring of light and love into the body of humanity.

The Great Invocation is a world prayer translated into over 50 languages and its importance cannot be over-emphasised as it expresses certain truths, i.e:
That there is a basic intelligence to whom we give the name God. That there is a divine evolutionary Plan, the motivating power of which is love.
That a great Being, called by the Christians The Christ – The World Teacher – came forth and embodied that love so we could understand that love and intelligence are effects of the purpose, the will and the Plan of God. That the Plan can only work out through Humanity itself.

The work of triangles is simple yet of deep spiritual significance. It is an act of service to Humanity.

Summary of Procedure
a) Link mentally with members of your triangle(s).
b) Visualise your triangle(s) as part of the worldwide network.
c) Visualise light and goodwill flowing around the points of your triangle, through the network and into human consciousness.
d) Use the Great Invocation, perpetuating the flow of spiritual energy.

The Triangles Network and the Reappearance of The Christ
From *Discipleship in the New Age. Vol II*, pages 170 – 172:

The work of the network of light and goodwill, focussed on the plane of mind, is the utilisation of this knowledge in order to affect the public consciousness. These are points which should be simplified and gradually taught, and in the clearest language, to all Triangle members. The work of the Triangles is to work with the minds of men, and with a factor which is used and exploited by leaders everywhere; the effort is to impress these minds with certain ideas which are necessary to human progress. People recognise the present darkness and misery, and consequently welcome light; men are tired of hating and fighting, and therefore welcome goodwill.

Let me touch for a moment upon another point of view. Just as stanzas one and four ((of the Great Invocation)) are related, so stanza two and the final line are also related. The Plan will be restored on Earth through illumination and goodwill, and when that takes place Christ *will* return to Earth. I would ask you not to misunderstand this phrase. Christ has never left the Earth and He said when bidding farewell to His disciples: "Lo, I am with you always, even until the end of the days." His Presence, however, is not recognised by the masses of men, and is only sensed and dimly hoped for by the orthodox religionist of all the world faiths.

As I have earlier pointed out, the return of Christ will be expressed, in the first place, *by an upsurging of the Christ consciousness in the hearts of men everywhere;* its first expression will be goodwill.

THE GREAT INVOCATION

From the point of Light within the Mind of God
Let light stream forth into the minds of men.
Let Light descend on Earth.

From the point of Love within the Heart of God
Let love stream forth into the hearts of men.
May Christ return to Earth.

From the centre where the Will of God is known
Let purpose guide the little wills of men -
The purpose which the Masters know and serve.

From the centre which we call the race of men
Let the Plan of Love and Light work out
And may it seal the door where evil dwells.

Let Light and Love and Power
restore the Plan on Earth.

In the second place, disciples everywhere will find themselves increasingly sensitive to His quality, His voice and His teaching; they will be "overshadowed" by Him in many cases . . .; through this overshadowing of disciples in all lands, He will duplicate Himself repeatedly. The effectiveness and the potency of the overshadowed disciple will be amazing.

One of the first experiments He made as He prepared for this form of activity was in connection with Krishnamurti. It was only partially successful. The power used by Him was distorted and misapplied by the devotee type, and the experiment was brought to an end; it served, however, a most useful purpose. As a result of the war, mankind has been disillusioned; devotion is no longer regarded as adequate or necessary to the spiritual life or its effectiveness. . . . When Christ again seeks to overshadow his disciples, a different reaction will be looked for. It is because of this that A.A.B. has so consistently belittled devotion and advocated spiritual independence. No devotee is independent; he is a prisoner of an idea or a person.

When Christ comes, there will be a flowering in great activity of His type of consciousness among men; when disciples are working under the recognition of the Christ, there will then come the time when He can again move among men in a public manner; He can be publicly recognised and thus do His work on the outer levels of living as well as upon the inner. For these three events, which are connected with the inherent divinity in man, the Hierarchy is working and preparing, and it will essentially register another of the results of the successful use of the new Invocation to aid in this task of preparation.

I think it was to this Christ Consciousness that Mary Lutyens referred in her book *Krishnamurti. The Years of Awakening*, page 134:

. . . and obviously (Krishnamurti) had great difficulty in putting his thoughts into words although he thoroughly prepared his lectures. His technique is now most impressive and he has complete command of his audience, but that is due, I think, more to the force of his personality than to his power of oratory. He always speaks in English, which a large proportion of his audience, at any rate in India, cannot understand, and yet they listen spellbound. I believe he speaks to some inner consciousness that is not dependent on words.

Nothing in Krishnamurti's sometimes difficult life tarnished the Christ consciousness in him, and it was to this that they responded. From the same book, page 96, we find:

This accusation that Krishna was influenced by 'the person that was nearest to him' is one that has followed him all his life. It has seldom been understood that the influence people have had on him, from time to time, has been entirely superficial. . . . . . . What is in him today, was there at the beginning. His true being was all the time slowly, secretly unfolding, hidden even from himself.

Part 3
FOR DEEPER
REFLECTION

For students who wish to
study the Ageless Wisdom
in greater depth.

CHAPTER 20

The Science of Meditation

*This chapter contains extracts from a pamphlet "The Science of Meditation",
by the Arcane School (Lucis Trust).*

What is Meditation? Why is it a Science?

Webster's dictionary defines the term "to meditate" as "to engage in
contemplation or reflection". This is an accurate description of one
effective form modern meditation can take. It goes beyond the
mystical method of seeking the ecstacy of union with the divine, or
with God, for its own sake. It transcends the goal of many modern
types of meditation which emphasise "peace of mind" by detaching the
mind from all its normal functions, often inducing a sense of mental
paralysis rather than peace. The mind is thus incapable of registration,
interpretation and application.

These three words probably supply the most accurate definition of
creative meditation – *registration*, *interpretation*, *application*. They
imply *mental activity*, involving cause and effect, contact with a source
of inspiration, and the consequent ability to use and apply the fruits of
meditation.

Meditation is a scientific technique which can be relied upon to
produce results if followed through with care and precision. While the
techniques of meditation can be learned, the way the techniques are
applied varies for each one. Each must find that way for himself, for it
is in experimentation that we gain experience in the right use of the
mind, bring the consciousness into alignment with soul energy, and
learn how to give right expression in meditation to the abundant
spiritual resources available in service.

Prayer and Meditation

Prayer and meditation are two distinct methods of approach to reality.
Both are equally legitimate and useful. Prayer is based on the concept
of *God Transcendent*, above and beyond the world of human affairs;
meditation, however, appeals to those who recognise *God Immanent*,

or within His creation. When we pray we speak to God; when we meditate we listen to God, or let God speak to us.

Both prayer and meditation are invocative in nature. They both call upon spiritual forces for the release of energies in answer to a voiced demand, and both methods work. Both methods are needed because much of humanity is still focussed at the emotional level.

Meditation is practiced by those who recognise that divinity – the "Kingdom of God" – is within, and that God-realisation is a natural process. The disciplined use of the mind, combined with service to others, is the means for attaining that realisation. "Christ in you, the hope of glory", is a reality to the meditator.

Redefining Spiritual Living

The idea of spiritual development has been associated almost exclusively with the religions of the world. The church rather than the human soul became the custodian of the spiritual life. Today the individual is the custodian of his own spiritual life and is in process of spiritualising his material life.

The word "spiritual" relates to attitudes, to relationships, to the moving forward from one level of consciousness to the next. It is related to the power to see a new vision and new and better possibilities. It refers to every effect of the evolutionary process as it drives man forward from one range of sensitivity to another; it relates to expansions of consciousness, to all activity which leads toward some form of further development. The discoveries of science, or the production of some great work in literature or in the field of art, are just as much an evidence of spiritual unfoldment as the experiences of the mystic or the registration by the disciple of a contact with his own soul.

Recognising one's own spiritual nature allows the individual to recognise divinity in others and in all forms of life. Learning to *think* of each other as souls, we begin to *act* accordingly. As each takes his own next step forward into a more inclusive and compassionate understanding, he helps to lift the human family nearer to its spiritual destiny – the establishing of the Kingdom of Heaven on earth.

Meditation : A Spiritual Discipline

The key word in spiritual development is *discipline*. A life that is self-disciplined mentally, emotionally and physically, can be depended upon by the soul.

The discipline of daily meditation as a means of contacting the soul and of developing soul consciousness and soul fusion, is a major means of spiritualising life on this planet and helping to externalise the Kingdom of God.

Work in meditation is required to harmonise the thinking and feeling faculties, to coordinate and integrate the mental and emotional bodies into a coherent whole, evoking the flow of energy from the soul. With the mind, the emotional and physical bodies under the guidance of spiritual purpose, inner conflicts are resolved and the integrated personality becomes a pure vehicle of soul expression, a means of releasing greater light and love into the world of human affairs.

Meditation establishes relationship between soul and personality. It is a cooperative relationship, leading ultimately to soul-personality fusion. The work is based on the simple premise that energy follows and conforms itself to *thought*. Correct use of the power of the mind will achieve any purpose, good or not so good. Occult meditation involves a focussed mind, the capacity to visualise, an ability to build thoughtforms and to use the creative imagination, plus an accurate grasp of the soul's intent.

This type of meditation enhances the quality of life. It creates a lighted way of relationship and communication between the subjective realm of the soul and its objective expression, the personality. As the personality adapts and surrenders to the dominance of the soul as the real Self, it is in turn redeemed by soul light and energy and all aspects of life on the physical plane are irradiated and uplifted.

The Value of Alignment
Meditation is, or should be, a deeply spiritual experience. It leads to right relationship with God and to right human relationships in everyday life. It is essentially the means *par excellence* of establishing *alignment* between the various aspects of planetary life which, from the angle of consciousness and of form, appear to be separate.

In meditation alignment concerns the mental body – the mind; the emotional/feeling nature – the heart; the etheric or energy body and the physical self. When these are integrated into a unity, they can be aligned with the soul itself, the spiritual Self. A channel of communication is thereby created linking the brain, the heart, the mind and the soul; the life energy of the soul, with its power to illumine and inspire, can then sweep through into activity, affecting every aspect of daily life. Once created in consciousness, the essential alignment is ever present, needing only a moment of directed thought to bring it to life as an active ingredient in the relationship between the inner and outer life.

Creative Meditation: A Planetary Service

Meditation is the single most effective means for transcending the binding, restrictive sense of separativeness and isolation which imprison the human consciousness and render it futile. Meditation is the outstanding creative agent upon the planet. The effect of human meditation at this time is to change conditions, to invoke the higher spiritual potencies, to work with concentration – both vertically and horizontally – within the world of men and within the kingdom of God. This vertical and horizontal activity holds the secret of creative meditation.

The intention to be of service to mankind is the essential motivation for all true creative meditation. Expansion of the human mind is based on the ability to love and to serve one's fellowmen. The ultimate result in the consciousness of the individual is illumination, wisdom and the will-to-good, and an expanding ability to co-operate in the creative and redemptive purposes of our planetary life. Meditation as a planetary service is both practical and effective.

Dangers and Safeguards of Meditation

The way of meditation is much like any other journey, in that one follows a path to reach a goal. And, as with any path, there are certain pitfalls that may face the traveller. Meditation is not harmful itself, but if misused or practised unwisely, it can create personal problems for the meditator.

The major safeguard in any course of meditation is simple common-sense, and a balanced attitude. Commonsense offsets over-zealousness, fanaticism or a rigid one-pointedness, which can lead to mental or physical strain. With a sense of balance, one realises that progress in consciousness is a long-term affair, and that changes do not occur overnight. This avoids the disappointment felt by the neophyte when great revelations do not come as promptly as desired.

One of the major pitfalls of meditation is also one of the best known: the case of an individual who becomes so lost in his own subjective world that he tends to withdraw from physical reality. Meditation should lead to a well-rounded life expression. Too much mental strain or over-stimulation can be corrected by *expressing* mental experiences as physical facts. This might be done by attempting to translate one's highest visions or ideas into some project or activity which will benefit others.

A second possible danger of meditation lies in emotional over-stimulation. Meditation brings an increased flow of energy into the meditator's life, which tends to accentuate both positive and negative qualities, and to bring them to the surface where they can be clearly seen. Each meditator is responsible for handling this greater energy flow. He has to discover his own emotional weaknesses and endeavour to maintain a balancing focus of attention on the mental plane.

The student of meditation should proceed slowly and cautiously. Anything worthwhile requires time and effort. The results that occur from a slow building process are more likely to endure than the results of work done hastily in hope of instant success. The student should also aim at regularity in meditation. Twenty minutes' work daily is worth more and is safer than four hours of work once a month.

The most reliable safeguard is to be found in a life of service. Meditation brings in energy and inspiration. If this is not expressed through some form of service, it can result in congestion or over-stimulation. Service is the right use of soul energy, vision and inspiration.

Group Meditation

This does not mean that individuals must work together in the same place or even at the same time. The true meeting place of the group is the plane of mind, or the mental plane.

In metaphysical terms, meditation takes place outside time and space, but what is important in group meditation is the sense of a common focus and interest, of group attention on the object of meditation. The individuals who comprise a group are united by a shared idea and interest, and not so much by a personal rapport. Groups may work together and meditate on many different subjects, but the underlying theme in group work is service to humanity. In this way the group plays its part within the planetary life. Groups may work to bring about a greater light in human affairs and to condition the subjective atmosphere of the planet. They work with such energies as light, love and the will-to-good, helping to relate these subjective energies to daily, physical life. Although these groups may be working to enlighten the human environment, they do not use force. *They do not, for instance, attempt to direct energy at the mind of some individual or group in the attempt to change or influence them.* But they make light available, or create a subjective condition whereby an individual or a nation can more easily stand in the light of its own soul. (Italics by author)

Participation in group meditation work often has side effects on the individuals involved. As one works in group meditation, one gradually gains a greater insight into one's own affairs, into world affairs, and into the nature of group interplay. Meditators develop a sense of integration with their co-workers, as well as a sense of identity and oneness with all those who serve humanity. In the process, participants gain a priceless knowledge: they learn from their own experience that there is a force for good in the world, that there is a Plan for human evolution, and that what they do in their own lives and contribute in service does make a difference.

Meditation at the Full Moon

Meditation at the time of the full moon is one important form of service. The full moon each month is a time of intensified energy and of heightened spiritual activity; a time of inspiration, of vision and insight, and of increased opportunity to serve. Meditation at the time of the full moon is a technique for effective contact with the light and love needed today in human affairs. At the time of the full moon festivals, the moon stands on the far side of the earth, away from the sun. This leaves a full, direct and unimpeded relationship between the earth and the sun, the source of our life, energy and consciousness.

Each month during the full moon the sun is aligned with one of the twelve zodiacal signs. The signs indicate the *quality* of the subjective energies available for transmission during that month. In the annual cycles humanity as a whole is exposed to the full range of experience. These energies and qualities stimulate the evolution of human consciousness; all zodiacal energies can be used by all individuals.

Conscious work with these various types of spiritual energy brings inspiration and ideas into the reach of human minds and hearts. Meditation, especially in subjective group formation, stimulates a new factor in human awareness – a growing *spiritual maturity*. This vast, planetary work of world service contributes to the task of spiritually civilising planet Earth.

The Sixfold Progression of Divine Love

The science of meditation is based on work with subjective energies. The skilled meditator is able to cooperate in meditation with others in distributing such energies where they are most needed through the power of thought. The primary energy underlying all life on this planet is the energy of love radiating from God, or the One in Whom we live and move and have our being.

Just as the human heartbeat sets the rhythm by which blood circulates through the body, the energy of love flows through life with its own rate and rhythm. In the case of our planet earth, the ebb and flow of love from the heart of the sun is indicated by the cycles of the moon. The time of the full moon is the high tide of the planetary flow

simply because the moon is out of the way; it is directly opposite the
sun. During the period of the full moon everyone can participate more
fully in the flow of divine love while the energy flow is at its peak. Each
full moon makes it possible to become a conscious part of a great
planetary process – the sweeping tide of energy known as the sixfold
progression of divine love.

This progression begins symbolically in the planetary head centre
(Shamballa), the centre of planetary purpose and will, the centre
where the will-to-good originates. This will-to-good is transmitted as
essential love. From the planetary head centre the stream of love
moves to the planetary heart, the spiritual Hierarchy. The Hierarchy is
the Kingdom of Souls, the fifth kingdom in nature or the Kingdom of
God. It is comprised of those who have passed beyond the strictly
human stage of evolution to what might be considered the superhuman
stage. The Hierarchy is the repository of planetary love and wisdom
and formulates the Plan of light and love which implements God's
Purpose and draws mankind forward.

As the flow of love reaches the Hierarchy it is focussed into a single
point – the heart of love within the Hierarchy, the Christ. This is the
living Christ, the teacher of angels and men, the eldest within that
great family of brothers, humanity. The Christ, standing as the head of
the spiritual Hierarchy, is the same great world Teacher who is known
by many different names in the major world religions. (The Bodhisattva, The Lord Maitreya, The Imam Mahdi, The Messiah, Krishna).

From the Christ, the stream of divine love flows into the new group
of world servers, a group of subjectively linked individuals working in
their own place and way to embody the light and love needed in the
world today. This group of servers transmits the flow of light and love
into the hearts of men and women of goodwill everywhere – those who
are responsive to love and to the idea of right human relations.

The flow of love finally emerges into physical expression by means of
various focal points through which the Christ can work. A focal point
might be, for example, a major planetary centre such as New York,
London or Geneva, or a significant world organisation such as the
United Nations.

This is *the sixfold progression of divine love* underlying all meditation. From the centre where the will of God is known, through the
spiritual Hierarchy of the planet, through the point at the heart of the
Hierarchy, the Christ, from the Christ through the new group of world
servers who, in their turn, direct it towards the men and women of
goodwill all over the world, and then into human activities on the outer
physical plane of life.

Everyone is a part of this living process. Anyone can become a conscious participant in this flow of love, in this subjective planetary reality which underlies the outer world of affairs.

Occult Meditation

There are essentially two types of meditation – mystical and occult. And both of these differentiate into various meditation techniques.

Mystical forms of meditation depend largely upon an active *feeling* nature and an intense desire for spiritual union.

Occult meditation, on the other hand, builds upon whatever mystical experience may have occurred, taking the whole idea of meditation a step further.

Today, when so much nonsense and inaccuracies are attributed to the term "occult", it is useful to bear in mind one simple definition. *Occultism is the science of energy flow and energy relationships*. Occult meditation is a means of consciously and purposefully directing energy from a recognised source to the creation of some specific effect. Effective occult meditation depends on the quality, the motive, the state of consciousness, the spiritual status and the defined purpose of the meditator.

Occult meditation is a mental activity, requiring a condition of alignment, or at-one-ment, between the three aspects of the mind: the lower or concrete mind, the soul, and the higher or abstract mind. This alignment integrates all three aspects of the individual meditator, spirit, soul and body, making available to him the spiritual resources of life, consciousness and form.

By way of this alignment the meditator is also united with the *life principle* in all things within the planet, and with the *soul or consciousness* of all manifestation. Thus, alignnment is dual; vertical and horizontal. And this creates the basic form of all truly spiritual occult meditation.

Today the most effective type of occult meditation is called Raja Yoga, the "kingly science of the soul." A yoga is a disciplined way of achieving union or alignment, and a measure of control on some plane of consciousness. Raja Yoga uses the creative imagination, the art of visualisation and the use of a seed thought to exercise and expand the mind into the world of meaning and significance. It is in becoming aware of life's meaning and significance that we train ourselves to function fully as souls in incarnation.

CHAPTER 21
Esoteric or Mystery Schools

This chapter consists of extracts from "What is an Esoteric School", published by the Arcane School (Lucis Trust).

The words "esoteric" and "occult" signify "that which is hidden"; they indicate that which lies behind the outer seeming and point to the causes which produce appearance and effects; they are concerned with the subtler world of energies and forces which all outer forms veil and hide. They deal with that which must be known before the initiate-consciousness can be developed.

Emphasis in the past has been upon subjective but nevertheless material forces (hidden within the human being), and frequently upon the psychic powers, such as clairvoyance and clairaudience which man shares in common with the animals. Physical purity has been enormously emphasised in the old schools and concerns the cleansing of the forms through which the soul must manifest. This cleansing is not esoteric in nature and is no sign of esoteric or of spiritual unfoldment. It is only a most necessary preliminary stage; until this purification has been undertaken, more advanced work is not possible. The physical disciplines are needed and useful, and must find their place in all schools for beginners; by their means the neophyte establishes habits of purity and builds the type of body required by the disciple when he starts true esoteric work.

This elementary training enables the neophyte to shift his consciousness out of the tangible world of daily living into the subtler worlds of his personality forces. He becomes aware of the energies with which he must deal and dimly senses that which lies behind them – the soul in its own world, the Kingdom of God.

The old schools have dealt with aspirants on the Path of Probation and Purification.

The newer esoteric schools are concerned with training and preparing the probationer to tread the Path of Discipleship.

The truly new schools which will appear in the twenty-first century, will prepare disciples to tread the Path of Initiation.

Teaching in Esoteric Schools

Schools in the past have done good preparatory work in bringing to the attention of the public, the nature of the *Secret Doctrine*, of esoteric teaching and the fact of the existence of the Masters of The Wisdom – as they work under the direction of the Christ.

Much knowledge has been imparted, bringing much mental stimultation and mental unfoldment, but frequently little real understanding.

The newer esoteric schools are promoting the growth of understanding.

The discipline to which the neophyte in the future should subject himself must be understood and the right techniques imparted.

Teachers will later appear, who will have a true understanding of the spiritual nature of authority. This will not be based upon claim-making and mystery but upon a life lived in accordance with the highest ideals, and upon the presentation of a teaching which will evoke both the respect and the intuitive response of the disciple. The teacher of the future will simply point the Way, tread the Way with the disciple, and emphasise the ancient rules but with their new interpretations.

The teacher assumes no authority over the group or over his helpers, except the authority of greater knowledge, wisdom and light; this makes him an immovable point of power against which the lesser interpretations and methods break and drop away. He teaches certain unalterable occult principles to which the entire group is trained to adhere, but they will do so easily and without controversy. It is those very principles which have brought them into the work.

All the time he lives among them as a learner and fellow student, treading the Way with those who must be taught. Humility is the keynote of the true esoteric leader, because humility indicates vision and a sense of proportion. These teach him that each step forward in the spiritual life reveals still more stages to be mastered.

The student is taught how to play his part in raising the consciousness of the race; this he does through a conscious, direct use of the trained mind, through his controlled emotional nature and his responsive brain.

He becomes proficient in playing the difficult, dual role of the disciple. This is to live as a soul in the life of every day.

The Nature of an Esoteric School

An esoteric school is one in which the relation of the soul, the spiritual man, to the personality is taught. It is the major line of approach for the student, and soul contact becomes his first great endeavour. He comes to know himself and struggles to work as a conscious soul and not just as an active personality. He learns to control and direct his lower nature through a technical understanding of its constitution and to pour through it the light, love and power of the soul. Through alignment, concentration and meditation, he establishes a permanent contact with his inner spiritual being and is then well on the way to become a useful server of humanity.

A true esoteric school works on four levels of service and of experience. This enables the disciple to make a complete approach to humanity and to use all of his equipment. In the true spiritual schools as approved and endorsed by the Masters, service to humanity is taught and not the need for the disciple to be in touch with a Master, as is the case in the majority of esoteric schools of the old order. Contact with the Master is contingent upon the measure and the quality of the service rendered by the disciple to his fellow-men. This is a point oft overlooked by teachers, who lay the emphasis upon the personal attainment of the individual and upon individual perfection. The new schools, now forming, are preoccupied with training men to meet world need and to serve spiritually, upon the following four levels of conscious activity:

a. *That of the outer world.* The disciple is taught to live normally, practically, effectively and spiritually in the everyday world. He is never a freak or a crank.

b. *That of the world of meaning.* The disciple is taught the why and the wherefore of circumstances and happenings – both individual and universal. He is thus trained to act as an interpreter of events and to function as a light bearer.

c. *That of the soul in its own world.* This makes the disciple a channel for divine love, for the nature of the soul is love. He heals and carries inspiration into the world.

d. *That of his Master's Ashram or group.* He is taught to co-operate with the hierarchical plan as it is gradually revealed to him and to arrive at the knowledge which will permit him to direct some of the energies producing world happenings. He thus carries out the purposes of the inner group* with which he is affiliated. (See Chapter 17, "Inner Groups and the Separated Self", page 127) Under the inspiration of the Master and His band of working disciples and initiates, he brings to humanity definite knowledge about the Hierarchy.

The Truths Taught in the True Esoteric Schools

It should be noted that many of the truths, hitherto imparted under the term "esoteric", have either not been so, or are now entirely exoteric.

The esoteric truths of the past are the exoteric fundamental truths of the present. During the past one hundred years, the esoteric doctrines and the secret teaching of the Ageless Wisdom – given to the public often under the pledge of secrecy – have become public property. The nature of man as taught in the mystery schools of the past has – under other names – become recognisable as modern psychology. The mystery of the astral body, of the etheric body and the mental body are now dealt with in our universities, in our psychological courses, dealing with the vitality of the human being, his emotional nature and the mind. The belief in the Masters was a closely guarded secret; now They are discussed from public platforms in all our great cities. The way of meditation and its techniques were closely guarded subjects and the public was taught that such teachings were dangerous; today, this idea is exploded and scores of people throughout the world meditate, make alignment and arrive at soul contact and knowledge. The truth has also been veiled and hidden by a vast body of secondary teaching which has sidetracked the interest of the enquirer, and engrossed his attention through the importance attached to phenomena. Posture, the use of ancient formulas, words and mantrams, breathing exercises, mysterious hints as to the raising of the kundalini fires, the awakening of the centres and other enticing aspects of secondary occultism have caused people to lose sight of the fact that much of the above, being in the realm of phenomena, is concerned with the physical body, its correct adjustment, its vitalisation and energising and that it deals with effects and not with the essential causes of the effects. All these phenomenal results will be demonstrated normally, safely and sanely as well as automatically when the inner man – emotional and mental – is en rapport with the spiritual world and is beginning to function as a spiritual being. This secondary approach to truth has done much harm to the cause of real occultism, and has properly disturbed the best minds in the spiritual field.

In the schools now forming, the emphasis is upon soul awareness, spiritual knowledge, and understanding of the higher forces, direct and first-hand knowledge of the spiritual Hierarchy which governs the life of our planet, a comprehension (progressively developed) of the divine nature and of the Plan which, in obedience to the will of God, is increasingly conditioning world affairs. The laws governing the individual, humanity and the kingdoms in nature are studied and the whole Science of Relations (as it is unfolded in our evolving world) becomes the practical interest of the disciple. As he establishes right relations with himself, with the world of spirtual being, in the world of human living and with all forms of divine life, the awakening of his own nature will *automatically* take place, his centres will become vital sources of spiritual power, and his entire constitution will swing into rhythmic activity and consequent usefulness. All this will happen, however, because of his correct adjustment to God and man, to his unfolding understanding of divine purpose and to his knowledge of the various scientific techniques and laws which condition all phenomena, man included.

NOTE: *Not all students wish to join an esoteric school, but the information imparted here should enable the reader to evaluate the quality of any teacher or group encountered in his search.*

In the best of the newer schools expenses and all overheads must be met, but profit making has no priority because the emphasis should not be upon material gain. They are seldom, if ever, a financial success.

CHAPTER 22

A Summary of the Lucis Press Books

This chapter consists of extracts from "Thirty Years Work" published by the Lucis Press Ltd (Lucis Trust).

It gives a summary of the contents of each of the Alice A. Bailey books. The titles of those written by Alice Bailey herself are marked by an asterisk, *. The rest were dictated by the Tibetan, the Master Djwhal Khul. The last two books are by Foster Bailey, husband of Alice Bailey.

The Unfinished Autobiography*

From her conservative British background, Alice Bailey's life led her in many directions, but always in one direction – towards the time when through drastic personal experience of many kinds she had acquired a synthesis of outlook and understanding, and an absolute conviction that one divine life pervades and animates the one humanity; that the Plan for man requires the cooperation and service of trained and dedicated human beings intelligently informed about world affairs, in collaboration with those who form the spiritual Hierarchy, the inner government of the planet. Her life work became an integral part of this synthesis and this realisation. Without in the least losing any of her very human qualities and involvement, her soul took up its commitment to her Master, and her personality provided full cooperation in the field of her accepted service.

Basically her work developed as a duality – her discipleship service to her own Master, Koot Humi, which included the establishment of the Arcane school; and her initially reluctant agreement to work with the Tibetan, the Master Djwhal Khul, in the writing of a series of books presenting the next phase in the continuity of the Ancient Wisdom teaching for the present and the immediate future.

This work with the Tibetan Master started in 1919. In his introduction to "A Treatise on Cosmic Fire", Foster Bailey remarks: "The story of many years of telepathic work by the Tibetan with Alice Bailey is revealed in her Unfinished Autobiography published in 1951. This includes the circumstances of her first contact with Him on the physical plane which took place in California in November 1919. Thirty years work was planned. When this had been accomplished and within 30 days after that period (in December 1949) Mrs. Bailey gained her release from the limitations of the physical vehicle."

The Consciousness of the Atom*
Seven lectures given by Alice Bailey are brought together in this book of seven chapters under the headings:
1. The Field of Evolution.
2. The Evolution of Substance.
3. The Evolution of Form, or Group Evolution.
4. The Evolution of Man, the Thinker.
5. The Evolution of Consciousness.
6. The Goal of Evolution.
7. Cosmic Evolution.

In these chapters the scientific relation of matter and consciousness is discussed as evolution progressively affects the atomic substance of all forms, subjective and objective. The purpose of the lectures was to present "the testimony of science" to this relationship and "to enable the hearers to observe the identical manifestation of these relations". Much progress has been made during this century in atomic science and in man's knowledge of the structure of the universe, the constitution of man, and the relation between the two.

The teachings and sayings of the Christ are quoted to cement the inescapable link between the scientific and the philosophical, or religious aspects of divinity. Each divine principle can be expressed in terms which relate to any human attribute or activity. Here is the synthesis of life in form.

The Destiny of the Nations
World problems are increasing in complexity as the population of the world increases, and as nations become inter-related and interdependent. It is important for the future of mankind that we understand and cooperate with the spiritual laws and forces at work within the interwoven structure of civilisation, so that the individual part – human and national – can be rightly related to the evolving whole.

A nation is subject, as a man is, to the impact of energies emanating from solar and cosmic sources. Different nations are more receptive to some energies than to others; and all nations, subject to the evolution of national consciousness, have a destiny before them which is literally based on the qualities and the principles of the particular ray energy seeking expression through the national soul.

In this book the ray energies affecting certain nations, world groupings and major cities are analysed in relation to meaning and purpose, and to the emergence of *ideas* appropriate to energy influences dominant at the end and at the beginning of an age.

Discipleship in the New Age – Volume I

How many would-be disciples are convinced of their worthiness to receive direct training from a Master of the Wisdom? How few are able to absorb the intense pressures of the experience and to profit from the opportunity! Included in these two volumes of *Discipleship in the New Age* are the series of personal instructions given to a small group of chelas over a period of 15 years, with related teaching on a number of subjects.

When the group effort was finally discontinued, the Tibetan Master remarked that while his purpose in establishing the group for Ashramic training had proved unsuccessful, the instructions and teaching given as a result of forming the group would prove of great and continuing value to increasing numbers of aspirants to discipleship; and certain important concepts were anchored in human consciousness through the group channel, including particularly the vital fact of the reappearance of the Christ. As the interplay between Hierarchy and humanity strengthens, many young disciples approaching the periphery of an Ashram are profiting from the experience of this group brought together for training by the Tibetan, and from the wealth of careful teaching and spiritual stimulation made available to them.

In the first part of Volume I of *Discipleship in the New Age* some of the requirements of the Hierarchical Plan and the place of service of discipleship groups are clearly shown in relationship. The "Six Stages of Discipleship" in the final part of the book show the sequence of growth in consciousness towards the center of an Ashram so clearly, that only the self-deluded can fail to identify his own place and his resulting opportunity.

Between these two parts of the book, training and teaching hints and personal instructions are given to each of 41 disciples and applicants for discipleship. In these direct and outspoken comments any sincere aspirant to discipleship can find himself and his own need understood and met, sometimes in drastic terms, from the deep spiritual insight, the knowledge and the love of a Master of the Wisdom.

Discipleship in the New Age – Volume II
This second volume contains the teaching given between the years
1940 and 1949 after the group had been reduced and reorganised into
one group, "the new seed group".

One of the main objectives of the new seed group was to "anchor"
some of the principles and seed ideas for the new civilisation of the
Aquarian era; and also to create an integrated group of trained
Hierarchical workers capable of providing needed cooperation with
activities initiated by Hierarchy to fertilise and prepare human
consciousness for the tremendous stimulation of the immediate future.
In this book, therefore, the personal instructions cover a shorter
period of time and only 22 individuals.

Two vitally important aspects of the life of discipleship are
emphasised from the standpoint of practical training techniques –
meditation and initiation. Meditation is shown not only as a way of
approach by the individual to the soul, and by the group to the Master,
but as the creative technique of the Lord of the World by which all is
brought into being.

The teachings on initiation are also given an essentially practical
presentation as "facts of life", to be understood and applied. The
glamorous idea of initiation as a reward for a good, self-disciplined way
of life, dissipates in the light of the reality. Neither has initiation for the
disciple anything to do with the internal, organisational "initiations"
peculiar to many occult orders and groups, which are meaningless
except in the context of the organisation itself.

Initiation for the disciple is the result of a conscious expansion into
"larger and larger wholes" – a progressive expansion into the actual
stream of consciousness of our planetary Life. These expansions in
consciousness are accompanied by a succession of revelations; and in
this volume of *Discipleship in the New Age*, five points of revelation are
discussed, with hints and symbolic formulas leading to a correct
interpretation of them.

Education in the New Age
Of the few specialised subjects included in these books by Alice Bailey
and the Tibetan, education is of primary importance. Today we are
losing the tendency to associate "education" only with the instruction
of the young and with academic matters. Education is, or should be, a
continuous process from birth to death concerned not so much with the
acquisition of knowledge as with the expansion of consciousness.
Knowledge of itself is a dead end, unless it is brought into functioning
relationship with environment, social responsibilities, historical

trends, human and world conditions and, above all, with the evolution of consciousness which brings the infinite vastness of an unknown universe within the range of the finite human mind.

To oversimplify, can we say that education is a continuous process of learning how to reconcile the human and the divine elements in the constitution of man, creating right relationship between God and man, spirit and matter, the whole and the part?

If this is education in the broader sense, it is more specific and more concentrated when considered in the light of child training. This book is so concentrated and specific. While presenting the need for wholeness – development of the whole person, spirit, soul and body as an integrated unity, and acceptance of the planetary whole as the area of personal experience and responsibility – the educational needs of the child today are set out in specific terms. Faults and inadequacies in the present educational systems existing in many parts of the world are enumerated, and methods for the future suggested.

The Externalisation of the Hierarchy

The subject of human free will has always contrived to set men's mental teeth on edge. The fatalist automatically resigns himself to whatever befalls him, seeing in effects no cause attributable to his own action – or inaction; but resigned always to the working of an inexorable fate.

The Christian counterpart tends to accept his lot as the working of God's Will in which he has no say or part.

At the other extreme stands the rebellious independent, determined to exercise his right to free, self-willed action.

This book, as one of its many values, shows the extent to which Hierarchy and other centres of life on the planet are dependent upon the unpredictable and often irresponsible factor of human free will. During the years leading up to the outbreak of World War II, every opportunity and every possible spiritual stimulation was offered to humanity in an effort to avoid precipitation of conflict on to the physical plane. Disciples and aspirants to discipleship were asked to give special cooperation to the Hierarchy, and to make an all-out effort to provide adquate leadership to human thought and decision. All were left free, however, to determine their own limits, if any, and to decide their own actions. According to law, the Hierarchy – even at danger point – could not infringe human free will and dictate or impose a course of action based on their own deeper knowledge and more profound insight.

Many of the spiritual factors surrounding the period of human history from 1919 to 1949 are presented in this book. The energies at work behind the world scene are shown; and the identity revealed of certain great Beings magnetically attracted in service towards this planet at a climaxing moment in the evolution of our planetary life.

These factors are an aid to our understanding of the interrelated energy patterns within the universe which operate according to law. But essentially they provide the esotericist with knowledge of available energy flow responding to planetary purpose and plan which can be contacted and given conscious and intelligent cooperation, particularly by those in whom the selfish, self-centred will has been transcended so that the spiritual will can be given more adequate expression. Some of these energy factors are particularly clear in the special "Messages" given over a period of many years at the time of the Festivals of Easter, Wesak and the Christ.

Many aspects of Hierarchical work, thought and planning are discussed in these Messages, with the Hierarchical effect shown of planetary evolution and initiation and its reflection into humanity. This achieved a climax at the time of the three Festivals in 1945, when a momentous decision was taken involving, among other results, the eventual externalisation of the Hierarchy and the reappearance of the Christ.

The final section of the book discusses the "Stages in the Externalisation of the Hierarchy". It is often difficult for the human mind to imagine the problems facing those liberated from the restrictions of form. It is even more difficult to contemplate the effects in those so liberated of a free choice to reassume such a limitation.

From Bethlehem to Calvary*

In her foreword to this book, the author remarks, "The conscious evocation of the Christ life in the human heart and our rapid integration into the Kingdom of God are the immediate tasks ahead, embodying our responsibility, opportunity and destiny".

The five expansions of consciousness by which this integration and evocation proceed are clearly portrayed here as the correspondences of the five climaxing experiences of the Master Jesus during His life in Palestine. These are the five initiations known as the Birth, Baptism, Transfiguration, Crucifixion, Resurrection and Ascension. Through these five stages on the Way, we follow the Master from Bethlehem to Calvary.

This is probably the factor of greatest value and service to the aspirant, setting his feet on the Path of Return; that the experience of the Master Jesus, including that of the Crucifixion, the Great Renunciation, reflects through the lives of all human beings. Through the divine life in us, and as the Christ principle unfolds in our heart and consciousness, the sons of men walk the Way of the Cross eventually to become soul-illumined Sons of God.

From Intellect to Intuition*

In this book *From Intellect to Intuition*, development of the intellect, while necessary, is shown as a means to an end and one step on the way to a fully awakened and active mental body.

Meditation is sometimes defined as "thinking in the heart"; correct meditation proceeds only when the heart and mind function together in unison. To touch the intuition, therefore, this blending of heart and mind is a necessity, since the intuitive sense is a faculty of the heart aroused by the activity of the integrated, three-fold mind.

"Meditation in the eastern sense is . . . a strictly mental process, leading to soul knowledge and illumination. It is a fact in nature that 'as a man thinketh (in his heart) so is he.' "

Glamour: a World Problem

Glamour is, of course, the result of a negative emotional focus; just as illusion results from a negative or unclear attitude of mind out of touch with the reality behind the outer appearance, so a man becomes the victim of strong self-created thought-forms built on personality forces and self-interest.

This book deals with the misconceptions existing on all levels of the personality life – maya on the etheric level; glamour on the emotional plane; and illusion on the mental plane; climaxing in the sum total of all three combined in the personality – the so-called dweller on the threshold.

The correct methods of working to dissipate world glamour and dispel world illusion, conform to modern psychological techniques accepted and practised for individual benefit. *A higher form of energy must be brought to bear* on the blocked condition. This means in practical terms, maya must be subjected to the inspiration and idealism of the emotional plane; glamour to the illumination of the mental plane; illusion to the light of the intuition, a buddhic energy; and the dweller on the threshold must be confronted by the Angel of the Presence, the soul.

"The need for the service of men and women free from illusion and glamour, has never been so dramatically present as it is today, and it is for these potential servers of a desperate necessity that I have written."

Initiation, Human and Solar

One of the great values of this book is that it does stretch the mind towards a new conception of the intense activity involved at all levels of consciousness on the planet to create conditions in which evolutionary growth can proceed. The work of the the planetary Hierarchy, and of some of the responsible workers within the Hierarchy, is outlined in a way which brings everyday human life into focus as an outer expression of qualified purpose through the Ashrams of the Masters. The three departments of Hierarchy form important planetary focal points of cosmic energy flow, each one imbued with purpose and responsible for an aspect of the Plan of God. The inter-relationship and interaction of the many kingdoms and centres of consciousness are revealed as tending towards the complete integration and alignment of our Planetary Logos within the systemic whole.

The detailed procedures of initiation rituals revealed here stimulate the imagination; but essentially the individual aspirant treading the Path of Discipleship is thrown back on his own inner spiritual resources as the only means by which progress can be made and consciousness expanded. This he does to the extent that he becomes sensitive and responsive to energy wielded and projected by Hierarchy.

The Light of the Soul

Many translations have been made from the original Sanskrit of the Yoga Sutras of Patanjali. They have become well loved, well used, and well applied by many in all parts of the world and of all religious beliefs. The Sutras have a power and a timelessness about them which demonstrate the accuracy with which they pinpoint the basic truths of human evolution from subservience to personality clamours to the serene freedom of the soul.

Many different training techniques have been available over the centuries, depending on the condition of human consciousness and the phase of spiritual growth to be accomplished. Each "Yoga" has had its place, fulfilled its function, and become an absorbed part of human experience.

In this book the factor of mind in meeting present-day needs is again given prominence as the agent of the soul, and the key to personality release.

These Yoga Sutras of Patanjali are based on Raja Yoga, the "kingly science of the soul": "Through the science of Raja Yoga the mind will be known as the instrument of the soul and the means whereby the brain of the aspirant becomes illuminated and knowledge gained of those matters which concern the realm of the soul."

Letters on Occult Meditation

We have a recognised cleavage to be bridged in the world today, usually known as the cleavage between "East and West", but termed more accurately between "Orient and Occident". Behind the differences in culture, tradition, religion, ideology and social customs, however, there is a growing interchange of thought and mental understanding. One powerful stimulation to this mental rapport may be in an increasing tendency for the westerner to cultivate the science of meditation long practiced in the East as an essential part of religious and spiritual experience. In this day and age, and as we move on into the mentally oriented age of Aquarius, with increasing numbers of men and women transferring from an emotional to a mental focus, the science of meditation as a mind training technique in concentration and invocation will become increasingly practised in the West.

However, there are deeper and more profound areas of life and consciousness to be penetrated and revealed in meditation. Meditation, in the occult sense, is not only a training technique for the mind, but a means of achieving alignment, union and identification with the soul, with the Christ, and ultimately with "the Father". As distinct from the experience of mystical union, occult meditation establishes a scientific process by which causes set in motion will produce identifiable effects, which can be repeated at will. This is a technique to be mastered by the mind; it involves intense mental activity followed by an absolute stillness, with the ability so to control and order the mind that it engages in action or becomes stilled to "reflection" at will.

The first purpose of this form of meditation is the conscious integration of soul and personality, so that the livingness of the soul may impress and influence the quality of the personality life. This draws a man steadily into that centre of consciousness within the planet we call the spiritual Hierarchy, the Kingdom of God; the spiritual Man then assumes control, and the divine potential is unfolded.

Since we are dealing in meditation with energy flow which is literally fiery and impersonal, there are pitfalls and dangers to be understood and avoided; these, too, are discussed. And also the colours and sounds corresponding to the various ray energies which, occultly speaking, are vibrations of different frequencies.

In looking towards the future, the author predicts the growing influence of the science of meditation, leading eventually to the establishing of schools of meditation under the guidance and instruction of initiated disciples. These schools will be of two kinds: one, preparatory; and the other actually training the student for initiation. The ultimate objective of these comprehensive training schools will be to provide qualified disciples for planetary service. In all training work inspired by Hierarchy the motif is service – the spontaneous effect of soul contact in the selflessly motivated disciple.

Problems of Humanity

Six basic problems . . . confront humanity with opportunity for progress: the psychological rehabilitation of the nations; the problem of the children of the world; the problem of capital, labour and employment; the problem of the racial minorities; the problem of the churches; the problem of international unity and the equitable distribution of the world's resources. From these many other social and economic problems arise, essentially resulting from growth in human consciousness and progress in many underprivileged countries and communities towards freedom, equality and interdependence in a modern world.

A perspective is shown here which relates the spiritual potential and subjective factors to the outer appearance of human affairs. Continuing cleavages in consciousness; psychological evaluations and reactions to world conditions; national, religious, class or racial prejudice; conditions of illiteracy, disease and poverty, and economic imbalance, are all responsible for creating and perpetuating conditions in which war is inevitable.

All men and women of goodwill are concerned with the solution of these problems. They are particularly the concern of those accepting the self-discipline of training for discipleship in the new age, those world servers capable of relating esoteric truths and spiritual realities to the field of service in which they are placed.

The esotericist of today is a practical worker. His illumined consciousness makes available to him a source of energy supply which is inexhaustible and which originates within the circulating energy of the One Life. He thus becomes a centre of energy transmission between Hierarchy and humanity, reflecting the soul, or Christ principle, throughout his service environment, illuminating and lifting the darkened areas of human consciousness.

The Reappearance of the Christ

There have been many messengers over the ages, manifesting through one or another of the great world religions or followed by a new form of religion based on the new revelation. Divine revelation and the periodic appearance of messengers, or Avatars, occur, however, according to cosmic law, when certain conditions exist within the whole scheme affected by, and affecting, every part, large and small.

Then a chain of events is set in motion which under law must eventually work out.

The imminence of the reappearance of the Christ is sensed and expected by many, belonging as He does to all humanity irrespective of differing religious dogma and doctrine. "He for whom all men wait" will Himself determine the manner and the timing of His appearance and the area of His work in a way which creates no divisions or separations between men, either religious, social or ideological. Not only does He come as the first Son of God, but as Head of the spiritual Hierarchy, the inner government of the planet. He is, therefore, a great world executive, representing the Kingdom of God, and fulfilling a definite function in the world of men. He is coming to establish through precept and example in world service the principles on which a united, interdependent and interactive world may create its new material systems and spiritual institutions for the new civilisation.

Preparation for the second coming is the responsibility of humanity; it is for those who know and accept the imminent return of the Christ to prepare men's minds and hearts to recognise and receive Him, and to create those conditions of balance and spiritual alignment which will ultimately draw Him forth into our midst. For no matter what message or revelation the Christ may embody when He comes, no matter what principle or energy He may anchor on Earth for human use, he is not coming to save humanity from the results of its own sins, but once more to show humanity how to save itself in the new conditions and new opportunities with which the world is faced.

The Soul and Its Mechanism*

It is an established and accepted occult fact that the soul works through the mechanism of the three-fold personality in stimulating the three worlds of human evolution – the mental, the emotional and etheric-physical planes of consciousness. In this book the method by which the soul and the personality vehicles interact and function together is clearly presented.

It is said that the aspirant to discipleship really needs to know only two things; the constitution of man and the next step ahead. In this book the way the human constitution actually functions in its component parts is made abundantly clear. It is an accepted goal for the aspirant that he learns to make of his personality equipment an instrument for the soul to use. Knowledge of the relation between the subtle and the dense bodies, the etheric centres and the physical glands, energy and force, the soul and its personality mechanism, can lift the process out of the vague haze which normally surrounds it, giving to it the clarity and precision of a scientific formula.

Telepathy and the Etheric Vehicle

Occultism shows that the scientific basis for the ideal of brotherhood rests on the fact of the one etheric structure underlying all forms within the solar system, energised and held in being by one life force. Mankind is, therefore, one in life and in form; he is merely unaware of unity in his own consciousness. And evolution is essentially the means by which he becomes progressively conscious of the Fatherhood of God and the brotherhood of man.

It is through this conscious, controlled use of mental energy that telepathic communication can be scientifically established with other minds by means of the etheric structure common to all. And by the same means the mind of the disciple, or of a group of disciples developing group consciousness, can be impressed by the clarity of thought and purpose of those members of the spiritual Hierarchy concerned with the working out of the Plan for humanity. The spiritual Hierarchy, we are told, works only through the minds of disciples, using the science of impression, and only for the purposes of the Plan. The impression is conveyed as a stream of ideas – those ideas inherent in the Plan for man – which the disciple or the group can then interpret and translate into self-chosen action.

The form of telepathy now developing within the spiritually awakened aspirants of the world is not, therefore, that of the solar plexus centre which is of the animal nature, but the result of a mental polarisation and penetration in consciousness towards the soul.

A Treatise on Cosmic Fire

Although this book was one of the first to be written by Alice Bailey in collaboration with the Tibetan, it is probably the most timeless, profound and least understood. *A Treatise on Cosmic Fire* deals with the underlying structure of occult teaching for the present era, with vast cosmic processes reproduced through all areas of life from universe to atom. It is, therefore, no book for the proof-demanding concrete mind, or for those who dabble in the spectacular and the phenomenal. The true student, however, the seriously applied aspirant, will find his mind stimulated and his consciousness expanded.

In her foreword to the book, the author mentions a five-fold purpose within its teaching; briefly: (a) To provide a compact and skeleton outline of a scheme of cosmology, philosophy and psychology which may serve as a reference and textbook; (b) As an elucidation of the relation between Spirit and Matter, demonstrating as *consciousness;*

(c) To show the coherent development of all that is found within a solar system and to demonstrate that *everything* evolves; (d) To give practical information about focal points of energy found in the etheric bodies of the Solar Logos, the macrocosm, and of man, the microcosm; (e) To give some information of the place and work of those sentient lives who form the essence of objectivity, and to indicate the nature of the Hierarchies of Existences who form out of their own substance all that is seen and known.

A Treatise on the Seven Rays

Vol. I Esoteric Psychology – 1

Five volumes have been written under the overall title of *A Treatise on the Seven Rays*. This sequence of books is based on the fact, the nature and the quality of the seven basic streams of energy pervading our solar system, our planet and all that lives and moves within its orbit. Of the specialised subjects presented in these books, two volumes are concerned with esoteric psychology – the first in relation to basic energy patterns and structures; the second particularly applied to the soul and the personality of man and to the working out of the Plan for humanity.

The "psyche" is, after all, the human soul, the centre of consciousness. Esoteric psychology begins with a consideration of the human being *as a soul*, manifesting in the form of a personality, consisting of mental, emotional and etheric/physical substance, and more or less in contact and control, depending on the stage of evolution in the personality consciousness.

The seven differentiated streams of ray energy play a significant role in this evolutionary process. A blend of five energies in a human being determine his goals, his problems, his available qualities and energy resources, and the correct method by which – according to his dominant ray influence – he may unfold his consciousness and make spiritual progress.

Vol. II Esoteric Psychology – 2

The second volume of Esoteric Psychology deals exhaustively with the ray qualities controlling the life, consciousness and appearance of a human being on the physical plane. Every man in his totality is subject to the laws of evolution by which he proceeds from the One to the many and back to the One, enriched by the experience of life in form and capable of contributing the results of that experience to the larger life which pervades him.

This book includes much comment and teaching of the utmost value to the disciple in training for world service, learning to take his place within that subjectively united and organised group of disciples discussed in this volume as "the new group of world servers". Group consciousness is a major goal for every aspirant to discipleship.

The first part of the book dealing with the Egoic Ray, includes sections on (1) The growth of soul influence (2) The seven laws of soul or group life (3) The five groups of souls and (4) Rules for inducing soul control. While the second part on The Ray of the Personality, contains detailed teaching on (1) The appropriation of the bodies (2) The coordination of the personality (3) Some problems of psychology and (4) Diseases and problems of disciples and mystics.

The final part of this volume on Humanity Today anchors these pervasive thoughts and energies within the world arena. The world situation is viewed from the esoteric and Hierarchical angle and in relation to the requirements of the dawning new age of Aquarius. A synthesis of thought and a unity of purpose must be established in the world in order to create conditions in which peace can prosper and the Christ can reappear.

Vol. III Esoteric Astrology

Astrology is described in this book as "the science of relationships" – the relationship existing between all living organisms within the universe. Not only the qualities of the ray energies affect these centres of consciousness, but also the quality and energy of the ruling planets and the zodiacal signs. Seen from the exoteric outside, astrology is a vast and most involved and complex subject. From the esoteric inside, while it is still vast, all-inclusive and complex, it is also possible to perceive the thread which unites and the pattern which prevails throughout the whole system. A basic simplicity in the grand design emerges, therefore, which can serve to interpret the whole.

The main chapter headings to this book provide the sequence in developing study: (1) The Zodiac and the Rays (2) The Nature of Esoteric Astrology (3) The Science of Triangles (4) The Sacred and Non-Sacred Planets (5) Three Major Constellations (6) The Three Crosses (7) The Rays, Constellations and Planets. In addition there is an appendix which summarises and tabulates many of the factors of fundamental importance to the study of esoteric astrology.

Vol. IV Esoteric Healing

There are probably more individuals and groups of people in the world of every shade of belief and capacity, devoted to the idea of healing than to any other single human need. Yet healing is an exact, and an exacting science; and in modern society no physician or surgeon may practice the ancient profession of healing without the personal qualifications legally recognised by the State for the protection of the public. No doubt prayer and invocation can be effective under certain circumstances, particularly when the one who serves is pure and harmless in motive, and has enough understanding to cooperate with the soul purposes of the individual, so permitting the healing energy of the soul to flow more freely and effectively through the personality, or to proceed with the process of withdrawal, if that is its immediate purpose.

Esoteric healing, however, includes far more than this; it is a science based on a number of requirements, including knowledge of the constitution of man and the nature of the various bodies, both dense and subtle. To this practical knowledge, the science of occultism contributes vital information of the energy factors, the karmic and ray influences, the psychology and astrology of the soul, and the laws and rules fundamental to the safe and successful practice of esoteric healing.

In this book the seven ray techniques of healing are described; the laws and rules of healing are enumerated and discussed; the requirements for healing are given in detail; and basic causes of disease are shown. We learn, for example, that much disease can be karmic in origin; that certain diseases are inherent in the soil and in the substance of the planet; and that many others are psychological, arising in the emotional or mental bodies. Hence the need for a total and comprehensive understanding both of the patient and of the correct and safe methods of healing.

We are also given a true understanding of death as the abstraction, or the withdrawal, of the soul from the body to continue life on its own plane without the limitation of the body, until a new cycle of incarnation and experience in form is necessary.

Vol. V The Rays and the Initiations
The final volume in this treatise on the seven rays contains the fundamental spiritual structure on which the next presentation of the Ageless Wisdom teaching will build. The book is in two parts; the first part enumerates and details the Fourteen Rules for Group Initiation. These are the rules for disciples and initiates, paralleling on a higher turn of the spiral, the rules for applicants contained in the book "Initiation, Human and Solar". The second part of this volume is concerned with the Rays and the Initiations.

Much of this teaching, while beyond the grasp of the average student today, is invaluable in expanding the mind to contemplate the larger patterns and processes in which the individual function may be viewed in perspective.

A Treatise on White Magic

Throughout the whole of this series of books runs a single thread uniting various aspects of life and specialised activities within the Plan for man. This is the thread of consciousness, evolving in man through the efforts of the soul to contact and control its personality equipment; and evolving within the planet as the centre Hierarchy becomes increasingly able to impress the Plan on the minds of men.

This book, therefore, contains the Fifteen Rules for Magic, and for soul control.

The power of the soul is always available to the one who seeks, as an aspirant to accepted discipleship, to become of practical service in his own peculiar times, state and environment.

The teaching in this book is based on four fundamental postulates which will:

1. Teach the laws of spiritual psychology as distinguished from mental and emotional psychology.

2. Make clear the nature of the soul of man and its systemic and cosmic relationships. This will include its group relationship as a preliminary step.

3. Demonstrate the relations between the self and the sheaths which that self may use, and thus clarify thought as to the constitution of man.

4. Elucidate the problem of supernormal powers and give the rules for their safe and useful development.

The book closes with a rousing call to the soul in all aspirants: "I close with an appeal to all who read these instructions, to rally their forces, to renew their vows of dedication to the service of humanity, to subordinate their own ideas and wishes to the group good, to take their eyes off themselves and fix them anew upon the vision . . . Let all students make up their minds in this day of emergency and of opportunity to sacrifice all they have to the helping of humanity . . . I call upon all of you to join the strenuous efforts of the Great Ones."

The Spirit of Masonry by Foster Bailey

This book contains five in a series of instructions the Tibetan Master intended to give to a group of Masons through the agency of Alice Bailey. However, due to time and other pressures in his work with AAB, the instructions were not completed. Foster Bailey was asked to take these five instructions and eventually to publish them. This he has done, with the addition, in Part II of the book, of the text of an article by AAB first published in the Master Mason Magazine, and of a lecture delivered by Foster Bailey to a Lodge in New Jersey. An Appendix on "Landmarks" compiled from the Encyclopaedia of Freemasonry by Mackey, completes an illuminating and stimulating book.

The books written by Alice Bailey with the Tibetan contain many references to the Masonic Craft; to its origins, the course of its history over the centuries, and to the significant part a revitalised and re-spiritualised Masonry can and will play in the future in carrying the light and the energy of the Mystery teachings through the Aquarian era.

"Masons have as yet much inner work to do with themselves. The time for the true Masonic recognition on a large scale is still distant. Masonry has still Masonically and spiritually to 'prove itself'. When this takes place and the spiritual purpose underlying all Masonic work is better grasped, then the Law of the Builders can make its influence felt. Then group work for the race can be done. Then the conscious cooperation of the Lodge at labour on High, will be seen. Then Masonry will be re-established as the custodian of the Mysteries of the spiritual life upon earth, and will prove itself to be the force of life which lies at the heart of all true religion."

Changing Esoteric Values by Foster Bailey
This book contains the edited and enlarged material presented by the author in four lectures given in London in 1954. Spiritual factors of value to esotericists today are included here with clarity and vision. Esotericism is shown as a practical science of service, in which the subjective and spiritual aspects of life can be related to human need and world affairs in effective ways. The old tendency in spiritually awakening people toward isolation from mundane daily life and to dependence on a so-called spiritual "authority" is ending. The esotericist is also a man of goodwill and a member of the new group of world servers, responsible for the well-being of the human race in conformity with the divine Plan. He learns and grows through the results of his own experience in relating spiritual principles to daily life.

These Alice Bailey/D.K. books are now widely accepted in Europe and America as the classic reference books for the New Age, have been translated into several languages, and are available from libraries and bookshops in most modern towns and cities. Further information on how to obtain them is overleaf.

It is not always possible, particularly at the beginning, to start by reading these from cover to cover: for instance, for many years I used *A Treatise on Cosmic Fire* only as a reference book, but can now read most of it with enjoyment. However, I recently met an undergraduate (reading physics at a local university) who had started with *A Treatise on Cosmic Fire*, reading it from cover to cover.

The well known scientist, Marcel Vogel, tells us that he found the same work unreadable until he turned to the index for subjects of interest to him, found a wealth of useful information, and went on from there.

Some readers have found it best to start with *The Externalisation of the Hierarchy*, as they found it so practical. However, as it is difficult, at first reading, to absorb all of the information contained in books of this calibre, it is advisable, over the years, to keep going back to them, each time finding something new and exciting to add to one's store of knowledge.

An outstanding compilation, *Master Index of the Tibetan and Alice A. Bailey Books*, was published in 1974, and is still available from the publisher:

Aquarian Educational Group
PO Box 267
Sedona
Arizona 86336
USA

This reference work I find invaluable, not only when studying these Lucis Press books, but also when checking on queries while reading any of the many excellent new books now available in this field. For me, D.K. always seems to have the answers.

Information on prices and availability of all the publications of the Lucis Trust can be obtained by writing to one of the three headquarters to find out the names and addresses of local groups and distributors. The headquarters are in London, New York and Geneva at the following addresses:

The Lucis Trust
Suite 54
3 Whitehall Court
London SW1A 2EF
England

The Lucis Trust
113 University Place
11th Floor
P O Box 722 Cooper Station
New York, N.Y.
U.S.A. 10276

The Lucis Trust
Case Postale 31
1 rue de Varembé (3e)
1211 Geneva 20
Switzerland

Glossary

The use of the *Master Index of the Tibetan and Alice A. Bailey Books* is recommended as saving hours of tedious searching, even when checking facts in other publications.

ABSTRACT MIND: That aspect of mind which exists on the higher levels of the mental plane (See Chart 1, page 25). It deals entirely with the higher values of the Spiritual Triad – is idealistic, illumined, and the presenter of ideas. It is the archetype or pattern building faculty of the mind which deals with the "blueprint" upon which the forms on the denser planes are modelled.

ADEPT: A Master. A human being, who has travelled the Path of Discipleship, who has entered upon the Path of Initiation, and no longer needs to incarnate into the three lower planes. An adept has completed the first five Initiations, and functions on the buddhic or intuitional plane in the fifth kingdom, which is the kingdom of God.

ALIGNMENT: The adjustment of different parts in order for them to work in unison as a complete whole. In meditation, to adjust the physical-etheric, emotional and mental bodies so that they can act as one, and can therefore be used as a channel for the soul in everyday living.

ALTA MAJOR CHAKRA: This is situated just below the base of the skull where the spinal cord emerges. It is the junction, gateway or link between the energies of the body and of the mind.

ANALOGY or LAW OF CORRESPONDENCES: The Law which interprets God in man – "As above so below". (See MACROCOSM, MICROCOSM)

ANGEL OF THE PRESENCE: It is the soul on its own plane, and it holds the three permanent atoms of the Higher Self, i.e. the spiritual, intuitional and higher mind. When an initiate becomes a Master, he transfers his focus to these three from the three permanent atoms of the lower self and from then on he functions on the intuitional plane.

ANIMA MUNDI: The subjective side, the underlying consciousness, of all forms in nature. The vast intricate sensory system of the planet. The soul of matter; the sentient (feeling) factor in substance itself. In other words, the responsiveness, the awareness, the *quality* which every form manifests.(See *A Treatise on White Magic*, pages 33 and 34.)

ANTAHKARANA or ANTASKARANA: The path or bridge between the higher and lower minds, between the higher self and the personality. This is built by the aspirant himself of mental matter. It is built out of the awareness of and response to higher spiritual energies.

ARC: Involutionary and Evolutionary – part of a circle or curve. The *in*volutionary arc covers the "Path of *descent*" or the descent of Spirit into ever denser matter until the lowest level in matter is reached. The latter half of the process is called *e*volutionary and marks the ascent or return of Spirit to its divine source, thus completing the circle. On the descending arc the spiritual is gradually embedded in the material and on the ascending arc Spirit slowly reasserts itself through the purification and redemption of matter. (See Chart 4, page 35)

ARCHETYPE: An original model from which anything is made. There are, on the mental plane, archetypes in mental matter of all the different forms which exist in the dense world. They are not merely models, but are living things, creative moulds, which fashion forms in their own likeness.

ARHAT: An Initiate of the fourth degree, which is the renunciation, the cross.

ARYAN: The name given to the fifth root race (see Chapter 3, "The Evolution of Humanity", page 32) This is the race that is developing the mind and has been in existence since before the time of the Lord Buddha. It is not confined to any one race but is the sum total of all the people scattered through all races East and West, on all continents, who are developing mental consciousness.

ASHRAM: A vortex of energy. The subjective spiritual centre to which a Master gathers his groups of disciples and aspirants for personal instruction and group service. A centre of living energy in the group life of the Hierarchy and a means of directing focused spiritual energy into the world.

"AS IF": "As a man thinketh in his heart, so is he." By acting "as if" one were a soul, it is possible more easily to work towards a true vision of soul and personality. This attitude brings into play the faculty of creative imagination which produces definite inner changes in a person.
(See CREATIVE IMAGINATION)

ASPIRANT: One who strives to attain a higher state of consciousness, and who achieves this state through a controlled mind, with purity of thought, motive and action.(See PATH, STAGES OF)

ASPIRANT, REQUIREMENTS OF:
1. To study the forces and energies within nature and within himself;
2. To learn how to wisely use these forces and energies;
3. To acquire soul knowledge;
4. To learn how to safely use the powers of the soul to control the personality (the mental, emotional and physical bodies);
5. To learn how to use spiritual will.

ASPIRATION: Seeking after knowledge of the soul. By the study and practice of rules and methods, an aspirant hopes to achieve the realisation of Spiritual consciousness. *Aspiration* must precede *inspiration*. It is a burning desire and a fiery determination, a purificatory furnace which destroys all that is base in the lower self, leaving the aspirant pure and refined.

ASTRAL AND MENTAL BODIES: These bodies, which exist on the emotional and mental planes are part of the equipment of the personality (mental, emotional and physical-etheric). They are composed of the elemental life of those planes and the whole struggle of the evolutionary process, which is the growth of consciousness, is between these elemental energies (which wish to follow their own tendencies) and the soul in its effort to control them. By steady purification of the mind and emotions, using dispassion, discrimination and detachment, these vehicles can be brought under control, and matter of a finer and more responsive quality to soul energy, can be built in.(See Chapter 6, "The Subtle Bodies of Man", page 55)

ASTRAL BODY: The vehicle through which all emotions, passions, desires and appetites act on the physical body and find their expression in the physical world. This body must be understood, controlled and trained to function under the domination of the soul.

ASTRAL PLANE: The subjective energy field in which the astral body exists. The world of emotions. The matter of this plane is fluidic, is more responsive to all life energies than is physical matter and is likened to water. It is in continual motion, changing in colour and form with the ever changing emotions. (See Chapter 6, "The Subtle Bodies of Man", page 60 and Chart 1, page 25)

ATLANTIS: A continent said to have stretched from Europe to North America, and now submerged under the Atlantic Ocean. It was the home of the Fourth Root Race, the Atlanteans. (See Chart 4, page 35)

ATOM: In the past the atom was regarded as an indivisible unit of substance; now it is looked upon as a centre of energy or electric force, which through its own internal make-up can give off energy, heat and radiation. It possesses the power to change from one kind of activity to another. To the esotericist the atom is a living entity, a positive nucleus of force or life, a little vibrant world, within whose sphere of life influence other lives are found. (See PERMANENT ATOM).

AT-ONE-MENT: (At-one-ness) To be conscious of oneself as a whole (Spirit, soul and body), the mind and soul functioning as a unit to express the will of the indwelling soul. That state is achieved when, through the ordered stages of meditation, the physical body is brought under the control of the soul. The emotional body reflects the Love nature, and the mental body expresses perfectly the Will or purpose of God.(See Chapter 21, "The Science of Meditation", page 140)

ATTRACTION, LAW OF: See chapter "The Law of Attraction", page 122

AUM: The Sacred Word. A triple sound: A. U. M. (AMEN is a derivation of AUM.) AUM and OM (a dual sound), sounded in different ways with intent, produce different effects. The sound of the AUM or OM sweeps energy into activity.

"He who lives under the sound of the AUM knows himself. He who lives sounding the OM knows his brother. He who knows the SOUND knows all." (*Esoteric Healing*, page 131)

This is a vast subject and makes a rewarding study.(See page 57 of the *Master Index of the Tibetan and Alice A. Bailey Books*)

AURA: The subtle bodies (etheric, astral and mental) vibrate at different rates or frequencies and all interpenetrate the physical body without displacing either it or each other. They extend beyond the physical: the etheric by about one quarter of an inch, the astral further, and the mental and causal further still. These extensions form what is known as the *aura*. The extent of the aura is dependent upon spiritual development. The higher the development the larger the aura.

AVATAR: (Sanskrit: from "ava", meaning down.) A freed soul, which means free from any attachment to the lower worlds, who incarnates (descends) in order to manifest on the physical plane some aspect of Divinity. An Avatar is a Being who is capable of reflecting some cosmic Principle or divine quality which will produce the desired effect upon humanity, evoking a reaction and producing a needed stimulation.Besides the Great Ones such as the Christ and the Buddha, there are many lesser, for instance, Leonardo da Vinci, Abraham Lincoln and Francis Bacon.

AWARENESS: A succession of expansions of consciousness, or the passing from one state of consciousness (or knowing) to another. It is the growth of that faculty of awareness which constitutes the predominant characteristic of the "Indwelling Thinker". It is the progress from the awareness, polarised in the personality, to that polarised in the Ego or soul; thence to a polarisation in the Monad, in Spirit, until ultimately the consciousness becomes Divine.(See UNDERSTANDING)

BHAGAVAD GITA: *The Bhagavad Gita*, one of India's most beautiful and popular spiritual poems, is an account of a dialogue, on the battlefield, between the great warrior Arjuna and the God Krishna, disguised as Arjuna's charioteer. Arjuna represents the personality, Krishna the soul, and the battlefield the astral plane of desire where humanity is struggling. At one point in the tale Arjuna is appalled to discover that the enemy against which he is preparing to fight, are all *members of his own family;* in other words, the negative aspects of his own character. These have to be transmuted and, as transmutation means the raising to a higher level, Krishna drives his chariot right between the two armies and advises, "Be one in self-harmony, in Yoga, and arise, great warrior, arise."

D.K. advises his pupils to study the writings of all the world religions, but states that only three are *needed:* the New Testament, the Bhagavad Gita, and the Yoga Sutras of Patanjali.

BODHISATTVA: Eastern name for the Christ. (See HIERARCHY)

BODIES (SUBTLE): Qualified energy fields of the mind and emotions. They are not bodies like the physical body but are reservoirs of particular types of force: collections of atoms vibrating at high speeds. Also known as "sheaths".(See Chapter 6, "The Subtle Bodies of Man, page 55)

BROTHERHOOD: A close unity – the Oneness of Life. The emerging world trend towards those things which will benefit all and not just a few. Brotherhood is a world-wide ideal. Love, understanding, co-operation, service, self-sacrifice, inclusiveness, freedom from doctrine and dogma, recognition of the divinity in all, are some of the characteristics of brotherhood. These things only come about when the individual strives not for personal gain, but works for the good of the whole.

BUDDHA: "The Enlightened" or "Light Bearer". Gautama Buddha, the Prince of Kapilavastu in Nepal, was the founder of Buddhism. The Lord Buddha taught that by the practice of detachment, dispassion and discrimination, man might learn the way of release from suffering. He formulated this understanding of the causes of world distress into Four Noble Truths:
1. That existence in the phenomenal universe is inseparable from suffering and sorrow;
2. That the cause of suffering is desire for existence in the world of phenomena;
3. That cessation of suffering is brought about by eradicating all desire for existence in this universe of phenomena;
4. That the way to cessation of suffering is by treading the Noble Eight-fold Path wherein are expressed: Right belief; Right intention; Right speech; Right action; Right living; Right endeavour; Right mindedness; Right concentration.

BUDDHIC PLANE: The Plane of Union or At-one-ment. The Christ world. Intuitional or Christ consciousness and group consciousness, are fully developed on this plane. (See Chart 2, page 30)

CAUSAL BODY or SOUL BODY: Throughout the long, long cycle of incarnations the soul remains on the third subplane of the mental plane, enveloped in a "bubble" of the matter of that subplane, like the yolk of an egg in its shell. This "bubble" is the causal body. This causal body is dissipated after the fourth initiation (the cross of renunciation), when the need for rebirth down into the lower planes no longer exists. The soul then rises to the Buddhic plane, the fifth Kingdom, the Kingdom of God.

CAUSE AND EFFECT, THE LAW OF: (Karma) The Law which governs "action and its coming into effect". In the mental, emotional and material worlds no good deed can escape its reward and no evil deed its fit penalty. "As a man soweth, so shall he reap." Perfect justice thus rules. By this Law, *our characters* are the consequence of our past evolution; therefore the future is *now* in our hands.(See Chapter 11, "Karma and Karmic Bonds", page 99)

CHAKRA or FORCE or ENERGY CENTRE: A junction on the surface of the etheric double where many strands of energy meet and pass each other, just like major railway junctions. They receive and transmit energy. They appear as dull, scarcely moving discs in the undeveloped man and as rapidly whirling suns in the developed man. They are duplicated in the astral and mental bodies.(See Chapter 5, "Evolutionary Sequence and the Chakras", page 43, and Chart 6, page 53)

CHANNEL: (See Concise Oxford Dictionary) "The course in which anything moves. Direction, line, medium, agency, (radio or television), band of frequencies sufficiently wide for transmission."The myriad strands of the etheric body are used in this manner i.e. as frequencies. In meditation we are trained to "act as channels" for the Christ Light: to receive it and to send it out via these fiery threads.

CHARACTER: The combination of all habits of thought and of feeling, representing the product of all past lives, thoughts, words, deeds and feelings. The channel through which the life forces naturally express themselves until the Higher Self assumes control of the personality.

CHELA: Eastern name for pupil or disciple of a spiritual teacher.

CHOHAN: (Tibetan) A Lord or Master. An Initiate who has taken more than five initiations.

CHRIST, THE: The Christ is the Light of the World, the Embodiment of Love and the Indicator of Divine Purpose. The Christ is the Way, the Truth and the Light.
There is the cosmic Christ, the planetary Christ of history, and the Christ in the human heart.
The Christ belongs to all humanity irrespective of nation, race, religion, social or cultural background. He is "the same great Identity" which those of different ideologies recognise under different names. He is The Messiah of Old Testament prophecy; the Son of God (manifested in the form of Jesus of Nazareth) of the New Testament; is known in the East as the Bodhisattva or Lord Maitreya; in the Middle East as the Imam Mahdi, and in India as Krishna.
The Christ is a Person, a Presence, a Principle. He brings together in one sweep of continuous energy flow, the cosmic fountainhead, the planetary manifestation and the human expression. He is power and livingness, love and wisdom, light and understanding. He ignites the spark of divinity within each human being.
He is the essence of divine truth and reality, the guarantor of ultimate spiritual achievement for "as He is so can we be in this world".

CHRIST CONSCIOUSNESS: Development of the Christ quality, which is love, in individual man, and in the human race as a whole. The conscious calling out of the Christ life in the human heart and our consequent integration into the Kingdom of God. "Christ in you, the hope of glory" (St. Paul). The attainment of Christ consciousness brings the complete subjugation of the lower to the higher, of the material to the Spiritual, of the personal to the Divine.

CHRIST, FOLLOWERS OF: Those who love their fellowmen irrespective of their creed, colour or race; whose love is of an inclusive kind, bringing international goodwill.

CLAIRAUDIENCE: The faculty (whether inborn or acquired by occult training) of hearing sound not possible of registration by the physical ear.

CLAIRVOYANCE: The faculty of the psychic power of extra vision, which sees that which exists in other than solid matter.

COMPASSION: Sympathy with, or understanding of, the suffering of others. Infinite Love, spiritual understanding and intelligence, or that subtle ability which recognises the meaning behind all events. The ability to empathise with others.

CONCENTRATION: One-pointed attention. To bring all thoughts to a common centre and thus intensify their action. Infinite patience to control and concentrate thought is essential in order to build a clear and powerful mental body able to contact the Higher Self and impress the wishes of the soul upon the waking consciousness.

CONCRETE MIND: The mind has two divisions, i.e. the abstract (higher mind) and the concrete (lower mind).The concrete mind is the critical, analytical, reasoning faculty functioning through the personality. It is the form-building faculty, the activity of the mental body, and the highest aspect of the lower personal self. It is materialistic and concerns the form side of things of the present moment. Matter of this lower mental plane is very active, impressionable, limiting and easily affected by vibrations of the emotional plane.
(See also ABSTRACT MIND)

CONSCIOUSNESS: Awareness of one's thoughts, emotions and actions – that faculty which enables man to be vigilant, observant, or to know. Consciousness is not only the sense of identity or self-awareness, but concerns also the sense of relationship of the "I" to all other selves.

CONSCIOUSNESS, EXPANSIONS OF: All-inclusive awareness which results in an increase of knowledge, wisdom and understanding. This is possible for all humanity through
1. discipline of life, reincarnation, the medium of the five senses, and the driving force of evolution;
2. specialised esoteric training, leading to a graded series of voluntary tests and initiations.
(See INITIATION)

CONSCIOUSNESS, GROUP: See GROUP CONSCIOUSNESS

CONSCIOUSNESS IN THE KINGDOMS OF NATURE: The growth of consciousness in man is expressed in the process of evolution. In the mineral, vegetable and animal kingdoms, consciousness is seen as attraction and repulsion.

The mineral kingdom: Evolves into vegetable consciousness – activity plus sensitivity (embryonic emotion or feeling);

The vegetable kingdom: Has the rudiments of a nervous system. This consciousness evolves into animal consciousness – activity plus sensitivity plus instinct (embryonic mind);

The animal kingdom: Develops a highly organised nervous system; astral matter becomes organised and feelings and emotions exhibit themselves. Instinctual consciousness, latent mind and the ability to use the senses. The animal kingdom evolves into that of man, who is the macrocosm for the three lower kingdoms; "A dog *knows* but doesn't *know* that he knows." (Teilhard de Chardin)

The human kingdom: Man demonstrates intelligent activity, can reason, is capable of emotion or love, and has added intelligent will. He is not only conscious but is *self*-conscious.

The highest points of evolution in the four kingdoms are:

The mineral kingdom: the brilliance of crystals and gemstones;

The vegetable kingdom: the perfume of the flowers;

The animal kingdom: the affection of a domesticated animal for its owner;

The human kingdom: Radiation.

CONSECRATE: The complete surrender of the whole personality to control by the soul. Sacrifice of the human personality will – man's own selfishness – to some special service. To devote one's life to some cause or ideal, great teacher, or service to humanity.

CONSTITUTION OF MAN: Comprises:

1. The personality : lower self
2. The soul or Ego : Higher Self
3. The Spirit or Monad : Divine Self

1. The personality consists of:

(a) A physical body which comprises two parts: the dense physical (solid, liquid and gaseous) and the etheric physical (four ethers). (See Chart 1, page 25)

(b) The astral or emotional body. This body reacts to forces and energies of feeling and desire which should be consciously controlled if growth in self-consciousness is to be attained.

(c) The mental body, which is made up of the substance of the lower mental plane. This body is not yet well organised in the majority of humanity. (See CONCRETE MIND and PERSONALITY).

2. The soul or Ego is the higher self in the causal body on the upper mental plane. Its quality is Love. It is the middle principle which links the personality and the Spirit or Monad.

3. The Spirit or Monad is the immortal part of each human being. Its energy is Pure Spirit and its quality is Divine Will. (See Chart 5, page 42, Chart 8 page

73, and Chapter 6, "The Subtle Bodies of Man", page 55
See also *Initiation, Human and Solar*, page xv)

CONTEMPLATION: (In meditation) To reach into the consciousness of the soul. *It is the soul which contemplates*. The mind becomes absorbed in that which is Reality and is unaware of separateness. In contemplation, the human consciousness ceases its activity and man becomes conscious of his essential oneness with Deity.(See Chapter 21, "The Science of Meditation, page 140)

COOPERATION: The act of working together with others in order to reach the same objective. A disciple is a "willing cooperator" for the good of the whole.

CORRESPONDENCES, LAW OF: See ANALOGY.

COSMOS: The system of things as ordered in the universe. Cosmology is the study of their origin relating to structure, motion and the essential parts of the system. Cosmic and Spiritual laws show everything to be a likeness to something larger, with only slight or minor differences. Repetition exists throughout the Cosmos and links the whole pattern of life. This is the secret of the unity of all life.
(See ANALOGY)

CREATION: An orderly act or process whereby things come into existence. It is by Divine Power (1st Ray), Divine Love (2nd Ray), and Divine Intelligence (3rd Ray), which existed prior to the creative act, that the qualities inherent in chaos were separated from one another, and forms originated.

CREATIVE IMAGINATION: The picture-making faculty or power to form an image or mental picture. First comes the thoughtform, then the desire to realise that which is imaged. By acting "as if", man deliberately invokes the creative imagination.

CRUCIFIXION: Loss of everything in Life which is of value to the *personality;* sacrifice even unto suffering and death as evidenced by the Lord Jesus who was fastened to the cross. By the time that this test is reached, the soul of the Initiate has become so strong and his character so expanded, his inner knowledge so great, his sense of values so changed, that he is quite willing to pay this price. (See INITIATION – the Fourth Initiation)

DANCE OF SHIVA: Shiva is the Eastern name for the Father of the Divine Trinity - the Creator – and the act of creation is known as the "Dance of Shiva". The oscillating circuit – Spirit and substance – is the cosmic dance in ordered pattern, the Dance of Shiva.

DECANATE: One of the three stages into which each astrological sign is divided.

DEDICATION: To give oneself as a soul and as a personality to the service of humanity, realising that each is but a part of the whole.

DETACHMENT: A state of impersonal observation. Through detachment one learns to withdraw one's interest and consciousness from the things of the senses and the calls of the lower nature. More and more one assumes the consciousness of the soul.

DEVA: Eastern word for angel. The devic or angelic evolution runs parallel with that of the human. Devas, or angels, exist in serried ranks from the Great Devic Lords (Archangels), down to the tiny nature spirits known to us through fairy stories and folklore (i.e. fairies, gnomes, elves, etc.). They are essentially motion, embody energy and build with energy – on all levels – all that is manifested. They are known as the greater and lesser builders. (Refer: *A Treatise on Cosmic Fire*, which is recognised as containing the most comprehensive study on devas available today.)

DHARMA: The working out of our karmic obligations in the place and circumstances where fate has placed us.

DISCIPLE: One who has attained a definite level of consciousness, whose main objective is to live and function as a soul, and to serve the Plan.
(See PATH, STAGES OF)

DISCIPLE, WORK OF: Through incarnations and during the course of evolution each aspirant encounters helpers, teachers and gurus. But when he reaches the stage of discipleship, two things happen. Firstly, he recognises that his own soul is his first master, and secondly, one of the teachers on the inner plane, seeing by the Light in him that he has reached the stage of discipleship, elects to take the aspirant into training. This teacher he recognises as his second master. The second master could be any more advanced disciple or initiate. A Master of the Wisdom takes only very advanced disciples as pupils.
(See PATH OF DISCIPLESHIP)

DISCIPLESHIP: The life of service under soul guidance and of conscious participation in the Work of God.

DISCRIMINATION: (In Sanskrit "viveka") The very first step on the path of occultism. To discern is to note differences – to discriminate is to *choose* between these differences: between the real and the unreal, between the Self and the not-self, between Spirit and matter, and to make the right choice of action.

DISPASSION: An attitude which imparts complete control of reactions to life, events and circumstances. Dispassion is acceptance of God's Will, and the ability to accept, *with understanding*, the circumstances of life.

DIVINE INDIFFERENCE: Non-attachment to form or the not-self. An impartial reaction is one of the quickest ways of releasing the Self from the personality. Divine indifference is based on a deep-seated *belief in the persistence of the immortal Being* within the form, so that personality problems and failings die from lack of attention.

DIVINE TRINITY: God the Father, God the Son and God the Holy Spirit. The Father, Mother, Son Trinity of all religions. The first, second and third Ray. (See Chapter 1, "The Seven Rays and the Solar System")

DOCTRINE: That which is taught. Religious instruction. Belief or tenets taught.

DOGMA: Tenet, doctrinal system as laid down by church authorities.

DWELLER ON THE THRESHOLD: Can be defined as the sum total of the forces of the lower nature, as expressed in the personality at any given time on the path of evolution. (See Chapter 4, "Incarnation", page 40)

EGO: In esoteric terminology, Ego (spelt with a capital "E") is another name for the soul. In the terminology of modern psychology, ego has different meanings, such as personality pride (e.g. ego trip).

EGOICALLY CENTRED: Working with the consciousness at Egoic (soul) level. Most of humanity is working with consciousness at the emotional level. (See Chart 4, page 35. See also "The Causal Body", page 70, in Chapter 6, "The Subtle Bodies of Man")

EMOTIONAL BODY: See ASTRAL BODY

ENDURANCE: The ability to "keep on keeping on" despite all circumstances or obstacles. Endurance (sustained perseverance and courage) is one of the characteristics of the soul. An essential quality in a disciple.

ENERGIES, MASTERY OF: Concerns the use and control of the centres of energy, the reaction of man to planetary forces: both his own and those from elsewhere in the solar system.

ENERGY: All is energy, vibrating at different rates on different planes or levels of consciousness.

ENERGY CENTRE (or FORCE CENTRE): See CHAKRA.

ENTITY: In the cosmic or esoteric sense, a synthesising, animating and intelligent Life. A Divine Livingness. Of the Spirit. In everyday language: a presence, an existence, or a creature. Sometimes used to describe those beings from the lower astral levels which possess human beings who have made themselves vulnerable to possession.

ENVIRONMENT: The place in which we are. The contacts which we make in our business life, home life and surroundings, in our social life, religious life and all other circumstances which condition our existence. Also our mental environment in which, by the power of thought, the mind can affect everything it reaches.

EQUIPMENT: This equipment (we are here referring to the energy field of a human being) is a series of subtle bodies which interpenetrate and surround the physical body. These subtle bodies are qualified energy fields of the mind (mental body), emotions (astral body) and etheric substance (etheric body). (The function of the etheric body is to vitalise the physical body.) These bodies are in reality electrical frequencies and we should train ourselves to think of them as such. In other words we are, each of us, equipped as is a highly sophisticated radio station: potentially capable of receiving and transmitting a vast range of energies on the different planes, from the highest on the spiritual planes to the lowest on the astral plane. We are "tuned in" according to the frequencies inherent within ourselves and contact is made at any given time according to the quality of the frequencies received and transmitted in the form of our thoughts and feelings.

ESOTERIC: The hidden inner spiritual meaning which lies behind all forms and all events, the understanding of which carries life and salvation to both the individual and to humanity. Occult or Wisdom Teaching; divine knowledge.

ESOTERIC SCHOOL: A training group or school where one is taught to work as a conscious soul in control of an active and intelligent personality.(See Chapter 22, "Esoteric or Mystery Schools", page 148)

ETHER: A kind of indivisible light substance which fills all space and acts as a transmitter of light, sound and electrical waves. Sound uses the third subdivision of the etheric plane for transmission. It is capable of being moulded by attractive force into forms and patterns. (See Chart 1, page 25, and Chapter 6, "The Subtle Bodies of Man", page 55)

ETHERIC BODY/ETHERIC DOUBLE: The vehicle of life force which substands, energises and vivifies the dense physical body, giving it warmth, motion and sensitivity. Every form has its etheric counterpart. Because the etheric is the finer substance of the physical plane, it is sometimes referred to as the physical-etheric. (See Chapter 6, "The Subtle Bodies of Man, page 57)

ETHERIC WEB: This fine network of fiery threads spreads itself over the energy centres or chakras, separating the two bodies, astral and physical, permitting the free flow of energies only through the two top subplanes, and acting as a barrier to the lower astral forces.(See LIFE WEB)

EVIL: Evil is the absence of good, just as darkness is the absence of light. It is that which separates us from God, that which opposes the evolution of consciousness.

EVOCATION: See INVOCATION.

EVOLUTION: The process which unfolds life and consciousness within all forms. A continual and increasing power to respond to something higher.(See Chart 4, page 35)

EXOTERIC: Outward, public. The opposite of esoteric or hidden. That which is taught openly.

FIRE: Fire is the most perfect reflection, in Heaven and on Earth, of the Divine Energy.
Electric Fire: 1st Ray. The Fire of Spirit. There is one Flame and countless undetached sparks shining in it.
Solar Fire: 2nd Ray. Fire of the mind: the fire of knowledge on the mental plane.

Fire by Friction: 3rd Ray. Fire of matter: the breath, or heat, of the Mother Aspect.

FIRE, PRANIC: That which is emanated via the etheric body. It corresponds in man to solar prana and to planetary prana.

FORCE: Any cause or active power which produces motion or a change of motion in a body. Specific energy as it expresses itself through a particular form i.e. as outgoing energy.

FORCE CENTRE: See CHAKRA.

FORM/FORMLESS: (referring to the mental plane) The *four lower* subplanes of mental matter are called the form subplanes, because the thoughtforms created here have definite shapes. The *three higher* subplanes are called "formless", since thought there does not precipitate into definite shapes but expresses itself as a complex radiating vibration. (See Chapter 6, "The Subtle Bodies of Man", page 70)

FREEWILL: The power of voluntarily directing one's own actions. It is not merely a choice between two courses of action.

GLAMOUR: An emotional, or astral, disturbance preventing or distorting the perception of truth. It refers to the world of emotional being and desire. (See also MAYA and ILLUSION). Maya, glamour and illusion are the misconceptions existing on all levels of personality life – maya on the etheric level, glamour on the emotional plane, and illusion on the mental plane, climaxing in the sum total of all three combined in the personality. The correct methods of working to dissipate world glamour and dispel world illusion, conform to modern psychological techniques accepted and practiced for individual benefit. *A higher form of energy must be brought to bear on the blocked condition.* This means in practical terms, maya must be subjected to the inspiration and idealism of the emotional plane; glamour to the illumination of the mental plane; illusion to the light of the intuition, a buddhic energy.

GOD IMMANENT: The concept of God as being within all forms, expressing divinity from within in all kingdoms in nature, including the human kingdom. (See Chapter 21, "The Science of Meditation", page 140)

GOD TRANSCENDENT: The concept of God as being above, outside of, or external to, His created world. (See Chapter 21, "The Science of Meditation", page 140)

GROUP CONSCIOUSNESS: (In spiritual work) Identification of the part with the whole; inclusive awareness of the group function; sense of responsibility towards assisting soul expression in others.

GROUP INTEGRITY: The consecration and united purpose of the group members enables them to put group work first, so that a common vision unites them all. By keeping personality affairs, criticism, private concerns and troubles out of group life, the group mind is steadied, cleared, and freed, thus permitting the work of the group to be uninterrupted.

GUARDIAN ANGEL: A White angel (angels are of different colours) who watches over each person, throughout each incarnation, from birth to "death". This angel can be termed a "reflection" of the soul, because it embodies as much Light as the person – at any given moment upon the path of evolution – can express.
(See Chapter 4, "Incarnation", page 40, and Chart 5, page 42)

GURU: A teacher of esoteric or spiritual knowledge.

HARMLESSNESS: An active, positive, dynamic quality: the will-to-bring-good-to- others. Harmlessness is achieved by watching every word, thought and deed, so that there is no possibility of injuring others. To be harmless is to have understanding and purity of motive. It makes for perfect relationships with others and is a quality of the Spiritual will.

HERMAPHRODITE: From the Greek Hermaphroditos who became one with the nymph Salmacis. A human being having normally both male and female organs. The *crowned* hermaphrodite is the true androgynous perfected person. This has no relation to what is known today as homosexuality. (See Chapter 5, "Evolutionary Sequence and the Chakras", page 49; *Esoteric Psychology Vol I*, page 278; *The Rays and the Initiations*, page 106).

HIERARCHY, THE: The Group of Masters who have achieved relative perfection and who constitute the invisible spiritual government of the Planet Earth. The Christ is the head of this Hierarchy and His work is carried out with Their assistance. The Masters of the Hierarchy are referred to in the Bible as "Perfected Men". They encourage and direct the evolutionary process: the furthering of God's Plan for Planet Earth. The Hierarchy is divided into three departments presided over by the three Great Lords:

		The present holders of these offices
1st Ray of Will	The Manu	The Vaivasvata Manu.
2nd Ray of Love-Wisdom	The Christ – the Bodhisattva (Head of the Hierarchy)	The Lord Maitreya.
3rd Ray of Active Intelligence	The Mahachohan	The Master Rakoczi.

(See PLAN, INITIATION).

HIERARCHY, THE WORK OF: This work can be studied from the angle of its relation to the four kingdoms (mineral, vegetable, animal and human) and the stimulation of inner qualities and their unfolding power, in each kingdom.

HIGHER AND LOWER SELF: There are two selves in man. The Higher Self, the Spirit, is immortal, imperishable. The lower, mortal, perishable self (the personality), is composed of the mental, astral, and physical and etheric bodies. (See Chapter 6, "The Subtle Bodies of Man", page 55). Contact with the higher Self is obtained through the technique of regular meditation.

HUMAN ENERGY FIELD: See EQUIPMENT.

ILLUMINATION: When the Light of the soul pours forth, man (on the physical plane) perceives in his brain consciousness that which was previously hidden from him. The illumined mind transmits soul knowledge.

ILLUSION: Is primarily of a mental quality and characteristic of intellectual types who have outgrown glamour as usually understood. Theirs is then the misunderstanding and wrong interpretation of thoughtforms and ideas. (See MAYA and GLAMOUR)

IMMORTAL: Eternal, everlasting; not subject to death. To continue existence after physical death or after the cessation of mortal form.

IMPERSONALITY: The ability to rise above the limitations of the personal self in both attitude and action.

IMPERSONALITY, GROUP: Serving from the soul and not from personality levels. Non-interference, non-criticism and the ability to mind one's own business whilst still maintaining service to others, or in constructive group relations. Impersonality is the normal attitude of the soul.

INCARNATION: An existence during which one is clothed with, or embodied in, flesh. Spirit incarnates only to gain experience in the three worlds (physical, astral and mental), in order to conquer and overcome the lower personal self and thereby attain self mastery. When all lessons have been learned and the experienced soul gains control in the three worlds, there will be no need for further incarnation. (See THREE WORLDS, Chapter 4, "Incarnation", page 36, and Chart 5, page 42)

INDIVIDUALITY: Existence as a single entity; that which is characteristic of a single person or thing; that which makes us distinct and separate from others in time and space. The distinction being that whereas the immortal and divine "individuality" prevails forever, the mortal human "personality" perishes.

INITIATE: The word is used loosely to mean anyone who is undergoing a transmutation of consciousness, which is an initiation. However, the occult Hierarchy of the planet consider the third initiation (the transfiguration) as the first true major initiation, and only after a person has taken this do they refer to him as "an Initiate". An Initiate has passed round and round the signs of the Zodiac, learned the lessons of these signs, climbed the mountain, been transfigured, and is now free to work universally for the Plan, as a superhuman being in a human body. (See INITIATION).

INITIATION: A fresh stage in the spiritual life. Part of the normal process of evolutionary development or progressive expansions of consciousness. Five of the Initiations relate to the five major episodes in the life of the Lord Jesus.

1. The Birth at Bethlehem	– The birth of the Christ child in the cave of the human heart;
2. The Baptism in the River Jordan	– The control of the astral body;
3. The Transfiguration on	–The soul shining through the medium

Mount Carmel	of a purified and developed personality: (an Initiate).
4. The Crucifixion on Mount Golgotha	– The Renunciation; the glory of the renunciation of all personality desire and the dedication to living service: (an Arhat).
5. The Resurrection and Ascension	– The consciousness transferred to the Fifth Kingdom (the Kingdom of God). The plane from which the Masters work: (a Master).

In order to achieve the Sixth Initiation, an Adept or Master has to undertake a very intensive course in planetary occultism.

6. A CHOHAN of the Sixth Initiation – a Lord
7. A CHOHAN of the Seventh Initiation – a Buddha
(Refer: *From Bethlehem to Calvary* and *Initiation, Human and Solar*)

INNER RULER: The Higher Self, the immortal Ruler who thinks, knows and feels through the threefold lower self, but is also capable of thinking in terms of the Divine.

INTEGRATION: The quieting of the lower bodies (mental, emotional and physical-etheric). To make these three parts one complete whole with the soul, in order that the soul may be in control of the personality.

INTERDEPENDENT TEACHINGS: Mutually connected with, or relying for support on, one another. The Lord Buddha of the East and the Christ of the West, gave the revelation of Divinity to their particular civilisations, and both worked for the eventual benefit of mankind. Their teachings are interdependent. Both embodied certain Cosmic Principles, and by their work and sacrifice, divine powers influenced mankind. The Buddha embodied Wisdom; the Christ taught "God is love".

INTUITION: Direct spiritual cognition. A form of knowledge arrived at apart from the reasoning mind – by the use of the higher or abstract Mind. Intuition is apart from, and beyond, the reasoning mind.

INVOCATION/EVOCATION: Asking and receiving, by use of the spiritual will. A form of spiritual, dynamic meditation. Invocation means "calling down" or "calling into" and is an inner action which includes and combines all the use of all our inner functions. It is simultaneously of the mind, of feeling, of the imagination and of the will.
(See Chapter 21, "The Science of Meditation")

INVOCATION, THE GREAT: A prayer which belongs not to any person or group, but to all humanity, and which is expressed in general terms, understandable by all.(See Chapter 20, "The Triangles Network")

INVOLUTION: The life wave of divine "Sparks" leaves "The Father's House" (the divine plane) to remain, known to us as monads, on the monadic plane, for the whole length of the involutionary and evolutionary period. The *in*volutionary arc is the term applied to the first part of this process. Each monad sends a thread of energy down into ever denser matter until the lowest point of concretion is reached. The second half of the process is the *e*volutionary arc. A well known expression of the entire process is the parable of the prodigal son. (See Chapter 3, "The Evolution of Humanity", page 32, Chart 4, page 35, and EVOLUTION)

JOY: A quality of the soul, originating in the soul, and finally realised in the triple personality. Real joy comes with the complete control of the personality by the soul. It is a soul essence which cannot be cultivated, but which emerges when the personality is in a condition through which joy can radiate.

KAMA-MANAS: From *kama*, desire, and *manas*, mind. During earth life, desire and the lower mind are so closely interwoven that they rarely act separately, and so are spoken of as kama-manas.

KARMA: See CAUSE AND EFFECT, THE LAW OF

KINGDOMS IN NATURE:
1. The mineral kingdom.
2. The vegetable kingdom.
3. The animal kingdom.
4. The human kingdom.
5. The kingdom of God; kingdom of souls.
6. & 7. "To these kingdoms no names have as yet been given because the possibility of their existence is only now just beginning faintly to penetrate into the consciousness of the disciple and the Initiate."
(See CONSCIOUSNESS IN THE KINGDOMS OF NATURE)

KNOWER: The soul. The one who understands or recognises with certainty. Meditation, plus organised discipline, facilitates union with the soul.

KNOWLEDGE: The sum total of human discovery and experience; that which can be recognised by the five senses. Knowledge deals with the building and developing of the form side, the material side of evolution (solar, planetary) in the three worlds of human evolution, and in the bodies of men. The result of the work of the senses, which, when interpreted by the mind, brings knowledge. Knowledge is the science of matter. Wisdom is the science of Spirit.

KUNDALINI: (Because of the interest now being shown in kundalini and the many invitations in current magazines to work with this tremendous force, and the general ignorance about the dangers involved, this entry is much longer than is usual in a glossary.)
Kundalini, in connection with the human form, is the force latent in matter itself. It is the integral life of each atom. In the human being this force lies quiescent, latent and potential in the lowest centre which is at the base of the spine. It is known as the "sleeping serpent".

This fire of matter first blends with the pranic fire (which is fed through the etheric spleen centre) and later with the fire of the mind. Its natural progress is to move slowly, at a uniform vibration, up the force centres or chakras in the etheric spine (NOT the bony physical spine), and geometrically, according to the ray type and development of the person.

The purpose of the ascending kundalini force, once it has been awakened and raised, is to destroy the enfolding, protective etheric webs which lie between the force centres or chakras along the etheric spine, thus allowing the freer flow of energies between the chakras.

"Should a man, by the power of will or through an over-development of the mental side of his character, acquire the power to blend these fires of matter and to drive them forward, he stands in danger of obsession, insanity, physical death, or of dire disease in some part of his body, and he also runs the risk of an over-development of the sex impulse through the driving of the force in an uneven manner upwards, or in forcing its radiation to undesirable centres. The reason for this is that the matter of his body is not pure enough to stand the uniting of the flames, that the channel up the spine is still clogged and blocked, and therefore acts as a barrier, turning the flame backwards and downwards, and that the flame (*being united by the power of mind and not being accompanied by a simultaneous downflow from the plane of spirit*), permits the entrance, through the burning etheric, of undesirable and extraneous forces, currents, and even entities. These wreck and tear and ruin what is left of the etheric vehicle, of the brain tissue and even of the dense physical body itself." (*Italics by author*) (*A Treatise on Cosmic Fire*, page 126)

The subject of "Kundalini", so fraught with potential danger, is treated very fully in *A Treatise on Cosmic Fire*. In addition, D.K. adds the following in *Esoteric Healing*, page 212:

"Another school of thought, branding themselves untruthfully as occultists, are equally in error. They work, or rather profess to work, with the centres, only fortunately for them nature protects them often from themselves. They endeavour consciously to vitalise the centres, to burn away the protective web, and *to raise the fires of matter before the fire of spirit has combined with the fire of the soul. They then fall victims to premature stimulation of the fires of substance before the balancing of the forces can take place*. Disease, insanities, and many neurotic conditions, plus serious pathological conditions, then occur. Some of the glands become overactive; others are overlooked, and the entire glandular system and the dependent nervous system are in a state of complete imbalance" (Author's italics).

LAW OF ATTRACTION: See Chapter 17, "The Law of Attraction", page 122

LEMURIA: A continent which preceded Atlantis and which is said to have been situated in the Pacific Ocean between the USA and Australia. It was the home of the third root race. Life on the evolutionary arc commenced in Lemurian times. (See Chart 4, page 35)

LIFE WEB: The life web (or etheric web or etheric body) is really a network of fine channels which are the component parts of one interlacing, incredibly fine, incredibly beautiful cord. This life web is composed of the intricate weaving of this vitalised cord. It is the body of vitality which underlies every form and links every part of that form with every other part. In the human being the web of life underlies the nervous system. This fine network of fiery threads spreads itself over the energy centres or chakras, separating the two bodies, astral and physical, permitting the free flow of energies only through the two top subplanes, and acting as a barrier to the lower astral forces.
(See ETHERIC BODY)

LOGOI: Plural of LOGOS.

LOGOS: See Chapter 1, "The Seven Rays and the Solar System", page 20, and Chapter 2, "The Seven Rays and Our Planet Earth", page 26 Planetary Logos – God of a planet. Solar Logos – God of a solar system.

LORDS OF THE RAYS: See SEVEN PLANETARY LOGOI.

LOTUS: The lotus is often regarded as a symbol of spiritual development. The roots grow in mud (physical man), the stem pushes up through the water (emotional nature) and the flower opens in sunlight (the mind). The three rows of petals in the flower itself also symbolise the threefold man enfolding the Divine Self – the jewel at the heart, or centre, of the lotus.

LOVE: The greatest creative, attractive force in the Universe. Love is magnetic, unifying; it creates understanding and is radiant. Love cannot be limited to one person as it flows constantly from, to, and through, everything. Christ revealed a "God of Love". Love introduces a new sense of brotherhood and unity. The fire of Love burns away all separatism.

LOVE OF GOD: The keynote of Christ – God is Love – proves Love to be the motivating power in the Universe. God, the spiritual and living Father, revealed Himself in His Son as love in Person, so that all men could grasp the great idea of LOVE.

LOVE-WISDOM: The quality of the second Ray. The second aspect of God. The Wisdom or Love aspect drives man on to perfection through the realisation of his oneness with all that breathes, resulting in service, through Love in activity.

LOWER MIND: See CONCRETE MIND.

LOWER SELF, NATURE OF: The threefold lower self is composed of a physical-etheric body, an astral or emotional body and a mental body.
See CONSTITUTION OF MAN.

MACROCOSM: The sum total in which we "live and move and have our being". The great universe, or God (the solar Logos) manifesting through His body, the solar system.

MAGIC, WHITE: A spiritual transformation effected by the soul-infused personality motivated by the will-to-good (first Ray), implemented by love-wisdom (second Ray), and activated with intelligent understanding (third Ray).

MAGICIAN, WHITE: One who uses energies for good. (One who uses the energies for selfish or evil purposes is a black magician.)

MAHACHOHAN: The Head of the third great department, or Activity Aspect, of the Hierarchy. He is the Lord of Civilisation and is an embodiment on the planet Earth of the Intelligence aspect of Deity (third Ray). (See HIERARCHY)

MAN (MANKIND): Man is an animal plus a living God. In man, highest Spirit and lowest matter are joined by intelligence – the principle of mind. He dwells on the physical, emotional, mental, intuitional and spiritual planes.

MANTRAMS: Verses from the Vedas (Hindu Scriptures). Mantrams are collections of words, phrases or sounds based on the Sacred Word, which by virtue of their rhythmic effects, achieve results that would not be possible without them.

MANU: The name of the great Being who is the chief, or ruler, of the human race. "Manu" – from the root "man" – to think. The Manu embodies the First, or Will, aspect of Divinity (first Ray). The Head of the First department of the Hierarchy. (See HIERARCHY)

MASTER: An initiate of the Fifth Degree. An adept, such as

The Master DK:	The Master Djwahl Khul, an adept on the second ray of Love-Wisdom.
The Master KH:	The Master Koot Hoomi, an adept on the 2nd Ray of Love-Wisdom.
The Master R:	The Master Rakoczi, an adept on the 7th Ray of Organisation and Ceremonial Order; also known as the Comte de St Germain, and, earlier, as Roger Bacon and Francis Bacon.
The Master M:	The Master Morya, an adept on the 1st Ray of Will.
The Master H:	The Master Hilarion, an adept on the 5th Ray of Concrete Knowledge.

(See *Initiation, Human and Solar*, pages 54 to 59, and "The Rays", page 23, in Chapter 1)

MATTER: Matter is energy. Matter and Spirit are one. Spirit is matter at its finest or highest level; matter is Spirit at its densest level. All life is formed on a system of delicately graded states of matter, of finer and finer atoms. There are seven states of matter: solid, liquid, gaseous, and four ethers. (See Chart 1, page 25)

MAYA: Complete identification with the outer appearance. In other words, identifying ourselves with our bodies instead of realising that we are souls *using* these mental, astral and physical bodies. (See GLAMOUR)

MEDITATION: Concentrated spiritual aspiration through the focused and controlled mind. The steady daily attempt to get consciously in touch with the soul or higher self. By meditation, man becomes aware of inner or higher states of consciousness, enters into them and functions there. Meditation enables man to become in outer manifestation that which he is in inner reality: to identify himself with his inner aspect.
(See Chapter 21, "The Science of Meditation", page 140)

MEDITATION FORM OR OUTLINE: A formula for the generation, concentration and distribution of ENERGY.

MEDITATION, THE PROCESS: It is divided into five parts:
1. Concentration – holding the mind firmly and steadily on the object of attention without wavering or distraction; learning to *focus* the mind and so to use it.
2. Meditation – the prolonged focusing of the attention in any direction and the steady holding of the mind on any desired idea. To *control* and *direct* the mind.
3. Contemplation – an activity of the soul (detached from the mind, which is held in a state of quiet).
4. Illumination – the result of Concentration, Meditation and Contemplation; involves the carrying down into the brain consciousness of the knowledge achieved.
5. Inspiration – the result of illumination, as it demonstrates in the life of service.
These five stages lead to union with the soul and direct knowledge of Divinity.
(See Chapter 21, "The Science of Meditation", page 140)

MENTAL BODY: The subtle body which is made up of the substance of the four lower levels of the mental plane. It is not yet well organised in the majority of mankind. It gives a certain character to the personal self, indicating habits of thought and reactions to the circumstances of life.
(See Chapter 6, "The Subtle Bodies of Man", page 62, and Chart 5, page 42)

MERGE: To absorb, fuse or blend. To unite with others (which involves service). To be at-one as brothers, blending with the group of souls to which one is spiritually linked.

MICROCOSM: Man, as a reflection of the great sum total. (See MACROCOSM) The little universe – man manifesting through his bodies.

MIND: It has three functions:
1. to receive impressions from the outer world via the five senses;
2. to reason, to discern and to discriminate;
3. to respond to impressions emanating from the subjective or spiritual world. This aspect is the abstract or higher mind.
(See ABSTRACT MIND, also CONCRETE MIND)

MIND OF GOD: See UNIVERSAL MIND

MONAD: The One in each of us. The threefold Spirit on its own plane. (See CONSTITUTION OF MAN. See also Chart 5, page 42, and Chart 8, page 73)

MONISM: "God is One" and "All Gods are One", are utterances of truth, and all enlightened people are monists. One Life pervades all forms and all those forms are the expressions, in time and space, of the Central Universal Energy.

MYSTERIES: See the introductory chapter "What is the Ageless Wisdom"? page 11

MYSTIC: One who seeks union with God Transcendent through the heart approach, involving feeling, sensory perception and emotional ecstasy.

MYTH: Traditional story or legend embodying ancient beliefs.

NOON-DAY REMEMBERING: A spiritual exercise. A brief, dynamic refocusing of the personality towards the soul as it seeks to use soul energy and to live the life of the soul on the physical plane. Undertaken at noon each day. Recollecting that one is a Spirit-soul-body and not just a body.

NOT-SELF: The personality expression of the soul in the three worlds.

OCCULT: The forces of Being and those springs of conduct or action which lie hidden in the purpose of life, whether solar, planetary or human. These subjective incoming and outgoing energies are neutral. They are used for good by the white occultist in serving God. The black occultist uses them in serving his own selfish personal ends. Unfortunately some religious groups are promoting the idea that all occultism is black.
(See ESOTERIC; also Chapter 12, "The Occultist", page 107)

OCCULTISM: Practical mysticism. It adds the intelligent use of the mind to the heart approach.

OCCULT RETICENCE: (Silence.) The making of no claims with regard to oneself or one's work; a withdrawal of attention to inner group purpose and plan. Disciples are taught to make light of their personality standing, while exalting the nature of their Inner God – identical in all people – and to refrain from speech unless it serves group purpose by stimulating the highest aspects in *every* person. Occult reticence leads to detachment from the form nature, and to identification with the soul.

OM: The dual sound of the sacred word significant of the relationship of Spirit and soul. This makes a rewarding study. (See AUM, and *Master Index of the Tibetan and Alice A. Bailey Books*.

ONE LIFE, THE: The divine, transcendent Deity within which all manifested life "lives and moves and has its being". The One Energy from which all other energies spring.

PAIN: The result of dis-ease, or dis-harmony, in one or more of the bodies (physical, mental or emotional). Indicates a lack of, or failure to achieve, balance. Pain is the upward struggle through matter and the added resistance which matter sets up when life seeks freedom from form.

PATH, THE: The way of discipline and enlightenment which everyone eventually treads on their way back to God. Man himself becomes the Path. (See Chart 4, page 35)

PATH OF DISCIPLESHIP: The path of self-discipline to be followed in order to achieve union of the personality with the soul. The conscious following of the Christ. The Way of Service. As the Masters of the Wisdom and their Initiates are very knowledgeable occultists, they make no attempt to guide an aspirant until they see, by the growth of the Light in him, that he is ready to respond, and make use of, any guidance given. (See DISCIPLE)

PATH, STAGES OF: See: ASPIRANT, PROBATIONER, DISCIPLE, INITIATE, MASTER OR ADEPT.
(See also Chapter 18, page 128)
In *"A Treatise on White Magic"*, pp 396, 397, D.K., when addressing disciples, describes the early stages of this path in the following words:
"The outstanding characteristics of those personalities who are not as yet soul-centered or controlled, are dominance, ambition, pride and a lack of love to the whole, though they frequently possess love for those who are necessary to them or to their comfort.
"You have therefore in the sequential development of humanity the following stages:
1. That of the animal consciousness.
2. The emotionally polarised individual, selfish and governed by desire.
3. The two above stages, plus a growing intellectual grasp of environing conditions.
4. The stage of responsibility to family or friends.
5. The stage of ambition and of longing for influence and power in some field of human expression. This leads to fresh endeavor.
6. The coordinating of the personality equipment under the above stimulus.
7. The stage of influence, selfishly used and frequently destructive, because the higher issues are not registered as yet.
8. The stage of a steadily growing group awareness. This is viewed:
a. As a field of opportunity
b. As a sphere of service.
c. As a place wherein sacrifice for the good of all becomes gloriously possible.
"This latter stage puts a man upon the path of discipleship, which includes, needless to say, that of the earlier phase, probation or testing.
"The problem consists in ascertaining upon which step of the ladder and in which phase one finds oneself at any particular time. Behind each human being stretches a long series of lives and some are now headed towards the stage of dominant selfish personality expression and are making themselves individuals in full conscious awareness. This is, for them, as much a step forward as is discipleship for all of you."

PATH, UNIVERSALITY OF: Every religion in the world which emphasises the need for treading the Path, or Way, lays down the same rules, is divided into similar divisions and stages, and holds out the same goal – reunion with the Divine. All roads lead to the centre.

PERMANENT ATOMS: These are literally small force centres around which the various sheaths or bodies are built.They are appropriated points of atomic matter kept permanently by the Monad for the whole period of manifestation. All consciousness, all memory, all faculty, are stored up in these permanent atoms.The permanent atoms are strung like pearls on the sutratma or life thread and those of the personality or lower self are stored, wrapped in the cord, in the causal body, between incarnations.
(See Chart 5, page 42 and Chapter 4, "Incarnation", page 36)

PERSONALITY, THE: This is composed of four bodies: the mental, astral, physical-etheric, and dense physical. However, because the physical etheric and dense physical are melded so closely together they are often regarded as one and the personality as threefold, composed of mental, astral and physical.
(See Chart 1, page 25)

PHENOMENA: See REALM OF PHENOMENA.

PHYSICAL-ETHERIC BODY: The body composed of the matter of the four etheric sub-planes of the physical plane. The etheric body is a body of vitality underlying and energising the nervous system of the physical body. (Because the etheric is the finer substance of the physical plane, it is sometimes refered to as the physical-etheric.) (See Chapter 6, "The Subtle Bodies of Man", page 57, and Chart 1, page 25)

PINEAL GLAND: Is attached to the back of the third ventricle of the brain; is connected with the head centre (see Chart 6, page 53; it should not be confused with the third eye.)

PITUITARY GLAND: This gland has a close connection with emotional and mental qualities. It is associated with the ajna centre, an energy vortex in the etheric body. It is in fact two glands in one and is located in the head, lying at the base of the brain behind the root of the nose. This gland is able to stimulate the brain cells and has a direct, important bearing on the personality. (See Chart 6, page 53; it should not be confused with the third eye)

PLAN: God's vision, as far as it is given to us, for the future of our planet. All the secrets of evolving life are at present hidden in this Plan (or Will), and these will gradually unfold into the "cloud of knowable things" as humanity evolves.

PLANE: A state of progressive experience. A plane is a complete series, or world, of substance under one law. Our planet is divided into seven planes which are each divided into seven subplanes which interpenetrate:
1. Divine
2. Monadic
3. Spiritual
4. Intuitional
5. Mental

6. Astral or Emotional
7. Physical.
The physical plane includes solids, liquids, gases and four ethers, i.e. seven states of matter which go to make up the densest expression of life. (See Chart 1, page 25)

PRANA: That vital force inherent in matter itself. This type of energy comes from the physical sun and works actively upon the vital body of every form in the natural world including those of human beings. In the human form it is absorbed by the etheric body through the etheric spleen centre.(See FIRE, PRANIC).

PRANIC FIRE: See FIRE, PRANIC.

PRINCIPLE: An aspect of the Divine Plan – a facet of the Will of God; a fundamental truth. A principle governs the action of the soul on its own plane.

PROBATIONER: One who, by purification and training, prepares for discipleship. (See PATH, STAGES OF)

PROBATIONARY PATH: The Path of aspiration, of purification. This is followed by the Path of discipleship.

PURIFICATION: The act of cleansing, or making wholesome, the bodies (physical and etheric, emotional and mental) by obedience to the laws of self discipline and of the Spirit. The probationary Path is the Path of purification.

QUALITIES: These are the attributes or characteristics of the soul: love, compassion, joy, serenity, courage, steadfastness, perseverance, confidence, stability, etc; soul qualities radiate through the personality.

RADIATION: Viewed by the inner eye, humanity consists of units which radiate light of varying degrees of brightness. "Radiation is the outer effect produced by all forms in all kingdoms when their internal activity has reached such a state of vibratory activity that the confining walls of the form no longer form a prison, but permit of the escape of the subjective essence." (*A Treatise on Cosmic Fire* page 1060)The Yoga Sutras of Patanjali state that "By mastery of the binding life comes radiance."

RAJA YOGA: The Kingly science of the soul. Union with the soul through the right use of the mind. (See Chapter 15, "Yoga", page 113)

RAYS (SEVEN): A Ray is one of the seven streams of force from God. Each is the expression of a great cosmic Being. There are:
THREE RAYS OF ASPECT:
1. The Ray of Will or Power
2. The Ray of Love-Wisdom
3. The Ray of Activity or Adaptability.
FOUR RAYS OF ATTRIBUTE:
4. The Ray of Harmony, Beauty, Art or Unity
5. The Ray of Concrete Knowledge or Science

6. The Ray of Abstract Idealism or Devotion
7. The Ray of Ceremonial Magic or Law.

REALM OF PHENOMENA: The realm of effects, not causes.

REDEEMER: To redeem means to liberate; to liberate from bondage; to rescue; to restore. Christ, our Redeemer, showed humanity the way to enter God's kingdom by liberating the power of the indwelling Christ within the personality aspect of mankind.

REINCARNATION or REBIRTH: Repeated earth experiences through birth in a physical body. This planet is a school of experiences through which we journey at intervals to undergo further unfoldment of the divine powers latent within us.(See Chapter 9, "Reincarnation", page 92)

RENUNCIATION: To give up, sacrifice or repudiate. To look away from the things of the personality. To ask nothing for the separated self. (See INITIATION)

RESPONSE: To answer to, or react to, stimuli, whether material or spiritual. A process of development by which we become consciously in tune with the soul.

RESPONSIBILITY: Acceptance and discharge of duty; obligation and opportunity to serve. A sense of responsibility is characteristic of discipleship.

RESURRECTION: The triumphant survival of the Spirit at the death of the body. Christ's manifestation in a spiritual body after the crucifixion and burial.

REVELATION: To remove that which conceals or obscures and brings clearly into the light, facts and reality. Revelation is the term covering all mental penetration into the life of the Spirit.

RIGHT SPEECH: The spoken word produces results which need to be considered. Right words should be used to express right thought. Silence at the wrong time, gossip and criticism, are destructive.

ROOT RACE: One of the seven races of mankind which evolve upon a planet during the great cycle of planetary existence. This cycle is called a world period. There are seven sub-races in each root race:
The 1st root race evolved on the Imperishable Sacred Land;
the 2nd root race evolved on the Hyperborean Land;
the 3rd root race evolved on the Continent of Lemuria;
the 4th root race evolved on the Continent of Atlantis;
the 5th root race (Aryan Race) is presently evolving (in consciousness) all over the world.
The first two root races were on the *down*ward *in*volutionary arc and were mindless. It was only during the third root race on Lemuria that man developed a physical body and spark of mind, and started on the *up*ward *e*volutionary arc.
(See Chart 4, page 35 and Chapter 3, "The Evolution of Humanity", page 33)

The sixth and seventh root races are yet to come. We are told that the sixth root race will be at its height approximately one million years from now.(Refer: *The Secret Doctrine* by H.P. Blavatsky)

SALVATION: Preservation from Spiritual destruction.

SANAT KUMARA: Eastern terminology for the One Life. God. The Ancient of Days. The God of Love.

SEED THOUGHT: A symbol or form of words which the mind earnestly studies and reflects upon, and which holds or hides an idea or truth of profound spiritual significance. In meditation, development of the seed thought is attained by holding the mind steady in the light of the Soul.(See Chapter 21, "The Science of Meditation", page 140)

SELF: Each human being has a lower personality self and a higher Spiritual Self.

SELF-FORGETFULNESS: Selflessness. The transfer of attention from the body to the soul within that body. Detachment from the personality self. Selflessness (altruism) is the opposite quality to selfishness.

SELF-RECOLLECTEDNESS: Recollection of ourselves as a whole. Constant remembrance that we are the soul.

SENSITIVITY: Alertness to soul impression. Aliveness to the impact of new ideas and to intuitive response. The ability to be alive, alert, keen to recognise right human relationship; quick to respond to need. To be mentally, emotionally and physically attentive to life and to develop the power of observation on all three planes in the three worlds (physical-etheric, astral and mental) at the same time.
(See INTUITION)

SEPARATED SELF: The personality. The lower self separated from the Higher Self (Spirit), or lower self as distinct from the Higher or Spiritual Self.(See Chapter 18, "Inner Groups, the Separated Self, and the Path", page 127)

SERVICE: To give and not to count the cost; to work without thought of regard or result or acknowledgement. Service is the immediate response of the personality to soul contact; the outflow of a loving heart and an intelligent mind.

SERVICE IN THE NEW AGE: The motive for service must be towards the general and the universal; the response of the group in answer to human need. The qualities of discrimination, keen analysis of motive, and the understanding of the nature and methods of right service, are of supreme importance.

SERVICE, THE STAGES OF: The *body temple* is to be kept clean and healthy by rhythmic working of the atoms of which it is composed. The *emotional body* aids the physical body by keeping rhythmic and stable and serving the soul as a

channel of force, and not as a waster of energy. The *mental body* serves by building in knowledge, in preparation for receiving the wisdom of the soul. The personality serves the soul by self-discipline and sacrifice.
(See TRANSMUTATION and PERSONALITY)

SERVICE, STRENGTH IN: This comes from the realisation of group unity. The foundation of the strength to step forward on a chosen path is "profound conviction". Balance is found by preserving stillness within the turmoil of the body, sense and desires, and by the power of the Higher Self to rule and control the lower self. Spiritual humility is spiritual strength.

SEVEN KINGDOMS: See KINGDOMS IN NATURE.

SEVEN PLANETARY LOGOI: These are The Seven Lords of the Rays. Also known as: The Seven Archangels The Seven Heavenly Men The Seven Spirits before the Throne. (See *A Treatise on Cosmic Fire*, page 233)

SHAMBALLA: The Centre where the Lord of the World, the Ancient of Days, Sanat Kumara, has his headquarters. It is *not* in dense physical matter, but located in the higher etheric levels over the Gobi desert.

SHEATHS: The bodies of the personality, physical, etheric, emotional and mental, which are used and discarded in each incarnation, are sometimes referred to as the sheaths.

SHIVA: Eastern name for God, as God the Creator.

SOLAR LOGOS: The God of our solar system. (See LOGOS)

SOUL: The Christ within. The soul is the mediator or middle principle. It is neither spirit nor matter, but is the relation between them. The soul is *group conscious* and is one with all other souls. The soul overshadows the personality and connects with man by a thread of energy (the silver cord of the Bible; see SUTRATMA) during the entire span of earth life. The personality is its instrument of expression.

SOUL GUIDANCE: The key to the entire process of unfoldment is *soul* guidance, leading or directing the conduct of the personality. The heart and mind are blended and merged with the soul, so that eventually Christ Will (1st Ray), Christ Love-Wisdom (2nd Ray), and the activity of the Christ Mind (3rd Ray), are consciously expressed.
(See SPIRITUAL UNFOLDMENT)

SOUL, THE WORK OF: To gain and maintain control of the lower nature through conscious adjustment of the bodies, so that they are directly aligned with the soul (See ALIGNMENT). Only in this manner can the soul impress the physical brain of the personality.
(See Chapter 21, "The Science of Meditation", page 140)

SPIRIT: Not material. The spiritual part of man. The Real; the Eternal; the One Life; the Monad; Energy. Spirit is the Life Breath which is the cause of all manifestation. Spirit lies behind consciousness.

SPIRITUAL LIVING: Living as a soul and not as a personality; clear mental perception and loving understanding applied in practical daily life. Attained by shaping our ideas to a definite pattern, by following the meditation process so as to find the quality of the soul, and by applying this for the benefit of all.

SPIRITUAL OBEDIENCE: Submission to the guidance of the soul – the first Master. Obeying the voice of conscience.

SPIRITUAL UNFOLDMENT: Results from the right use of emotional and mental energies, which expand and develop the latent spiritual powers. To respond to the soul and to learn thereby to love and serve humanity.

STAR, FIVE-POINTED AND SIX-POINTED: These are of very ancient origin and signify many different things. In man, the five-pointed star flashes forth above the head of the initiate at the first initiations. The mystic longs to become the centre of a five-pointed star. Worship, the attitude of the mystic, must give place to the raising of the three lower energies (a triangle pointing upwards) and their evocative response to the three higher energies (a triangle pointing downwards), thus producing an eventual unity of the two interlaced triangles: the six-pointed star, best known to us as King Solomon's Seal.

SUB-HUMAN: All lives in all forms *below* the human kingdom.
(See KINGDOMS IN NATURE)

SUN, THE: The Sun, in its aspect of Light, is the symbol of the soul.
Esoterically, the Sun is regarded as triple:
1. The physical Sun: Body; Intelligent form.
2. The heart of the Sun: soul; Love.
3. The central spiritual Sun: Spirit; Life or Power.

SUPER-HUMAN: All lives above the human kingdom; therefore all lives in the Kingdom of God, and all grades of being above the human.
(See KINGDOMS IN NATURE)

SUSHUMNA: The subjective channel in the spine.

SUTRAS: Set of maxims in Sanskrit literature (rules of conduct).

SUTRATMA: Also known as the life thread or the silver thread; it is a dual stream of energy, of life and consciousness, linking the personality with the Higher Self. It passes from the monad down through the soul body to the personality: mental, astral and physical. On it are strung the permanent atoms. (See SOUL)

SYMBOL: The expression of an idea, or a thought, by means of an image or picture in the mind. A symbol always embodies an idea having a meaning or value. Lama Anagarika Govinda describes the symbol as a bridge between the literal world and the direct experience of God.

SYMBOL, INTERPRETATION OF: The spiritual ability to recognise the meaning of that which lies behind the form. (See Chapter 16, "Dreams")

SYNTHESIS: To be unified and brought into harmonious relation, as when the separate aspects of the human being blend with each other and with the soul, their Creator, their source of energy and their active power. The work of the Hierarchy is directed towards synthesis and understanding.

TECHNIQUES, IN PREPARATION FOR SERVICE:
1. TECHNIQUE OF THE PRESENCE OF GOD – concerns the *soul*. It is the *Way of Contemplation*. It is reached by way of identification with the soul because it is the soul that contemplates.
2. TECHNIQUE OF LIGHT – concerns the *mind*. Knowledge, when acquired, is offered for use *by* the soul via the process of "holding the mind steady in the light". It is the *Way of Meditation* whereby one becomes a "light bearer" and reflects light.
3. TECHNIQUE OF INDIFFERENCE – concerns the astral plane. The control of the emotional nature by the practice of divine indifference - complete impersonality; the *method of harmlessness* – when, behind all thoughts and actions, there is freedom from emotion through guidance from the soul.
4. TECHNIQUE OF SERVICE – is related to the *physical plane*. It is the *Way of Spiritual Outgoing*.

THIRD EYE: A special inner organ which develops gradually with the expanding consciousness, and which registers the finer vibrations of the superphysical world. Sometimes called "The eye of the soul". It exists in etheric matter in the centre of the forehead in the form of an eye looking out between the two physical eyes. It is an energy centre manifested as the result of the vibratory interaction of a triangle of force:
(a) the pituitary body
(b) the pineal gland
(c) the alta major centre.

THOUGHTFORM: A mental formation visualised and externalised on the mental or kama-manasic plane. When a man thinks, a vibration is set up in his mental body. This activity causes the matter of the mental plane to be moulded into a thoughtform. The colour and life of this form is dependent upon the emotions which accompanied the original thought. A thoughtform is a temporary living entity, which vibrates and persists in mental substance for so long as it continues to be energised by the mind.
(See section "Thoughtforms", page 66, in Chapter 6, "The Subtle Bodies of Man")

THOUGHTFORM, IN MEDITATION: A "lighted" thoughtform is produced by memorising the meditation outline and adding to it an understanding of its purpose. This is essential if the astral body is to be controlled. According to the quality of the vision and thoughts of the man, so will be his desires and his outer actions – "As a man thinketh in his heart, so is he".
(See MEDITATION, OUTLINE)

THREE WORLDS: These are the worlds of physical existence, emotional experience and mental endeavour and understanding.
(See Chapter 4, "Incarnation", page 30)

TIBETAN, THE: The Master, Djwhal Khul (D.K.); an Adept of the Second Ray of Love-Wisdom. He is known as "the Messenger of the Masters". He is very learned regarding the Rays and planetary Hierarchies of the solar system. Most of the books written by Alice A. Bailey were dictated to her by D.K.. A large portion of *The Secret Doctrine* was dictated by him to Madame Blavatsky. He communicated mentally with both of them while they were fully conscious.(See Chapter 14, "Channelling", page 110, and *The Unfinished Autobiography*)

TRANSFIGURATION: The third initiation. The physical man illumined and transformed by the brilliant radiance of the indwelling Divine Life.

TRANSITION: A shift of consciousness from one plane, or standard of values, to another; from one way of looking at life to another. To pass from what has already been achieved to something better and higher.

TRANSMUTATION: The process of change whereby any substance can be speeded up to a higher vibration and thus shifted into a subtler dimension. The changing and redirecting of the energies of the mind, of the emotions and of the physical nature, so that they serve to reveal the Self. The passage from one state of being to another, higher state of being.

TRINITY: See DIVINE TRINITY

UNDERSTANDING: The faculty of the Thinker (the soul) to appropriate knowledge as the foundation for Wisdom. That which enables man to adapt the things of form to the life of spirit; to link inspiration arising from Wisdom, with knowledge. Knowledge deals with the not-self, whilst understanding is a quality of the soul – the Thinker. In the life of the spirit, understanding is the *cause of revelation*.

UNION: The act of making one. Combination or harmony of agreement between parts. Through an ordered process of soul unfoldment, a conscious union (at-one-ment) is brought about between the lower or personal self and the higher or divine Self. Dualism is replaced by unity.(See Chapter 21, "The Science of Meditation", page 140)

UNION, STAGES OF: The Union to be progressively achieved is:
1. Union of the threefold man (physical-etheric, emotional and mental bodies).
2. Union of the lower man with the soul – the interplay between the soul and the personality via the physical brain.
3. Union of the personality, soul and Spirit, so that they function as one upon the physical plane.

UNITY: At-one-ness; wholeness. To know God as the Eternal Cause and Source of all. To recognise the Whole; to become one with God by becoming

one with our immortal Self. The consciousness of the individual soul is the consciousness of the Whole. Separativeness, divisions and distinctions fade away in the knowledge and realisation of One-ness.
(See MACROCOSM, MICROCOSM)

UNIVERSAL MIND: The Mind of God. The One Mind that contains all minds. It includes all states of consciousness. It is All Knowledge, All Power and Ever Present. The Universal Mind, or Divine Thinker, is the Intelligence Principle which makes itself known in man through the lower concrete mind, the abstract mind and the intuition.

UNIVERSAL RELIGION: All religions spring from the One Source. The teachings of the East and of the West need to be fused and blended before the true and Universal Religion – for which the world is waiting – can appear on Earth.(See section, "The New World Religion", page 88, in Chapter 9, "The Reappearance of the Christ")

VITAL BODY: See ETHERIC BODY

WEB: See LIFE WEB

WESAK: A festival which takes place in the Himalayas at the full moon of May (Taurus); it is said that at this festival, at which all members of the Hierarchy are present, the Buddha returns, for a brief period, to His association with the work of our planet.

ZODIAC: Astrology is based, curiously enough, upon illusion, for the zodiac is the imaginary path of the sun through the heavens, as it appears from the standpoint of our planet. The sun is not in any sign of the zodiac but only appears to be as it passes between our Earth and the constellations at any particular time or season. Although largely an illusion, at the same time the constellations exist, and the streams of energy which pass and repass, which intermingle and interlock throughout the body of space, are by no means illusions, but definitely express eternal relationships.

Bibliography

The Holy Bible – King James version.

Bailey A.A.

Books by The Tibetan (The Master Djwhal Khul) through Alice Bailey
Initiation, Human and Solar 1922
Letters on Occult Meditation 1922
Glamour: A World Problem 1950
A Treatise on White Magic 1934
A Treatise on Cosmic Fire 1925
The Reappearance of the Christ 1948
The Externalisation of the Hierarchy 1957
Discipleship in the New Age Vol. II 1955
The Light of the Soul 1927
A Treatise on The Seven Rays Vol I Esoteric Psychology Vol I 1936
Vol II Esoteric Psychology
Vol II. 1942
Vol IV Esoteric Healing 1953
Vol V The Rays and Initiations 1960

Books by Alice A. Bailey
From Intellect to Intuition 1932
From Bethlehem to Calvary 1937
The Labours of Hercules 1974
The Unfinished Autobiography 1951
The Soul and its Mechanism 1930

Compilations by Students
Ponder on This 1971
The Soul the Quality of Life 1973
Serving Humanity 1973
Master Index of the Tibetan and Alice A. Bailey Books 1974
A Compilation on Sex 1980
Death: the Great Adventure 1985
London and New York; Lucis Press Ltd/Lucis Publishing Company. These are
first publishing dates; There have been many reprintings since.

Alder V.S. *From the Mundane to the Magnificent*. London: Rider. 1979, 1988.

Bayley H. *The Lost Language of Symbolism*. London: Benn. (No date) (Alternative publ. London: Williams and Norgate. 1912, 1951)

Blavatsky H.P. *The Secret Doctrine, 2 vols*. America: Theosophical University Press. 1952.

Capra F. *The Tao of Physics*. London: Wildwood House. 1975, pb London: Fontana (Flamingo). 1976, rev 1983, 1987.

Capra F. *The Turning Point*. London: Wildwood House. 1982, pb London: Fontana (Flamingo). 1983, 1987.

Chopra D. *Quantum Healing. Exploring the Frontiers of Mind/Body Medicine*. New York: Bantam Books. 1989.

Cirlot J.E. *A Dictionary of Symbols*. London: Routledge & Kegan Paul. 1967.

Cooper J.C. *An Illustrated Encyclopaedia of Traditional Symbolism*. London: Thames & Hudson. 1978.

Eastcott M.J. *The Silent Path*. London: Ryder. 1969, repr. 1979, 1989.

Ferguson M. *The Aquarian Conspiracy*. Los Angeles: J.P. Tarcher. 1980.

Fortune D. *The Esoteric Philosophy of Love and Marriage*. London: The Aquarian Press. 1967.

Fuller J.G. *The Ghost of 29 Megacycles*. London: Grafton. 1985

Greaves H. *Testimony of Light*. London: World Fellowship Press. 1970.

Gris H. and Dick W. L. *The New Soviet Psychic Discoveries*. London: Souvenir Press. 1979.

Harding M.E. *Journey Into Self*. New York: Longman Green & Co. 1956.

Hodson G. *The Miracle of Birth*. Madras: The Theosophical Publishing House. 1985.

Joy W.B. *Joy's Way*. Los Angeles: J.P. Tharcher, Inc. 1979.

Jung C.G. *Answer to Job*. Princeton: Bollingen Press. 1952.

Jung C.G. *Memories Dreams and Reflections*. London: Collin Routledge & Kegan Paul. 1963.

Jung C.G. *Man and his Symbols*. London: Aldus Books. 1964.

Jung C.G. *Synchronicity. An Acausal Connecting Principle*. London: Routledge & Kegan Paul. 1972.

Jung C.G. *Dreams*. Princeton: Bollingen Press. 1974..FF

Karagulla S. *Breakthrough to Creativity*. Marina Del Rey: DeVorss. 1985.

Karagulla S. and Kunz DvG. *The Chakras and the Human Energy Fields*. Wheaton, Ill.: The Theosophical Publishing House. 1989.

Leadbeater C.W. *The Science of The Sacraments*. Madras: The Theosophical Publishing House. 1920. 1980.

Leadbeater C.W. and Besant A. *Thought Forms*. Madras: The Theosophical Publishing House 1901. 1911.

Lutyens M. *Krishnamurti. The Years of Awakening*. London: John Murray, 1975.

Neal V.P. and Karagulla S. *Through the Curtain*. Marina Del Rey: DeVorss. 1983.

Peterson R. *Everyone Is Right*. Marina del Rey: DeVorss. 1986.

Powell A.E. *The Etheric Double*. London: The Theosophical Publishing House. 1925. 1930.

Powell A.E. *The Mental Body*. London: The Theosophical Publishing House. 1927. 1956.

Roerich H. *Letters of Helena Roerich*. New York: Agni Yoga Society, Inc. 1967.

Roerich H. *Fiery World III*. New York: Agni Yoga Society, Inc. 1948.

Tansley D.V. *Radionics and the Subtle Anatomy of Man*. Saffron Walden, Essex: Health Series Press. 1974.

Wachtmeister C. et al *Reminiscences of H.P. Blavatsky and the Secret Doctrine*. Madras: The Theosophical Publishing House (A Quest Book). 1976.

Wynne-Tyson E. *The Philosophy of Compassion*. London: Centaur Press.1970.

Yogananda P. *Autobiography of a Yogi*. Los Angeles: Self-Realization Fellowship. 1974.